To Phil Moseley

with all my best

Frank Gilroy

# THE KHRUSHCHEV PATTERN

# THE
# KHRUSHCHEV
# PATTERN

by Frank Gibney

DUELL, SLOAN AND PEARCE

New York

*To*
*Edna and Joe*

# AUTHOR'S NOTE

I should like to thank the Lenox Foundation of New York for its material assistance in making this book possible. Owing to its help, I was able to avail myself of the services of bureaus and correspondence of United Press International for much of the reporting and research necessary to this project. Although the concept of the book and the material stem from my own studies of Communist affairs and my experiences as a reporter overseas, the UPI reports furnished both invaluable updating and, often, stimulating insights into areas where I lacked the vantage point of first-hand experience. For whatever errors may have crept into the finished product, however, I must accept full responsibility.

I should like also to thank Allan Forsyth, without whose research and reporting help the book could not have seen the light of day. His work in preparing and condensing the Appendix, in particular, was indispensable.

Some of the material on Latin-American affairs appeared in different form in an article written by Peter Deriabin and myself in *Life in Español,* and I thank the editors for their courtesy in allowing me to reproduce it here.

# CONTENTS

# THE KHRUSHCHEV PATTERN

# CHAPTER I

# LENIN INSIDE OUT

"One cannot ignore the specific situation, the changes in the correlation of forces in the world, and repeat what the great Lenin said in quite different historical conditions. . . .

"If we act like children who, studying the alphabet, compile words from letters we shall not go far. . . .

"One must not only be able to read but also correctly understand what one has read and apply it to the specific conditions of the time in which we live, taking into consideration the existing situation and the real balance of forces."

—NIKITA S. KHRUSHCHEV

THE above statement, made by the Premier and Party leader of the Soviet Union in Bucharest, on June 21, 1960, is a convenient summary of one of the major shifts on the scene of modern history. The change was Nikita Khrushchev's formal repudiation of the Leninist doctrine that a general shooting war was inevitable before Communism could in the end overthrow the forces of "imperialism" and "capitalism" in the world. For a world Communist leader to turn his back on this basic traditional prop of Communist doctrine was a huge achievement, a prodigious risk, and an act impelled only by the most dire necessities—most immediately the development of weapons that could blow both Communism and capitalism off the map of the universe. Even more remarkable was the success which this change produced, from the Communist point of view.

It is the purpose of this book to describe the impact of this change on the world in the period between 1955 and 1960—which we can conveniently label the "Era of Peaceful Coexistence"—and to show the way the change worked and how it was used by the world's various Communist movements and their allies. The break with the Leninist tradition was first publicly admitted by Khru-

3

shchev in 1956, in a speech at the Twentieth Congress of the Communist Party of the Soviet Union. But it had already been prefigured in the tactics of Khrushchev's governance, since he became First Secretary of the Party.

The first phase of the "era" terminated in the spring of 1960, after the U-2 spy plane and the collapse of Summit negotiations in Paris. On an inter-governmental level, it was then obvious to the Soviet leadership that few further concessions could be exacted from the West on the basis of a friendly face and the repudiation of Lenin. The Chinese Communists, less worried than the Russians about the danger of nuclear warfare, were pressing for an openly aggressive policy. And, as we shall see, there were forces opposed to further "peaceful coexistence" within the U.S.S.R. So a half-turn in Soviet policy took place, and the movement was reflected in the behavior of Communists throughout the world. The same Khrushchev who had lauded Eisenhower as a "man of peace" began saber-rattling over Cuba and over the Congo. Anxious to follow up the political advantages realized from the crash of the American U-2 aircraft at Sverdlovsk, the Russians went to the length of staging another shooting incident. But this time it was an American reconnaissance plane, an RB-47, that was shot down over international waters in the Barents Sea in a crude and deliberate Soviet provocation.

Although these warlike activities contrasted with the general tenor of the five preceding years (barring Hungary, of course, which almost upset Khrushchev's calculations), we need hardly be deceived about the true purpose of peaceful coexistence. It was a tactic and not a new strategy—even though it necessitated a break with Lenin's principle. But at various points and in various ways it proved extraordinarily effective. For in this five-year period Khrushchev's skillful reading of the "specific conditions of the time in which we live" drastically revived the fortunes of his movement.

In 1955 the world mechanism of Soviet Communism had the look of a collection of damaged parts badly rusted by exposure to the open rains. Inside the Soviet Union Nikita Khrushchev was hard at work reforming a faction-ridden Communist organization, the while cementing his own hold on the throne left vacant by Stalin's death. Outside the U.S.S.R., in the sixty-odd Communist parties scattered over the world, the damage done by the death of Stalin was there for all to see. Factional struggles for power mirrored those going on in Moscow. A wave of inner doubt and irresolution continued to wash over both the Party's leadership and the remaining faithful.

The next year saw the doubt and disturbance brought to a climax. Khrushchev's own speech at the Twentieth Congress of the Communist Party of the Soviet Union stripped bare the decades of crimes against the Russian and other peoples by Stalin and the Soviet leaders who served him. Khrushchev had complied in these crimes and approved of them as wholeheartedly as Beria, Malenkov, Zhdanov or any of the others. ("Hail the greatest genius of mankind," Khrushchev had shouted at the Eighteenth Party Congress in 1939, "teacher and leader, who leads us victoriously to Communism, our own Stalin. . . .") That he was forced to admit them in public shows the deep inner trouble of his Party and the Soviet people.

Fired by these anti-Stalin revelations, literal revolutions broke out in the Soviet dominions. The earlier revolt in East Germany, and to a lesser degree in Czechoslovakia in 1953, was eclipsed by the revolution in Poland and the bloody struggle of the Hungarian people in 1956. These troubles in turn begat more. Soviet suppression of the Hungarian freedom fighters produced a revulsion against Communism and Communists throughout the world unprecedented in modern times. If there were apologists galore for the Moscow purge trials in 1938, few outside the U.S.S.R. were anxious to defend Hungary.

Among the world's Communist parties, Hungary acted as a temporary dissolvent. The Italian Party showed a massive fissure in its structure, which time has still not healed. There was indignation in

Japan. The co-leader of the Party in Brazil walked out—a particularly damaging blow since he was in charge of Party fund-raising. What was left of Communist or fellow-traveler support in the United States was severely shaken. If the shock of Hungary was not felt so strongly at the time in most of Asia, and sadly obscured by other events in the Middle East, it had ultimately a delayed impact of great importance.

On the network of Soviet-run front groups throughout the world—the complex of boldly named organizations which fight for "peace," "democracy," "rights" or "justice" as Moscow pronounces them—the twin blows of the Stalin revelations and Hungary seemed almost catastrophic. The World Federation of Trade Unions, most powerful of the front groups, groaned in its iron harness, as thousands of once misguided union members—and their leaders—began demanding to know the embarrassing truths behind their sloganry. Only in Asia again, did the line hold firm. And this was a hollow comfort to a Russian leadership increasingly plagued by the overt competition of the Chinese.

Yet by 1960 this picture of world Communism in trouble had totally changed its shading. The Soviet Union, wrapped in a comfortable web of summit conferences, international visits, exchange delegations and folksy Khrushchevian statements to the international press, had not looked more respectable to the outside world since the transitory honeymoon of the New Economic Program in the 'twenties.

While the peaceful coexistence policy continued, the praises of Soviet science and invention whirled around in the same orbit with the aptly-named Sputniks, the gross satellites propelled by the world's heaviest-thrust rockets. American school children—or their social studies teachers, at least—veritably doted on schemes for Russian pen-pals. No manager of a raw new hotel in one of the underdeveloped countries could consider his hostelry complete without the familiar dark suits and wide trousers of the visiting Soviet trade delegation. If Mao Tse-tung's China still stood in the eyes of the world as a bad boy, prone to aggressive acts, there were many to point out that he was merely retarded in his evolution. Khrushchev and the Russians, after all, had reached a point where Communism, as it was noted, desired only to compete peacefully. Was it not true that Communism and capitalist democracy—each mellowing in its own way—would some day coalesce in a happy mass of international unanimity?

This change in Communism's world stature and fortunes over five years was accomplished without any corresponding substantive change in its aims, methods, content or leadership. If Khrushchev's Russia was more relaxed and confident-seeming than Stalin's, exactly the same apparatus of police controls remained at the ruling Party's disposal. They had merely been loosened. Even the extent of the loosening was highly debatable—a leading foreign authority on the Soviet Union was surprised to find himself under far more heavy surveillance on a Moscow visit in 1959 than he had been in 1956.

The Communist Party had a tighter hold than ever over the rulership of the Soviet state (see Chapter II). The ruling Party of the Soviet Union in turn dominated the world's Communist Parties and their subsidiaries with a control broken only by the necessity of admitting Chinese junior partners in certain Asian areas. The aggressive aims of Communism continued to be visible through all the window-dressing. As Khrushchev said to a visiting Japanese correspondent: "We are convinced that sooner or later capitalism will perish, just as feudalism perished earlier. The socialist nations are advancing towards Communism. All the world will come to Communism. History does not ask you whether you want it or not."

Apparently few people in the world listened to him in this context —judging by the surprise when the U.S.S.R. turned "aggressive" again in 1960. Yet millions had applauded his homely witticisms, his boasts about Soviet scientific achievement and his occasional granting of a passport to a Latvian long separated from his family in the outside world.

Getting a new reputation for the same old product this way is quite a trick. In the American public relations business, where this trick is performed or attempted almost weekly, the process is known as "acquiring a favorable image." It happens regularly to soup, steel mills, labor unions and political candidates and the steps taken are not unfamiliar. But never in recent history has this job been done in such major, heroic proportions. Khrushchev gave a favorable image to a Party, a movement, a country—it is hard to separate them in this regard—which only a few years previously had been denounced as an international pariah. It was an impressive achievement for a political group which scorns the very word public relations, albeit conversant with propaganda.

Under Khrushchev the international influence of Communism grew greater than at any time since Lenin. Its following has never been larger, nor its potential greater for making converts—or at least insuring that increasingly wide sections of the earth's population emerge favorably disposed to the movement.

Historically, the hard core of Communist believers have always needed a spongelike mass support around them, to swell their triumphs and to cushion their adverse moments.

Lenin first coined the term "useful idiots" for them. First applied specifically to the Socialists, it is a good phrase for describing the Communist follower, whether he is a left-wing Socialist in Japan, a member of the Chilean Popular Front, a professional humanitarian like Jean-Paul Sartre, or an idealistic student from Guinea who plans to organize a new chapter of the World Federation of Democratic Youth.

There was another period in recent history, culminating in the late 'thirties, when the Moscow Communists were able to forge a Popular Front of impressive dimensions through a great deal of the civilized world. In Europe, for a time, the old Popular Front government seemed to sweep all before them, and the movement spread to Latin America and Asia. The Anglo-Saxon democracies were not immune to its appeal. Harry Pollitt's British Communists were a force to be reckoned with in the 'thirties. In the United States—a day most of us have conveniently forgotten—there were the youth congresses on campuses, the students' unions, the Communist-line labor groups, and debates that raged through the pipe-smoke of hundreds of faculty rooms over whether the Marxist way ("... and all right, I admit that they are ruthless sometimes ...") was not after all the only real hope for democracy's progressive evolution.

The Popular Front of those days foundered of course on many rocks and shoals, and some knew its illusions before others. George Orwell could smell its fakery in Spain and that peasant hero of the Spanish Loyalists, El Campesino, was to learn its perfidies in Soviet prisons. Finland and the Baltic states saw the illusions explode first, and although the final disillusionment was postponed by the false euphoria of the World War II alliance, the perils of dealing with Communists were borne in upon the academic theoreticians sitting across the Atlantic—in a way so crushing as to explain why the only campus radicals found in the United States in 1960 were probably the anti-liberal members of the local Edmund Burke Society.

From the Communist point of view, the old-time Popular Front failed because its only strength lay in taking advantage of a common menace: fascism. When fascism as an organized world movement exploded with the World War II victory—if indeed it had not quietly died a long time before—the Communists were left standing out in the daylight with the dusk of the "menace" removed. They had no positive platform other than their own preachments, so their true features speedily became visible.

The new popular front of the Khrushchev era was quite different. Its strength has not depended on the negative appeal of "the common danger." It is rooted in the common hope for a better world. The Soviet propagandists have learned enough to base their new front on a popular appeal. The appeal may be broken down as follows: 1) the glories of Soviet science, which "alone" has the qualities of leadership and concentration to lead mankind to earthly bliss; 2) the appeal to nationalist revolution, in a world of liberated black, brown and yellow men, where a chorus of "down with colonialism" supplies the same useful theatrical backdrop of the old Shakespearean mob in Julius Caesar shouting mechanically, "We'll hear the will; we'll hear the will . . ." 3) the spurious agape of Communist brotherhood, which last includes the dinning, boring, but on the whole effective repetition of slogans for peace and against atomic war.

These appeals would not be so successful if the advance of Communism were concentrated on Europe, as it was in the 'thirties. But Europe has not interested Khrushchev as much as it interested Stalin or others. The Europeans know Communism well. They have been through it for many decades. Many, in fact, have grown dangerously contemptuous of the power of its message on other continents by measuring it with their own well-worn yardsticks.

In Asia and Africa the atmosphere is more receptive. The horror of Hungary, or the history of earlier Soviet inhumanities like the Katyn massacre or the 1938 purges have not impressed themselves strongly enough on the Asian mind to outweigh the fact that the Soviet Union was never at one with their former colonial "oppressors." Add to this the fact that the mass movements of Communism with its sudden forced industrializations, its systems of targets, goals and disciplines are attractive to the hard-pressed leaders of countries with little practice at non-authoritarian modes of government. Their large, hungry populations have problems so vast that the processes of parliamentary democracy, if used to decide them, must seem to many like time-wasting frustration. This explains why democracy has been virtually abandoned in Indonesia and elsewhere.

It is congenial to the peoples of the new nations to hear Khrushchev say, as he did at the critical Twentieth Party Congress in Moscow, that "the disintegration of the imperialist colonial system, now taking place, is a post-war development of world-historical significance. The complete abolition of the infamous system of colonialism has been put on the agenda as one of the most acute problems."

It is even more heartening when the Communist-front groups, at their international congresses, incorporate planks into their "campaign" platforms like this one of the World Federation of Trade Unions:

"In colonial countries the working class should demand trade union rights, democratic freedoms and better living and working conditions. All this the foreign monopolies would resist with bitter hostility. But if the national bourgeoisie stands firm and the entire people is ranged behind it, and if it does not hesitate to accept all possible aid from the Socialist camp, it will be possible to force the colonialists to retreat."

Here we have the message of the new Khrushchev popular front. It is not an all-inclusive message for the world, hardly guaranteed to win friends and influence converts in many of the western countries. But Khrushchev, like a good political general, realized the virtues of the concentrated attack in one quarter. Where the Popular Front of the 'thirties beamed its message at those useful idiots who were worried about Fascism, the popular front of the late 'fifties and the 'sixties was directed at those who worried about want and nationhood itself.

The underdeveloped countries are greedy for immediate improvement. They are impatient with the cautious restraints and measured approach of the western democracies when dealing with international alliances and aid programs. Except for a few far-sighted leaders they are not interested in the long-term implications of the Soviet credit programs or the student exchanges with Moscow. If it is a Faustian bargain, they are willing to strike it. When people are starving now on the front-doorstep of the new capitol building, there will be time enough to worry about paying the Devil later.

With a speed that owes much to the suppressed energy of a nation confined for two generations in a rigid isolation, Russian advisors have come along with the Soviet loans into the strategic areas of the Middle East, Asia and Africa. Working on parallel levels come the good-will ambassadors of the multitudinous "front" groups, hoping to capitalize on the desire of the newly emancipated to be treated like flattered members of an international club.

Take one example of the "front" groups' swift growth in Africa: the spreading affiliates of the World Federation of Democratic Youth. Since 1953 the WFDY has enrolled the following African youth organizations: the Union of Sudanese Youth; the Rural Youth League of Togo; the Working Youth of Ubangui-Chaii; the Association of Moroccan Students in France; the Democratic Youth of Madagascar; the African Youth League of the Ivory Coast; Togoland Youth Movement; Maaband Youth Association of Ghana; Congo Youth Union; Niger Youth Union; Union of South Africa Indian Youth Congress. A few years ago the new countries thus favored by the WFDY were barely names in Moscow. It says much for the vigor of Khrushchev's front movement that they were so quickly organized and welcomed into the Socialist camp.

The World Peace Council is more universally effective, because its appeal is so unexceptionable on the surface. Even in countries where Communism is virtually a proscribed word, it has not been hard to find signers for the appeals against nuclear testing, the ban on military bases overseas (U.S. bases, that is) and other honest-sounding articles of the new Communist line. But in the underdeveloped countries of Africa and Asia, almost any variety of front movement can take root, sometimes blossoming with great speed.

The new Communist emphasis on recruiting the useful idiots— and as many as possible—stems partly from the fact that the actual Communist parties in the underdeveloped countries are new, weak and often prone to nationalist heresy. Moscow has never forgotten extreme situations like Burma, where at one point there were four different Communist parties in the field—all militantly opposed to each other—or Iraq at present, where the government has artfully sponsored a splinter from the loyal Communist Party group. In the circumstances, it is often more reliable to direct a steadily pro-Communist trend from Moscow, Prague or the other front headquarters, allowing the student groups, trade unions, and the like to carry the banner.

There are real, deep and often fascinating differences between the Party and the front groups, as they are organized in various countries. But several common denominators show through the entire world complex. The principal appeal continues to be directed at the intelligentsia, or whatever passes for such in a country, and the workers. But the workers are often not to be found in any great numbers. Many of the promising unions organized by the WFTU in the underdeveloped countries will have to wait for some factories to appear before they can start fomenting any real political trouble. Often, taking a leaf from the book of the Chinese Communists, the fronts try to mobilize farm workers as a substitute for the militant factory workers of Soviet folklore. Especially where these farm workers are herded together on large plantations, as in some areas of Brazil, they have had striking successes.

The intellectuals, on the other hand, are apt to be more important to the Movement in the underdeveloped countries than they have been in any other area. Education was not a strong point of most colonial governments. As a result, with certain partial exceptions like India and the Philippines, the newly independent nations have little or no educated electorates; their destinies are in the hands of small groups of university-trained intellectuals, most of whom got their learning the hard way and already flirted with Marx somewhere along the road. In some countries, also, the desire for sudden education has turned out comparatively large numbers of unemployed lawyers and bachelors of arts, while skimping on the quantity of doctors and engineers. Among these discontented intellectuals, as with the generally poor student populations, the Khrushchev leadership has found a fertile field for recruiting useful idiots by the bushel. In a largely anti-Communist country like Japan, for instance, the most effective pro-Communist demonstrating is done by university students and the left-wing teachers' union.

Because of the value of intellectuals in the newly free nations, the numbers in the front groups they join are deceptive. There may be only two members of the International League for the Rights of Man in a tree-shaded village somewhere south of the Equator. But if they share local government between them, and in addition are the only citizens who can read, they may muster quite an influence.

In building the new Popular Front, the Soviet leadership has been able to rely on props more solid than emergent needs and idealism in Ghana, Indonesia or Iraq. The Soviet primacy in the fields of space and missiles has been dinned into the world's ears with regularity. Although precisely-mannered gentlemen may sit in Washington and assure their Congressional committees and the world that the overall military strength of the United States equals or is in fact greater than that of the Soviet Union, their voices have never been able to drown out the crashing impact of the first Sputniks. Power counts in the calculations of new countries' leaders probably more than idealism. And one of the great successes of the new Soviet image has been to suggest that its power is now decisive. That this is not true is incidental to the point. Many believe it to be the truth and it is their beliefs which influence policy, not the correctness of them.

Another factor in the modern Khrushchev pattern has been the trade offensive. Between 1955 and 1959 the Soviet Union and its satellites tendered more than $3 billion in loans, credits and—but rarely—outright grants to certain of the world's underdeveloped countries. The total trade volume of the Soviet bloc with the underdeveloped countries increased from $861 million in 1954 to $1.8 billion in 1957, and it has steadily grown since. Almost 5,000 technicians were sent abroad by Moscow to assist various countries, again principally in Africa and Asia.

The Soviet credit program has been, to say the least, highly selective. It has concentrated on certain countries whose friendship was critical to Soviet policy—Afghanistan, Iraq, the United Arab Republic, Indonesia and India. In the four-year period ending in 1958 three-fifths of the Soviet aid and credit total was in the form of arms, delivered to the U.A.R., Iraq, Afghanistan, Indonesia and the feudal kingdom of Yemen. In other areas, notably Latin America, loans and credits have been used to establish a bridgehead of Soviet influence.

The worth of the Soviet aid and credit programs is debatable. Moscow not only buys and sells for its own needs, but uses an intensified form of "preclusive trading," simply for the purpose of attracting a country into its own orbit or weaning it away from further connections with the West. Barter is a favorite device. Cotton has been bought from Egypt and Syria and rice from Burma— only to be sold back to other countries at prices which sadly undercut the world market. And the Communist cause in Bolivia and Malaya has hardly been furthered by the wholesale dumping of tin on the world market.

But, countering these drawbacks, Communist aid has the advantage of speed. Khrushchev need worry about no Congressional approval if he promises a country a new steel mill. And the superficially low interest rates on loans—unlike the United States, the Soviet Union almost never gives grants-in-aid—serve to foster the illusion of self-respecting brotherhood, so energetically created.

The extent to which the U.S.S.R. will go to win friends through aid and trade was illustrated by the *reductio ad absurdum* of a recent note to the government of Iran. Iran is a country which the Soviet Union has tried alternately to invade and subvert since the end of World War II. In line with the new image projected by Khrushchev, Soviet trade representatives signed an agreement in 1956 to exchange Russian sugar for Iranian rice. Since few modern granaries exist in Iran, the merchants of the Caspian littoral delivered their rice to the Soviet trade commission replete with the droppings of the mice who live in their open rice barns and storehouses. After a series of conferences, the Soviet trade representative in Iran, Peter Gordeytchik, announced in December 1957 that his government would continue to take delivery of the rice, but he called on Iranian exporters to "please keep the mouse-droppings to a minimum."

". . . Rice with mouse-droppings," the Soviet representative noted, "is not suitable for consumption and according to the views of the Soviet Ministry of Health this kind of rice is even injurious to the health and hygiene of the Soviet people. Consequently the sale of rice which contains mouse-droppings is legally prohibited . . .

"Although the (Iranian) Ministry of Monopolies and Customs undertook by the agreement it signed to deliver rice without mouse-droppings, mouse-droppings were very much in evidence from the samples taken from the first consignment . . .

"In accordance with the agreement signed, we would be justified not to take delivery of the rice; but, since the governments of Iran and the Soviet Union desire to improve and expand the commercial relations of the two countries, we reported the situation to Moscow and requested permission, as an exception for this year alone, to take delivery of rice with mouse-droppings . . .

"Although the Soviet Union buys rice from three other countries, it never takes delivery of rice with mouse-droppings from any of them, and at present, Iran is the only country that will deliver rice with mouse-droppings. . . . Soviet trade representatives at the port of Pahlevi have been instructed to take delivery of rice only with a minimum quantity of mouse-droppings, namely, not more than two mouse-droppings in each sack. . . ."

This policy of pleasing, which surely reached a new high in the Iranian rice incident, has been successful, if clumsy, in regularizing Soviet and Communist relations with many countries. In the old Popular Front days, local fellow travelers and Party members had nothing to advertise except the military might of the U.S.S.R., which was all too often being used in the wrong direction. Now, thanks to Khrushchev's widely advertised trade program, they have gained an added respectability and usefulness in being the contractive agents for dams, wheat and steelmills.

# CHAPTER II

# THE NEW SOVIET UNION
# AND THE SOCIALIST CAMP

"I prefer a bad character that can grow wheat to a good character that can't."

—N. S. KHRUSHCHEV

NO IMAGE can be manufactured out of nothing, and national policies are no exception. The new image of Khrushchev's Communism on the international scene is a direct reflection of what has happened inside the Soviet Union. And for the last five years in Soviet history—a baffling amalgam of change and stabilization, release and repression, exploding energy and stunted prosperity— there is no better symbol than the First Secretary of the Party, Nikita Sergeyevich Khrushchev.

The paradoxes in this man are a tempting field for any journalist or historian. He has twisted Communist ideology like a pretzel and he admits it, frequently justifying his heresies by references to established Communist scripture. "If Marx, Engels and Lenin could arise now," he once chortled, "they would laugh at those bookworms and quoters who instead of studying the life of contemporary society and developing life creatively try to find among the classics a quotation about how to act in connection with a Machine Tractor Station in such and such a district . . ." He has changed the ground rules of both Soviet and international Communism more than any leader since Lenin; yet he was able to say confidently on one of his foreign tours (in India in this case): ". . . We say to the gentlemen who are waiting to see whether the

Soviet Union will change its political program—wait for a blue moon! And you know when that will be . . ."

Although Khrushchev's own five-foot shelf of books on the theory and practice of Communism has replaced Stalin's as required reading for Russian Party members, he is by his own admission no ideologue. He is essentially the model of a good political boss, the sort of man whose principal talent lies in a brilliant capacity to adapt and discipline circumstances, however surprising. In 1955 he found himself in a certain set of circumstances, and out of them he built an altered political, social and economic platform for the Soviet society, plank by plank. The word "altered" is used advisedly. Despite all his flexibility, Khrushchev has never broken with the principles of Party control, police power and massive industrial direction. These remain the staples of Communist society and they are likely to remain for some time. As a recent Harvard University study (made for the Foreign Relations Committee of the U. S. Senate) noted: ". . . though it is always dangerous to insist rigidly that nothing has changed in Russia (thereby often promoting policies calculated to delay any incipient change) it would be at least equally dangerous to ignore the consideration that during the next decade Soviet policy is likely to remain totalitarian, led by a doctrinaire Communist Party and dedicated to a radical change of the international order."

Khrushchev rose to power over the heads of Stalin's other successors because he correctly grasped the degree to which the premises of authority in the Soviet state had changed. Under Stalin, rulership of the state was quite literally ordered on a Byzantine model. Stalin came to power through his leverage on the Communist Party, but he was contemptuous of it. He kept power, once he had seized it, by concentrating it all in his hands. His chosen instrument for so doing was the State Security, the secret police organization, which served him the way similar organizations had served emperors in the long-dead past. He ruled through terror and mystery. So great were these attributes, and so strong his personal control, that a single successor was quite unthinkable. When he died, the tensions built up within the Soviet people by years of terror, compounded by years of destructive war, obviously cried for some sort of release.

When Georgi Malenkov had his brief moment of power in late 1953 and after, he tried to relax the tensions of the Soviet state too sharply and too quickly—that is, if one wanted to save the Communist system and its firm control over the population. Malenkov worked towards a detente in his foreign policy, encouraging an easement of tensions throughout the world. Putting through the Korean armistice, which it is doubtful the Chinese Communists wanted, was an excellent example. In his domestic policy, he sought to satisfy the long-husbanded craving of the Soviet citizenry for more economic freedom, for consumer goods and a raised standard of living. In working towards these goals he was supported by the rising class of managerial people in the Soviet Union, technicians and (albeit in the Communist statist sense of the word) businessmen.

These people had lost interest in the Communist Party as such through the terror-ridden days of Stalin. They tended to be impatient with its dictatorship. They seemed to be the wave of the future. Their ascent to power, through Malenkov and his immediate supporters at the top, promised for a time even to strip off the apparatus of Communist Party control which threads its thin steel way through every element of the Soviet ruling bureaucracy. It appeared that the head of a government department, rather than the local Party boss, was finally to be the real boss of his department, and so on down through the hierarchy.

Another feature of the Malenkov policy was an urge to increase consumer goods production at the expense of a vast arms establishment. In a way strikingly like the "More bang for a buck" reduction of arms instituted by the Eisenhower administration's businessmen in the United States, Malenkov's Soviet businessmen sought to concentrate on "high-yield" strategic nuclear weaponry. The Soviet Army naturally opposed this trend.

Although Malenkov's policy may have presaged eventual

changes of rule within the Soviet Union, he was ahead of his time in the early 'fifties. For his reforms weakened the remains of the Stalinist power state without putting anything in its place except more canned goods and an itch for efficiency. Had the Malenkov reforms continued, forces for a real democracy might have developed within the Soviet Union, in the manner of biological matter rapidly evolving into higher forms of life under pressure of favorable circumstance. Khrushchev saw the danger at once; few statesmen of our time have been more keenly alert to any dangers threatening a totalitarian order. He began a campaign against Malenkov waged on grounds of ideology. In a denouement, he attacked Malenkov's policy of abandoning the Soviet priority for heavy industry as "nothing but slander of our Party . . . a belching of the rightist deviation, a regurgitation of views hostile to Leninism . . ." Malenkov was dismissed as Premier in 1955 and began his slow descent to obscurity.

Malenkov was the front-runner in the Soviet power struggle. To strike him down, Khrushchev needed the help of others; his hand was at once strengthened and concealed by the comforting anonymity of the pack. Now began Khrushchev's rapid assumption of power into his own hands. To old Bolsheviks (that is, to the few of them left alive for rehabilitation) Khrushchev's march to power had an eerie resemblance to Stalin's. Like Stalin, he worked his way up through the party, building not only on his position in the Ukraine, but on his former job as Party chief in Moscow. Against Khrushchev's new, tough brand of *apparachik,* both the rising manager class and the older, more conservative Party men gave ground. Indeed, Khrushchev attracted many to him by his very drive and informality, such a contrast to the Stalin ideal. It was not the first time that informality had been mistaken for liberalism.

Using as a sort of shield the politically half-lifeless body of Bulganin, Malenkov's successor as Premier, Khrushchev had consolidated Party power in his hands by 1955. He had relied heavily on the prestige of Marshal Zhukov during this delicate period, with the implicit endorsement from the Soviet Army that the

Zhukov alliance implied. By 1957 he felt strong enough to move against all his rivals. He struck down Malenkov on the left and on the right the conservative old-line Party faction of Molotov and Kaganovich, who had remained true to a rigid "dogmatist" view of Stalinist orthodoxy. With characteristic ingenuity, he christened both the liberals and these super-orthodox Communists the "anti-Party group" and brushed them off the board. He then moved against Marshal Zhukov himself, playing upon intra-Army jealousies to reduce the most popular soldier—and quite possibly the most popular public figure of his day, the Eisenhower of the Soviet Union—to the same position of obscurity in which he had languished during the last years of Stalin.

Khrushchev was still in the process of securing his own base of power when he proceeded to shake the Communist world with his denunciations of Stalin's dictatorship, the cult of personality, in his famous secret speech to the Twentieth Party Congress in Moscow in 1956. The great Soviet purges, the murders, the vicious practices of the State Security were all laid bare, indeed with an enthusiasm which Khrushchev and his henchmen may well have later regretted. The words of the speech echoed in the hall where they were pronounced like heresy being preached from the pulpit of St. Peter's—"It became apparent that many Party, Soviet and economic activists who were branded in 1937-38 as 'enemies' were actually never enemies, spies, wreckers, etc., but were always honest Communists; they were only so stigmatized, and often, no longer able to bear barbaric tortures. . . . Confessions of guilt of many arrested and charged with enemy activity were gained with the help of cruel and inhuman tortures. . . . Stalin personally called the investigation judge, gave him instructions, advised him on which investigative methods should be used; these methods were simple—beat, beat and once again beat. . . ."

The ensuing convulsions of anti-Stalinism shook the Party to its core and, in the satellites, paved the way for the Polish and Hungarian revolutions. But in Khrushchev's terms, the need for such a drastic remedy was amply borne out by the results later achieved.

For a quarter of a century the Communist Party of the Soviet Union had been crusted with the weight of the Stalin personal dictatorship. Khrushchev liberated the Party from this shell, so that he might better be able to use it as his own vehicle of power, and the stabilizing force in what he saw to be an era of critical change for the Soviet people.

Going back to "Leninism" with the zeal of a backwoods preacher getting back to the Bible (and despite the fact that he had already scrapped some of Lenin's basic premises) Khrushchev called for a sweeping reexamination of Party goals and premises. Internally, he revived the Malenkov plan of increased concessions to the consumer and made it more dynamic. He tied it up with national pride and the urge to rival the wealthiest of the capitalists, i.e., the United States, not only in prestige and power but in creature comforts. "We do not intend to blow up the capitalist world with bombs," he told one of his audiences as early as 1957. "If we catch up with the United States in per capita production of meat, butter and milk, we will have hit the pillar of capitalism with the most powerful torpedo yet seen." This was the domestic side of his "competitive coexistence."

He was careful to hang on to the police power, and concentrated it in his own hands. His substitution of Aleksey Shepilov, a trusted Party functionary, for the veteran State Security boss, Colonel General Ivan Serov, in December 1958 strikingly paralleled Stalin's replacement of the professional NKVD boss Genrikh Yagoda by the Party functionary Yezhov more than twenty years before him. But he realized that police and terror rule in the Soviet Union had reached a point of diminishing returns. He reinstituted the rule of the Party, but made it more flexible and hence workable through a marked tendency to decentralize power (within the limits of safety, that is, for what remains a dictatorial government).

Having thus restored Party discipline, he found no need for the naked terror of the State Security. In a country where Party disapproval can mean loss of a person's job, his living quarters and all hope of improving his station, a policeman need not be visible on every corner if the Party organization is vigorous and competently directed.

The new Khrushchev Party proceeded to gain further strength by its flexibility of approach. Khrushchev smashed some of the historic setups of the Soviet politico-economic system on the grounds of simple efficiency, e.g., the Machine Tractor Stations which had been established in the countryside more for political control of the agricultural populations than for economic efficiency. He adopted at least ostensibly the criteria: "will it work?" and "how best can it achieve our goal?" (When workability was thrown out the window in favor of bureaucratic needs or the need to maintain the Party dictatorship, he was careful to disguise the fact.) The Khrushchev combination of reform and control was often striking. His ideas for opening the virgin lands and revising the systems of collectives marked breaks with established Soviet tradition. Yet at the same time such institutions as his proposed "agrogorods"—farm cities—in their centralized scheme of living would take away even the last vestiges of independence, the tiny individual plots of land, still allowed to *kolkhozniks*.

In releasing political prisoners, loosening the bonds of police control and allowing on occasion a dash of free discussion Khrushchev displayed a calculated boldness. And his gamble worked. By exuding confidence himself, he aroused confidence in his "new" goals. By encouraging flexibility of approach, he gave talent a new outlet. By dwelling on the new strength of the Soviet Union, he stimulated Russian nationalism to work ever harder in the peaceful "race" with the Americans. As an American authority, W. W. Rostow, noted in a recent book: * "Outside the area of high politics and the control over policemen and guns, the new disposition of executive authority released many new trends in thought and aspiration within Soviet society in the post-1953 period—from the Presidium's Secretariat, to the university students, down to the millions of Soviet citizens in forced labor. The immediate operational

* *The United States in the World Arena* (New York: Harper & Brothers, 1960).

effect, however, was to bring to bear on the making of Soviet policy at home and abroad younger and fresher minds whose views had been suppressed by the heavy-handed rigidity and omnipresence of Stalin in the postwar years. In many ways the years after 1953 have been a golden period for the generation of soldiers, technicians and bureaucrats whom Stalin educated and trained to operate a modern industrial and military system, but who had worked under severe restraint and inhibition as well as human fear so long as Stalin was alive."

It must not be forgotten that the keystone of the Khrushchev Era's expansion has been the words "peaceful," as in Peaceful Competition. Most of the belligerent shouts of "we will bury you" are reserved for foreign consumption. This is not to say that saber-rattling is taboo before Soviet audiences. Extensive threats and maledictions were uttered after the public discovery, in May 1960, that American high-level reconnaissance aircraft had indeed been able to fly high over the Soviet Union with impunity for some years' time. This was thought necessary to quiet any doubts of the populace about Soviet armed strength. Yet Khrushchev's great popular success inside the Soviet Union lay not in warlike threats, but in dramatizing the post-Stalin improvement in living standards and concretely setting up goals of better living, more creature comforts and increased leisure time—a practice hitherto unknown in Soviet society.

In short, Khrushchev accented the positive. By admitting foreign tourists, and even letting selected groups of Soviet citizens go abroad, by dwelling on concrete achievements of Soviet technology, he publicly invited competition with the "capitalist camp." The strides of Soviet science have been particularly effective in this regard, and he has been most careful to see that scientists and their technical help labor under the most favorable circumstances with a minimum of official interference. He points to the early-rising Sputniks as evidence of the inevitability of Communism's world triumph and to someone living inside the Soviet Union they must seem very telling evidence. The new image is one of apparent frankness, with all the apparatus of deception and coercion swept carefully behind the door.

On occasion, this veneer is rudely bruised or scraped away, and the harsh outlines of a totalitarian state show through. Such a moment was the Boris Pasternak crisis in 1958. Then the Soviet Union, Khrushchev's Soviet Union, was forced to admit that the work of its own Nobel Prize-winning novelist, Pasternak, was too dangerous, ideologically speaking, to be published within the country. Actually, Pasternak's book was by no stretch of the imagination actively anti-Soviet or anti-Communist. It was merely not pro-Soviet, a state of "negativism" which neither a Fascist nor a Communist state can tolerate.

Yet the treatment of Pasternak was in itself significant. He remained free and working until his death in 1960, although laboring under an official cloud. In an earlier period he would not have died so peacefully.

The Khrushchev innovations in Communist ideology and control, thus begun in the Soviet Union, were carried to the satellite countries. There, as has been noted in Chapter I, the first reaction to the death of Stalin and the Twentieth Party Congress seemed sheer catastrophe to the Communists. The old Stalinist satraps, like Rakosi in Hungary and Bierut in Poland, were engulfed, along with their henchmen, in the discontent let loose over eastern Europe. It was apparent that the former overtly colonial relationship between the Soviet Union and the satellites, in force through the Stalin period, could not be reimposed without severe trouble, even bloodshed.

For this problem, too, Khrushchev had an answer. In a most disarming way, he scrapped the insistence of Stalin that the road to Communism, as followed in the Soviet Union, was the only possible ideological traffic artery, and must be tracked through without a single deviation. Specifically, he energetically wooed Tito, the arch-enemy of Moscow orthodoxy. ". . . the roads and conditions of socialist development are different in different countries," the joint Soviet-Yugoslav declaration noted in Moscow in June 1956, ". . . any tendency to impose one's own views in determining the roads and forms of socialist development are alien to both sides."

From Khrushchev's point of view, a greater flexibility was inevitable. He was attempting to restore the supremacy of Communist ideology to replace the power rule of a national dictatorship with several foreign subsidiaries. If for all practical purposes the Khrushchev regime proposed to exercise—and does exercise—virtually the same domination over the satellites that the Stalinists enjoyed, the distinction was nonetheless important. In the changed conditions of 1955 and thereafter, it would be far easier to enforce obedience to a set of principles than to a prescribed Russian rulebook which gave directions about how countries in the "Socialist camp" should regulate the smallest details of their societies.

Khrushchev moved too late to forestall the revolution in Hungary and his brutal intervention there did much to remind the world that the leopard, after all, cannot change its spots, even though it may sound and walk differently. Nor was he able to bring Tito to terms, despite what amounted to abject overtures. (Tito finally realized that the new Soviet definition of partnership, although admitting of many interesting nuances, was still spelled in Russian.) Only in Poland could he stabilize the situation. It is certainly true that an attempt at enforcing a return to Stalinism there after October 1956 would have meant open war. In allowing the Poles to overthrow their homegrown Stalinists and substitute the government of Wladyslaw Gomulka, a Communist previously jailed by his Party for "nationalist" and hence anti-Soviet deviation, Khrushchev took a gamble which few other statesmen of this day would dare make.

Poland remains something more like an ally of the Soviet Union than a mere satellite. The freedoms won by the Poles in their bloodless October Revolution have been severely clipped by Gomulka, a man of authoritarian disposition, but some of the most significant ones are still in effect. Khrushchev has exerted continual pressure on the Poles to conform to Russian patterns, but nothing like the pressure exerted on satellites by past Soviet governments. He is guided in his policy towards Poland by the premise that an orderly, Communist-run country with significant—and from the orthodox Marxist point of view, appalling—deviations in its policy towards private agriculture, the Church and free speech (by and large, it is permitted) is preferable to a rigidly run Communist country whose people are on the point of rebellion.

The satellites of Romania and Bulgaria have given the Russians comparatively little trouble, nor has the orderly and prosperous manufacturing country of Czechoslovakia. East Germany, although lately built up by Khrushchev's policy, remains a factor of doubtful political stability given any crisis or disaster which anti-Communist forces could take advantage of. Hungary, too, carries within itself the seeds of rebellion; although the Kadar government which was imposed after 1956 has made some significant concessions to its people, notably in agriculture.

None of these countries could be said to have a large body of believing Communists. Quite to the contrary. For while in the Soviet Union Russian nationalism lends strength to the Communist ideology, in the other countries local nationalisms work against it. Communism is universally regarded as something foreign, even after fifteen years of occupation and control. Tito himself, independent of Soviet control, has had to go through a most interesting set of gyrations in Yugoslavia to attempt to convince his people that his variety of Communism is a native product. There is as yet no strong indication that the Yugoslav people have been so convinced.

Facing the situation in Eastern Europe realistically, Khrushchev decided to let economics do his work for him. What would it avail the Poles, for instance, to have their own "road to Socialism" markedly different from the Russian road, so different as not to be "socialism" at all, if their factories were nonetheless dependent on the Soviet Union for their raw materials, part of an interlocking group of national economies? So where Stalin had merely exploited the satellite economies, Khrushchev set out to integrate them. His success has been thus far considerable. The Council for Mutual Economic Assistance has worked to blend the economies of the bloc into a working unity, with a characteristic Khrushchev goal to strive for. In a speech given in East Germany in 1959 * the Soviet First Secretary ran on like this:

"With the victory of Communism on a world-wide scale, state borders will disappear, as Marxism-Leninism teaches. In all likelihood only ethnic borders will survive for a time and even these will probably exist only as a convention. Naturally these frontiers, if they can be called frontiers at all, will have no border guards, customs officials or incidents . . . the future development of the Socialist countries will in all probability proceed along the lines of consolidation of the single-world Socialist economic system. The economic barriers which divided our countries under capitalism will fall one after another. The common economic basis of world socialism will grow stronger, eventually making the question of borders a pointless one. . . ."

Thus, in the world of the East European satellites as well as within the U.S.S.R., Khrushchev staved off an explosion with his new program. As contrasted with the Soviet Union under Stalin, Khrushchev's version of Socialism was every bit as radical a departure from the immediate past as the New Economic Program of the early Soviet days, when the desperate Communists were forced to revert to capitalistic incentives to keep the country from economic disaster. But Khrushchev took great pains to avoid the appearance of any sudden policy shifts. There was merely a reversion to Communist Party control combined with an increase in consumer goods and popular freedom, a stressing of ideology in the abstract combined with a pragmatic willingness to make ideology jump through hoops if the situation required.

As it developed, however, there were a great many people within the Soviet hierarchy and Party leaders elsewhere in the Communist world who did not think the ideology could stand much

* As quoted by Zbigniew Brzezinski in *The Soviet Bloc: Unity and Conflict* (Cambridge: Harvard University Press, 1960).

more of Khrushchev's hoop-jumping. They were opposed to the "peaceful coexistence" concept. When the U-2 incident and the Summit breakup occurred in 1960, without the hoped-for concessions from the West, they were in a position to make their opposition felt. It was true that the satellites in Europe were quiet for the time, their peoples and their leaders temporarily stilled by Khrushchev's interesting combinations of coercion and compromise. For the long term, however, Khrushchev, or more properly his successors, would have disturbing problems to face.

Stalin had laid down ideology as a formal doctrine, of which he was the sole Pope. But Khrushchev's very flexibility of approach, while necessary and inevitable, lent itself to discussion. The intellectuals and theoreticians all through the Communist camp had at varying times made the discovery that Marxism without a dictator interpreting it is like a crustacean pulled out of its shell: formless and extremely unsatisfactory. In Poland Kolakowski and other young Marxian philosophers had started out from Marxist premises and reasoned their way into something like a free democratic society, before the government managed to suppress at least the more dangerous printed parts of their observations. In the Soviet Union intellectuals like young Vladimir Dudintsev wrote material that explored the premises of Marxism to about the same purpose. Even Mao Tse-tung, while propagating his short-lived "let many flowers bloom" policy, had discovered that *his* intellectuals could talk themselves out of Communism as easily as a Pole or a Russian, given the chance for even a little free discussion.

In his long speeches and exhortations Khrushchev had shown himself aware of the importance of keeping Communist ideology alive as a unifying force—or at least of exhuming it for that purpose, on the analogy of the old Hussites who made their favorite general's skin into a drum, after he died, and marched confidently into battle. Khrushchev had put tremendous pressure on Wladyslaw Gomulka merely to admit that the Soviet Union was not only "the oldest and mightiest Socialist State," as the Polish Communists conceded, but the nation which must play a special, and unique, if not, as expressed before, the "leading" role in the happy Socialist camp. Such pressures, noted and known, ill accorded with the boasts of Communist fraternal democracy.

There was also the materialism of the Soviet people to reckon with. The growth of consumer goods in the U.S.S.R. since the death of Stalin was impressive by any standards. The production of refrigerators, for instance, had risen from 49,200 in 1953 to 426,000 in 1959, that of washing machines from 3,500 in 1953 to 724,000 in 1959. Soviet health magazines, significantly, had begun to feature articles about keeping one's weight down. The Soviet consumer was, within limits, growing a bit choosy. There are few American "status-seekers" who could out-elbow a modern Russian in his search for the appurtenances of the good life.*

To keep up home front production of essentials as well as the new consumer items, Khrushchev found it necessary to demobilize a good part of the huge Soviet Army in 1959-1960, including 250,000 officers who by no means appreciated the loss of their caste status. Every aid program overseas, also, meant a bite out of the domestic Soviet economy. Unless conspicuous results could be shown for the new image of the helpful U.S.S.R. as a helpful international partner, there would be questioning and half-spoken discontent. Better than anyone else, Khrushchev was in a position to know that he was pushing a world revolutionary program with a most unrevolutionary-minded population.

While Khrushchev was smoothing and straightening the Communist bloc at home and in Europe, he had to meet from another direction the most severe ideological challenge in the history of Soviet Communism. This was the claim of the Communist Chinese to have virtually achieved the hoped-for goal of any "Socialist" state: "the realization of Communism in our country." The claim

---

* As a case in point, Soviet motor scooters and motorcycles lay unbought in many stores, despite their availability; since the average Soviet citizen would prefer to wait for the infinitely greater status symbol of a car.

was bound up with Peking's assertion that the entire policy of peaceful coexistence represented a dangerous abdication of true Leninist principles.

Behind this split was the fact that Mao Tse-Tung regarded himself, after Stalin's death, as the leading surviving Leninist disciple. He had looked with great suspicion on Khrushchev's denunciation of Stalin in the famous secret Party speech in 1956, the more so since any criticism of the "cult of personality" struck at his own theory of rule. Maoist China is exactly like Stalinist Russia in the amount of veneration given the single dictator.

Where the Soviet Union since the death of Stalin had tended to relax its police hold on its people, the Chinese People's Republic of China was in the middle of its own bitter struggle period, the same sort of herculean drive to industrialize and communize society which the Soviet Union itself had made in the bloody 'thirties. Mao's version of Communism, in the full tide of its revolutionary fervor, was distinguished by an even more uncompromising doctrine of war and violence than its Soviet antecedents. In a sense, the Chinese had become the Anabaptists of the Communist movement.

At the outset of the Khrushchev regime, his insistence that the roads to "the dictatorship of the proletariat" may vary enabled the Communists on both sides of the Sino-Russian border to avoid an embarrassing ideological split, due originally to the differences between Mao's ideas of agrarian Communist revolt in Asia and the standard Russian model of a worker's revolution. Later, during the Polish and Hungarian disturbances of 1956, the Chinese took the position of a liberal intermediary, treating between Moscow and its restive satellites. In this role Mao did much to stabilize Khrushchev's hegemony. But the more the Russians seemed to take "competitive coexistence" seriously, the more annoyed were the militant Chinese.

At a time when Khrushchev was increasing the supply of consumer goods in the U.S.S.R., Mao Tse-Tung was entering on his experiment with the "communes," the fiercest attempt made in history to use human beings as drafted chattels, for the sake of production goals. The communes—or "people's communes" to give their exact name—received a blare of publicity in Asia. The Chinese announced that these schemes in which thousands of families were alternately herded together and separated on vast work farms were the very factor that had brought China close to the transition to pure Communism. There was significant silence about the communes in most of the Soviet press. Khrushchev went so far as to pour contempt on the whole idea himself, in a talk to some Polish workers.

The Chinese for their part brooded with increasing anger on the pattern of exchanges and meetings at the Summit which Khrushchev was busily weaving with his enemies in the West. By 1960 the Chinese Communist press had burst forth with outright denunciations of this "soft" approach. For them the only real approach to the "capitalists" remained war. The new image of Soviet policy seemed far too faded for their fancy.

The controversy thus joined was as inevitable as the first Soviet conflict with Tito, the only other Communist ruler who had established the Party in his country by his own efforts, apart from the help of the Soviet Union. Khrushchev, who probably would never have made the mistake of breaking with Tito in the first place, had nonetheless learned enough from sad experience to handle the Chinese very gently. The Chinese, in turn, dependent on the Soviet Union for whatever outside help they received, were equally inclined to go easy in the ideological clinches. But the split was noticeable to everyone and the passage of time did not ease it.

By the spring of 1960 the Chinese were furiously rocking Khrushchev's diplomatic boat. Peking was re-defining the aggressive nature of Communism through the border aggressions against India and further suppression of the Tibetan people. And countries like Indonesia, with large populations of overseas Chinese, were made to feel the full weight of Mao's imperialist interest in all Chinese, wherever they may be. Nor had the drive to capture Formosa by military invasion abated one whit. While Moscow was talking about

Lenin's idea of "peaceful economic competition" between the two systems, Peking was citing and reciting Lenin's texts saying exactly the opposite. "The contradiction between the oppressed nations and the imperialists is a life and death contradiction," said Vice Premier Lu Ting Yi in June, "Between them there can be no such relations as live and let live, active coexistence and friendly cooperation . . ."

Peking damned Moscow by implication for being "revisionist." Moscow came back to denounce the "infantile left deviationism" that was so bold as to criticize the leader's peaceful coexistence theme.

At the Bucharest conference in June 1960 the differences were patched up. The Chinese agreed apparently to cease their attacks on peaceful coexistence; the Russians conceded that armed violence had an equal place, in the proper circumstances, with any peaceful methods in subverting capitalism. Khrushchev's supremacy in ideology was re-affirmed. And opponents of his "peaceful" methods within the Soviet leadership, as well as Peking, gave ground.

Yet the very shift of Soviet policy to the hard line, since the U-2 incident, suggested the amount of concessions required to preserve Moscow's and Khrushchev's primacy. For the moment the threat was over. The Chinese and the Russians were too wise to keep airing their own disputes in public. At the same time, their differences of approach would continue to have a powerful influence on world Communism.

These were the tensions within the Communist bloc during and after the era of "peaceful coexistence." Yet there was no doubt, as we shall see in the following pages, that the Khrushchev pattern had revived Communism as a serious factor abroad, more serious in the countries that knew it least. As regards the Western countries Khrushchev's constant visiting and commenting had done something which Stalin had never accomplished—not that he had wanted to. It had injected the Soviet Union into the international dialogue. Where Stalin was known as an aloof Oriental despot, Khrushchev was demonstrably the kind of a fellow who, if he saw an unfriendly article in *Die Welt* or the *Daily Express* or *Le Monde* or *The New York Times,* would likely as not argue with it in print the next day. His motives could be seen through by the West, denounced and resisted; but in a curious way he had injected both his governmental and personal image into its discussions. Not so with many of the discredited Communist parties and front movements of the West—and Khrushchev knew it.

But in the rest of the world, the revival of aggressive Marxist ideology had an appeal that was all the stronger for its reinforcement by the obvious progress of the Soviet Union. The underdeveloped countries in particular looked with interest on the country which could claim to have raised itself from virtual barbarism, to hear the Communists tell it, to the status of a ranking industrial power in forty years' time. As history can tell us, the cleverest frauds are the most plausible, and they take the longest time to discover.

# CHAPTER III

# THE MUDDLED MIDDLE EAST

"We were, in my opinion, like a patient who had spent too long a time in a closed chamber. The heat inside the closed chamber became such that the patient was almost suffocated. Suddenly a storm raged and wrecked the windows and doors. Cold draughts rushed in, lashing the body of the patient, still soaked in perspiration. The patient was in need of a breath of air. Instead, a violent cyclone burst upon him. . . ."

—GAMAL ABDEL NASSER,
*The Philosophy of the Revolution*

"WE are not Communists, but we have no quarrel with the Communists. What are the Americans trying to protect us from? The Russians, if anything, have a better record than you, for they have not been linked with the colonial powers. No, our own problem is right here, in the Arab countries. We are fighting reaction and entrenched feudalism—the same fight that Europeans had a long time ago. We can take care of our own Communists; if, as you say, they are part of an imperialist movement. But this I do not believe . . ."

The speaker was a highly intelligent professional man in Amman, Jordan, a Palestinian Arab by birth, bitter about the Israeli seizure of his old home, but full of idealism for the new pan-Arab world he would build in a popular front of workers and intelligentsia. He was a member of the leftist, but very definitely non-Communist Ba'ath Party, then gaining strength rapidly throughout the Middle East. His unconcern with Communism was typical of his political generation. In Syria, Lebanon, Egypt and Iraq other well-educated and well-intentioned people like him were saying

36

much the same thing, unwittingly reenacting the same cycle of hope and disillusionment already played out by Europeans in the 'thirties and Chinese in the 'forties. The time was 1957—and the young Arab leaders were talking "popular front."

Three years later, the Ba'athist's dream was smashed indeed. Instead of creating a working popular front, Communism's invitation into the Middle East had brought new factions, bitterness and bloodshed. Communists working in Syria, the Ba'athist headquarters, had finally become so obvious a threat to the country's independence that the Ba'athist leaders in panic turned to the lesser of two evils. They brought their country into its dreary union with the rough but at least anti-Communist Egypt of Gamal Abdel Nasser. The Communists in Iraq, after the 1958 Revolution against the authoritarian Nuri as Said, had tried energetically to control its course—so much so that Iraq remained tense and threatened by civil war, living in a perpetual state of emergency. In Egypt, Communist activity brought sharp punitive action from Nasser, who remained in the curious and temporarily satisfying position of extracting heavy aid sums from the Russians, while persecuting their brethren inside his country.

Saudi Arabia had its quota of agitators. In the west of the Arab world, the Maghreb, Communists in Morocco, Tunisia and Algeria were attempting, as yet unsuccessfully, to identify themselves with the new revolutionary nationalism. As for the professional man in Amman, he had been jailed after the failure of a prematurely formed plot to take over the little desert kingdom. The moderate revolutionary Ba'athist Party for which he had held such high hopes was virtually shattered.

All in all, the last decade in the Middle East has offered a striking illustration of Communism's successes and limitations in exploiting a real revolutionary situation. The successes were predominant, and they were successes that the comparatively rigid policy of Josef Stalin could never have achieved. Khrushchev had used his native Arab Communists at every turn to assist the larger objective of his "peaceful" war on democracy, but with determined

orders to use the "soft sell." In the Stalinist tradition he had sacrificed local parties, temporarily, to avoid giving offense to countries he wished to cultivate. But, unlike Stalin, he had given his
overseas Communist parties an extraordinarily favorable image
to work with, the image of a Soviet Union strong, but resolutely
peaceful, bent on scientific and economic progress.

The image was smudged principally because the various Communist parties and front groups moved too quickly. As a result,
Soviet policy found itself grappling with some uncomfortable and
unprecedented dilemmas. The West was on the run in the Arab
world. But the Russians and their Chinese friends were having their
troubles trying to direct, or even influence, that world themselves.

The background for the spurt of Communism in the Arab countries was almost made to order. World War II had brought to a
head the Arabs' discontent with their client status vis-à-vis the
West. Rashid Ali Gailani's 1941 rebellion against the British in
Iraq, for one, showed how close to success an anti-colonial revolt
could come. Its lesson was not lost. First Nazi Germany, then the
Soviet Union, making its first noisy demands at San Francisco in
1945, stood plainly visible as alternatives to Arab dependency on
Britain and France. This offered to the fertile Arab imagination a
host of possibilities.

By the 'forties, also, an emergent intelligentsia had developed in
all the Moslem states of the Middle East and North Africa, from
Casablanca to Teheran. It was western-educated, but impatient
with western modes of government, which it identified with colonialism. (Interestingly, all but one of the leaders of the Communist
Parties of Syria and Lebanon were educated in the American University of Beirut.) The extreme solutions of Marxist thought registered heavily with many of the rising young teachers, lawyers, army
officers and diplomats of this generation.

Communist parties had been known in the Middle East since
early after the October Revolution. In Egypt, Syria and Lebanon
local parties had been started by Moscow-trained Arabs in the

early 'twenties. But not until the period after World War II did
they find so many to read their pamphlets, if not to endorse their
methods.

There was real discontent for the Communists to feed. For the
rule of the West, only technically beneficent, had raised more questions than it answered. In the field of public health alone, advances
here as elsewhere in the world had kept down the death rate and
increased sanitation and health marvelously; but the Western doctors were unable to provide accompanying plans to feed the mouths
they had saved. The restlessness of the times, also, communicated
itself to the mass of people—the normally docile body of farmers,
tradesmen and artisans which through Arab history has been capable of suddenly aroused outbreaks of violence. In 1945, as in 1845
or 1045, "the street," as the mob in action is known, was a factor
to be reckoned with. And with each new set of political promises
its discontent increased.

There was another factor which Communism finds congenial:
the crumbling of the entire cultural pattern, which for centuries had
been founded on the religion of Islam. Since Mohammed came riding out of the Nejd in the seventh century, Islam had covered the
Arab countries like a great cultural and spiritual blanket, sometimes shielding, sometimes smothering. By the end of World War II
it had long ceased to hold much of an appeal to the intelligentsia
or the leadership of these countries, barring a few significant exceptions. The new Arab university student felt lonely and uprooted
by his apostasy—whatever his outward aspect. This crack in the
Arab's culture was all the more serious because Islam had been so
comforting and all-embracing.

It is admittedly hard to generalize about modern Islam. It sleeps
in Saudi Arabia, insofar as concessions to the modern world are
concerned, although it retains great power—at least until recently
the strict Koranic punishments were used by the Saudis for civil
offenses. In Pakistan, thanks to the pioneering work of modern
Islamic scholars like the late Sir Muhammed Iqbal, Islam has been
strenuously brought up to date. While making Islam the official

religion of the country, Pakistanis have tried to interpret the Koran's injunctions, and transfer them to a modern context. In Egypt, although Islam is strong in the villages and boasts a rather sophisticated center of learning at El Azhar in Cairo, there has been no such dynamic re-working of Islamic thought. Egyptians are the world's most casual Moslems; Gamal Abdel Nasser goes to the mosque on feast-days, with his photographers, in much the same spirit that similarly secularist European rulers present themselves at the local cathedral.

In none of the Middle Eastern countries, however, is Islam anything like an active counter against Communism. Its influence, where it is exerted, is passive. It resists, rather than attacks. The sheikhs can be counted on to oppose Communism for the most part; but they are conscious that their influence has its limitations, and they use it cautiously.

Most of the faithful of Islam, including its clergy, are naïve politically. In Iraq and in Syria members of the Islamic clergy all too readily accepted the claims of Communist front organizations like the World Peace Council, through ignorance of their real objectives. Their prestige made the front groups, of course, all the more valuable to their owners. The carefully staged pilgrimages of Soviet Moslems to Mecca have brought some dividends to the Russians. Faced with these smiling and carefully coached "pilgrims," pilgrims from elsewhere in the Moslem world find it hard to believe the stories of the actual repression going on in Central Asia against Islam.

Since the 'thirties, in fact, the Communists of the Middle East have made efforts to exploit Islam itself as well as the fact of its decay. The democracy of Islam, and its sharing of wealth and goods have been used to buttress the claims that Communism is just twentieth century Islam, just as various western folk in the hazy 'thirties used to refer to Communism as "twentieth century Christianity." Such a message has doubtless made few converts. It is true, however, that the unitary nature of Islam—not merely a religion but a religion, a state and a way of life rolled into one—

makes Moslems better prepared psychologically than many others for the unitary state that is Communism.

The second unique factor speeding Communist success in the Middle East was the establishment of Israel. The origins of the Israeli-Arab dispute are deep-rooted, even in its modern incarnation. So many rights and wrongs have been committed and argued on both sides that the morality of the whole dispute—which is continually argued on moral grounds—is shady. The fact remains, however, that the Israelis did set up a Jewish state on land which the Arabs believed to be their own, and where Arabs—Christian and Moslem—had been living for the long intervening centuries since Titus destroyed the Temple at Jerusalem.

The effort of the Arab states to destroy the Jewish state by force in 1948 failed, despite their superiority in populations. Their armies (only excepting Jordan's Arab Legion) were poorly led, ill-equipped and inefficient. Out of this failure came not only resentment but an acute consciousness of backwardness and inferiority, feelings which led directly to the revolution in Egypt and ultimately to that in Iraq.

This resentment was directed toward the Western powers, whom the Arabs blamed for Israel's creation and success; and it provided a fertile field for Communist agitation. Realizing this, the Soviet Union quickly reversed its original position on Israel, which had been cautiously favorable, and became the outspoken champion of the Arabs. Needless to say, local Communists throughout the Arab world were able to exploit this attitude very handily for their own purposes. In no other area were the Communists handed such a beautifully built-in grievance.

There was no one more eager or better qualified to exploit such grievances for Communism than a man named Khalid Bakdash, a veteran Party organizer who has justly earned the title of "Mr. Communism" for the Middle East. Bakdash, like most of the Party leaders in this area, is a member of the local intelligentsia, the son of a wealthy Kurdish family in Syria. Although only 48, he has

30 years of active Party experience behind him. He became a Communist as a law student in Damascus and traveled to Moscow for his Party indoctrination in the early 'thirties. He became Secretary of the Communist Party of Syria and Lebanon in 1937, at the age of 25.

Bakdash is a political gymnast of proven ability, and he has carefully revised the Communist message for Middle Eastern consumption. More than any other major Communist leader, he has made concessions to the religious background of his area, anxious to capitalize on Moslem sentiment and always ready to invoke the memory of past Moslem patriarchs. "Omar Ibn Khattab," he once wrote, typically, "was a simple Bedouin and yet his opinion has remained important for all. How is it that workers, peasants and intellectuals in our days are not permitted to express their opinions on their country, on affairs of the nation and on the government?" He went to special pains, and with success, to bring Moslem sheikhs and even some Christian Arab clergy into his peace movements and other front groups.

Through the years, Bakdash became a popular public figure in Damascus and Beirut—when he was not exiled from one or both, as at present—and he changed the Party line to fit the affairs of the moment. In 1944, he made a memorable bit of Communist electioneering. ". . . We have not demanded, do not demand now and do not even contemplate socializing national capital and industry . . . We promise the big landowners we shall not nationalize their land. . . . we promise the big merchants that we shall not demand the nationalization of their trade . . . We shall support the small merchants. . . ." After the new popular front movement got under way following World War I, Bakdash even had to caution his own followers, at one point, that they were still really Communists. "Certain comrades think that our support of the partisans of peace means that we are abandoning certain slogans of ours," he said. "This is a serious and disastrous error."

Until the death of Stalin, Bakdash had, however, been forced to conform his party publicly to the continual twists of the Moscow line. After 1954 he was let off the leash. The emerging Khrushchev regime even permitted him to desert his pro-Moscow policy and adopt the more profitable line of neutralism, with the major denunciations of course falling on the United States and other western powers.

In Syria this policy paid off handsomely. After the fall of the semi-military dictatorship of Colonel Shishakli, Bakdash brought his small group of militants out of hiding and went into parliamentary competition. In the elections of 1954 he was voted into the Syrian Parliament, the first Communist ever to take national parliamentary office in an Arab country. Others of his party were kept out only through desperate coalitions of other parties.

For the next three years, Bakdash reaped the rewards of his patient cultivation of non-Communists. In 1950 and 1951 he had succeeded in enrolling a great many non-Communists in the Syrian and Lebanese branches of the "Partisans of Peace." The majority of the Syrian Parliament signed the Stockholm Peace Appeal. The familiar front organizations bloomed—like the Democratic Lawyers' Union, the Syrian Democratic Youth, the Artists' Association, the Association of Syrian Republican Students. All these had been suppressed by Shishakli. Now, with the dictatorship overthrown, Bakdash was able to revive such fellowships. The Communists made common cause with the newly emerged Ba'ath Party. They dominated the councils of a group of so-called independents, led by Khalid Al Azem, the perennial Party-liner who enjoyed the added distinction of being Syria's richest landowner. It was not for nothing that Moscow hailed the 1954 elections as a turning point in Syria's history.

With the way thus prepared inside Syria, the Soviet Union began a three-year cultural and trade invasion of almost unparalleled intensity. A Soviet film festival opened in Damascus. Visiting delegations—doctors, agricultural experts and students—poured in from Moscow, and Syrians in turn were cordially invited on expense-paid tours to the Soviet Union. The first trade agreement between Syria and the U.S.S.R. was signed in November 1955.

Others followed with the satellites. An arms deal was concluded shortly thereafter. The Syrian Army, still smarting from the 1948 disaster, was able to roll down the roads towards Jordan in new or at least only slightly used Soviet tanks.

Syria in 1957 looked like Castro's Cuba three years later. In January there were mass arrests of pro-Western leaders. Newspapers were forbidden to make statements critical of Communism, Communists or the Soviet Union. Radio Moscow chimed in with the local mood by constantly repeating warnings of Western plots against Syria, usually linked with the conveniently situated Israelis. Moderates in the Army command were replaced and a pro-Communist officer, Afif Al Bizri, placed at its head.

The "national front" of the emerging leftist dictatorship received solid Communist backing as "a union of all the forces of the country against imperialism, and for the cooperation of the Arab states in the field of economic development." Speaking for his Party, Bakdash declared himself first and "above all an Arab nationalist."

By late 1957 Bakdash's form of "nationalism" was transforming Syria into a Soviet satellite. Bulgarian engineers were building new military airfields in restricted areas and more Soviet and satellite advisors were packing up for the trip south, ready to consolidate the gains. The Socialist Ba'athists, aware that the next step was formal Communization of their country, took their only line of retreat when they invited the popular Gamal Abdel Nasser to accept the political union of Egypt and Syria.

Union was declared in 1958. It brought an extension to Syria of Nasser's own repressive policies against the Communists of Egypt (see below). Colonel Abdul Hamid Serraj, the pro-Nasser G-2 of the Syrian Army, overthrew his pro-Communist bosses and moved in with his security men to prepare for a wholesale roundup of Communists. "The Communist Party has shown its real self," he told a Syrian audience late in 1958. "Its attitude is treason to the Arab cause and a dagger's stab directed by people who do not represent the real face of the Syrian region."

Syria itself had paid heavily for its Communist flirtation. Not only had the government's anti-Western policy wrenched Syrian economics out of their natural trading orbits with the West, and committed them to a series of ultimately unprofitable Soviet barter deals, but the union with Egypt in the United Arab Republic, the only antidote to a Communist take-over, proved a harsh purgative. Essentially, this proud, willful and professionally cantankerous segment of the Arab people found itself no more than a colony of Cairo's, ripe for economic and political spoliation.

By this time Bakdash was on the run again, commuting between the Soviet Union and Red China. Many of his lieutenants were in jail, the rest in hiding. His unofficial staff headquarters he moved to Beirut, sending out orders through the small Lebanese Communist Party, of which he is also Secretary-General. Communism has declined in Lebanon since reaching its high-water mark in 1950 —its principal remaining strength is concentrated in six Communist-dominated unions. But the relatively free atmosphere there permits the continued publication of Communist literature and a certain amount of message and courier work. Although the Party is proscribed and persecuted in Damascus, Beirut is after all only two hours by car over the mountains.

What the Communists lost in Syria they more than made up in Iraq. As of this writing they remain the hump on the back of the Iraqi revolution. They barely missed capturing it completely. The Communists, through their multitude of front organizations and sympathizers, are beyond question the most powerful political force in the country. In any other country but Iraq, in fact, they would have assumed formal control long since; but Iraq, as Moscow is finding out, is a most peculiar country.

The Communist Party of Iraq grew up in the mid-'thirties. At times nothing more than a loose alliance of wayward intellectuals, it made up for its small size by the complexity of its internecine disputes. Its first Central Committee was not formed until 1944. It never gained legal status under its own name; but by 1946 three different Communist groups were operating in the guise of independent political parties. For a time they were all licensed by the government.

Until the Iraqi revolution of July 14, 1958, the country was governed by a tight clique representing its big land-owning, tribal and commercial interests. Premiers came and went through a political revolving door—being decided on according to the temper of the times. ("There are times," one of them once said, "when you need a soft man; then there are times when you need a hard man, or a statesman, or an economist. We have them all.") The strongest of all, perennially returned to power whenever a hard ruler was needed, was Nuri as Said.

Nuri was an early Arab patriot, who had given up his commission in the Turkish Army to fight with Lawrence of Arabia in World War I. But he never lost the mannerisms of a Turkish military man. He was a long and faithful ally of Britain, and he had a clear-sighted view of the political future. He was by any standards one of the ablest Arab political men of modern history. But he made no concessions to the changing times. He had sound plans for the development of Iraq, itself a hodge-podge creation of World War I, whose oil revenues made it the richest of the Arab countries. But they were long-range plans. And he let few of his fellow countrymen in on his secrets. He ruled alone. The nominal ruler, King Feisal, who was later killed along with Nuri during the revolution, was an amiable young man who had gone to Harrow and liked fast cars.

Nuri's repression made the Communists popular. Since he was in the habit of identifying all opponents of his unpopular regime as Communists, this hitherto unknown party began to rise in public esteem. Executions of Communists through the years excited the country. When one imprisoned Communist leader died following a hunger strike in 1951, there were mass demonstrations in Baghdad. In 1954 the Communists were able to form a National Front with two other parties, the left-wing socialist National Democratic Party and the rightist Istiqlal Party. In the elections held that summer— the same year when Bakdash was returned to the Syrian Parliament, this three-party front managed to elect fourteen candidates of its own. Shortly after this Parliament was dissolved.

Through the 'fifties, Nuri's policies grew steadily more hated by the population. His unpopularity rubbed off on the Western allies, due principally to his outspoken fidelity to the Baghdad Pact, that legalistic idea of the late John Foster Dulles. The United States, the principal architect of the pact, failed to bolster it even by the simple expedient of entering it. And Nuri complained with some justice that he received no concessions from the West to make his foreign policy popular. "I can't hold this position down alone," he said not long before his death. But meanwhile he went ahead with his old policy of putting in jail everybody who opposed him.

When Major General Abdul Karim Kassem, a career officer, carried out his revolutionary coup in 1948, there was rejoicing in "the street," among the intelligentsia and among the desperately poor farmers—or those of them who had the strength left to cheer. Order was restored after the mob enjoyed a brief savage time of riot through Baghdad, killing several Americans and Europeans along with Nuri and other officials. It was a small irony of history, all too familiar to Americans who had seen the same drama unfold in China a decade preceding, that the first shot fired in Kassem's revolt came from a 108mm American recoilless rifle made in Charles City, Iowa. It was part of the $50,000,000 worth of arms the Iraqi received from the United States in the four years before the revolt.

Kassem himself is a Puritanical soldier. An idealist about his country, he believed that the revolt would give rise to an immediate surge of popular enthusiasm, united behind the pure goals of *his* revolution. He had roughly the same hopes which Nasser and his fellow officers carried into the Egyptian revolution and he demonstrated an even greater lack of political planning. There were two organized forces supporting him. One of them, including quite a few officers and many of the ill-fated Ba'athists, hoped for a pan-Arab union with Nasser's United Arab Republic. The second force was the Communists, and despite their past disunity they were the better prepared.

The Party's Central Committee telegraphed Kassem its unconditional support the day of the revolt. Both the Soviet Union and Communist China extended recognition to Kassem's new government just two days afterward, with the satellites crowding right behind. The swiftness of this recognition suggested the close touch between Moscow and its unofficial Iraqi representatives.

The Communists mounted the crest of the wave with amazing rapidity. Front organizations, long organized on a clandestine basis, came out into the open. Besides the familiar Partisans for Peace and outfits like the League for the Defense of Women's Rights, two organizations appeared which threatened to become the cadres of a Communist state. The Popular Resistance Force, a paramilitary home guard, roamed the streets, well-armed with rifles and Sten guns, checking cars, investigating and take quick vengeance on Communist opponents. For just as Nuri had labeled any foe "Communist," the Communists were quick to tag any foe of theirs as a partisan of Nuri's and the "imperialists."

More sinister than the Popular Resistance Force were the Committees for the Defense of the Republic. These were made up of Communists or pro-Communists in almost every walk of life. In government offices, business houses, or farms or in industry, these committeemen kept watch over the loyalty of their fellows to the revolution. During the first year of the revolution hundreds of people were arrested solely because they had been reported in these Communist loyalty checks.

Among them these front organizations had little trouble mobilizing "the street" in Baghdad and other towns for the "spontaneous popular demonstrations" beloved of their craft.

The split between the Communist and the non-Communist supporters of Kassem, the "sole leader," began to develop early. The first threat to Kassem's rule, real or fancied, came from the latter. His lieutenant, Brigadier Abdul Salem Aref, was at the head of those demanding a union with the U.A.R. But Kassem was increasingly cool to the idea of playing second fiddle to Nasser's noisy brass section in Cairo. In November 1958, he imprisoned Aref on charges of plotting with Nasser against him. "You can understand how the poor fellow must have felt," said an Egyptian official at the time. "Here Kassem had spent almost his whole adult life plotting and scheming for *his* revolution. He brings it off and whose picture goes up in all the Baghdad shop windows—Nasser's."

The following March other army officers broke out in rebellion in the northern city of Mosul, in the middle of the oil region. Although they revolted because Kassem seemed to be favoring the Communists, it is probably true that the Communists provoked them to a premature rising. The Communist militia helped loyal troops crush the Mosul plot, thus becoming stronger than ever. They now called for a National United Front—a multi-party union suspiciously like some of the Communist-led groupings in the European satellites just after World War II. When Kassem frowned on the idea, the Communists suddenly soft-pedaled it, along with their demands for cabinet representation. It was clear that Moscow, mindful of the failure in Syria, was desperately pulling back on its adherents' coat-tails.

Kassem was by this time alarmed himself over the Communists' gain in strength. With Aref and the Nasserites out of the picture, there was no nationalist force around to counter their influence. The Revolution was losing its balance. In June he ordered the Communist militia to lay down its arms. The next month, the Communists underlined his fears by staging a bloodbath in the city of Kirkuk. For three days they and their allies ranged the streets killing off all the Nationalists they could find. At least 200 were slaughtered—some of them buried alive.

Kassem had hitherto been unfailingly indulgent to the Communists; even this time he did not cite them by name for the Kirkuk excesses, preferring to denounce "anarchists" and "greedy people."

For the next six months Kassem tried to steer a middle course between the Communists and the Nationalists. He felt himself unable to trust the latter. In October, he was almost killed when a band of armed men riddled his familiar drab station wagon with submachine-gun bullets. In the trial staged after his recovery from his wounds, Ba'athists and pro-Nasser elements were blamed. At the same time the Communists were losing their brief popularity. Agitation began for Kassem to take more steps against *them,* as well as the Nasserites.

In August the official Communist paper *Ittihad al Shaab* (*Unity of the People*) published an abject apology for its over-eagerness. The party had made mistakes, it said, "due to the drunkenness of victory and the conceit caused by its great achievements." Admitting that many of its members had been enrolled too hastily to permit adequate indoctrination, the Party announced that it was suspending recruiting activities for the time being. Barely a week before this the military governor of Baghdad, Kassem's new chief assistant, Major General Ahmad Saleh al Abdi, ordered the Committees for the Defense of the Republic dissolved. They had, he admitted, been "terrorizing" Government officials and employees.

It should be clearly understood that such steps were not part of a concerted anti-Communist policy, or at least they have not yet been so. On the contrary, they were desperate measures taken to prevent the Communists from taking over the revolution lock, stock and barrel. Any effort to root out the Communists completely would be a tremendous undertaking. By 1960 the Communists had expanded their front organizations to take in virtually every walk of Iraqi life. There were the usual friendship societies—Iraqi-Soviet, Iraqi-Chinese, even an Iraqi-Bulgarian Friendship Society. There were the occupational groupings like the Engineers' Union, the Iraqi Journalists' Association, the General Union of Peasants, associations for economists, writers, and surveyors.

Some of these the Communists took over bodily; in most they were content to pull the strings. In other groups control was divided between Communist and anti-Communist factions. The unions, for one, fell easily to the Communists. By the end of 1959 the General Federation of Iraqi Trade Unions had formally enrolled itself in the Communist World Federation of Trade Unions. One Ali Shukar, head of the pro-Communist Railway Workers' and Employees'

Trade Union, was elected president. The federation's new monthly bore the original slogan on its cover: "Workers of Iraq, unite!"

The Communists were especially efficient in colonizing the Iraqi press and radio. By early 1960 there were only two anti-Communist daily papers left in Baghdad. The rest exhibited varying shades of red. Most papers got their foreign news from Tass or the New China News Agency. The latter maintained a staff of some twenty-five persons, largest of any news agency in Iraq. For in Iraq, as elsewhere in Asia, it was already quite clear that the world contained not one but two Communist headquarters.

While the local sympathizers tried to take over the machinery of society within Iraq, the Soviet Union and the other members of the "Socialist camp" rushed into the void left by the discredited "imperialists," with the studied air of a professional Santa Claus. Santa's bag was packed with the usual goodies—trade agreements, visiting delegations, aid projects, technical advisors and tons of guns, tanks and small arms. In nine months, the Russians had already sent in enough equipment to outfit two of the Iraqi Army's five divisions. By the end of 1959 Iraq had signed treaties or trade agreements with almost every Communist country.

Through this period trade with the West also continued. In 1959 Iraq realized over $242,000,000 from its share in the crude oil extracted by the British Iraq Petroleum Company. Britain, the United States and neighboring Kuwait still led the list of Iraq's export customers. A ban on Western goods was finally revoked when it became apparent that the members of the "Socialist camp" were unable to supply their like. In late 1959 Iraq resumed its practice of importing large quantities of used American clothing—the visiting Soviet technical experts were among the most avid buyers. Baghdad's traditionally freebooting taxi drivers stopped shouting "anti-imperialist" slogans long enough to force the government to resume importing American cars.

But such backing and filling could not minimize the degree of Communist advance. By the end of 1959 some 250 technical "experts" of various sorts, eighty of them Russian, had been imported. They more than filled the void left by the departure of Iraq's old Western advisors. The usual steel mill was promised. Two hundred Soviet military advisors had arrived to help out the remodeled army. This was four times the number of British and American military advisors who had worked with the old regime. In February 1960 a sixty-man Russian engineering delegation came on the scene to survey a new Iraqi railroad. In the same month—the *reductio ad absurdum* of "showcase aid" in a country at Iraq's scientific and industrial level—six Soviet scientists arrived, equipped with the standard treaty, to discuss "peaceful uses of atomic energy."

Soviet and satellite trade fairs multiplied. Iraqis could view Czech fashions, Hungarian farm implements and Romanian canned foods. The Russians themselves opened two permanent exhibition rooms for automobiles and television sets on a main Baghdad boulevard. Cultural agreements were signed with North Korea and Albania. Although many Iraqi students continued to go to Europe or the United States for their higher education, English being their only foreign language, arrangements were made to send as many as possible to Moscow and other Communist cultural centers. The Soviets promised, further, to establish ten vocational and technical schools in the country. In December 1959 to point the way for the agricultural reformers (and clear up any illusions the Iraqi peasant may have had about owning his own land) the Iraqi government announced that the U.S.S.R. had consented to set up five model state farms there. All in all, Iraq was becoming almost a copybook example of Communist penetration.

Some of the Iraqi leaders who arranged these deals were out-and-out Communists, others merely Party-liners. Ibrahim Kubba, Minister of Economics and Agrarian Reform, played a leading role in shifting the country's dependence to the East, and his two ministries were loaded with pro-Communists. Communist sympathizers continued to exercise an effective news blackout of the country through their control of radio, TV and other communications functions under control of the Ministry of Guidance. Others bored into the Ministry of Education.

Although most of the Army remained either straight nationalist or nonpolitical, a few highly political officers wormed their way into positions of prominence. Chief among them were the notorious "four colonels." Colonel Mahdawi, and his military colleague, Colonel Majid Amin, ran the proceedings of the People's Court. In nightly televised court sessions which rivaled the later performances of Fidel Castro in another hemisphere, the colonels used the trials of members of the Nuri as Said regime as forums for the foulest language against the accused and the "imperialist camp," and the most extreme sort of Communist propaganda. Both of them, although not officially party members, were on the Central Committee of the Partisans of Peace. Practically speaking, this amounted to the same thing. (Amin was apparently a secret card-holder in the Party itself.)

Another Communist colonel, Fasfi Tahir, had been Nuri as Said's *aide de camp* and figured prominently in the old man's dethronement and murder. Now installed as aide to Kassem, this dedicated Communist was serving him with about the same degree of loyalty. He had close connections with the Soviet embassy in Baghdad, and was assumed to be one of the principal bearers of instructions to the local Party leaders. His brother gained the strategic position of chief military censor for foreign press and publications. That is to say, he supervised the distributions of Tass and New China News Agency dispatches to Iraqi newspapers.

The activities of such people represented a sharp disillusionment to the genuine nationalists who had hoped for much through the revolution. In February 1959 seven ministers in Kassem's cabinet resigned in protest over Communist influence. Theirs and similar protests—notably those of the anti-Communist General Abdi—finally took effect. In February 1960 the most prominent of the pro-Communists, Minister Kubba, was removed from all his portfolios "in the public interest."

The popular revulsion against the Communists began to make

itself felt. Dr. Faisal Samir, the pro-Communist Minister of Guidance, was shouted down while delivering a speech of Kassem's to the Society of Islamic Ethics. Some of the anti-Communist Shi'ite sheikhs began public preachments in the mosques against this foreign doctrine. What was left of the anti-Communist press, now gently let off the leash by Kassem, quickly accused the Communists of sabotage, crimes, barbaric actions and (somewhat unjustly in view of the Communists' virulent anti-Semitism) of conspiring with "international Jewry." Kassem's own National Democratic Party received more favored treatment.

At the beginning of the year the simple soldier showed some surprising tactical shrewdness when he brought off a trick which more distinguished statesmen on several continents had been vainly attempting for two generations: he split the Communist Party. The stage was set by the Communists themselves. As soon as they gained power, they resumed the multitude of intra-party disputes which had plagued them in the times of persecution and exile. The leading schismatic was one Daud Sayigh, an intellectual—and a born Roman Catholic, incidentally—who had been recurrently booted out of the Party for indiscipline. As January 8, 1960, drew near—the date on which Kassem had promised to license political parties—both Daud and the orthodox Communist leader Abdul Qadir Ismail, filed for permission to establish the "Communist Party of Iraq." By careful prearrangement, Kassem's Ministry of the Interior licensed Daud, but refused the request of the orthodox Party leadership. When Ismail announced in desperation that he would seek to register the Party under the name of Unity of the People Party, this application, too, was turned down. The Ministry said it was not only illegal, but that the whole group seemed in conflict with the government's stated objectives of independence, unity and republican government. So the sole legal Communist Party of Iraq is now run by the local Trotsky.

As a by-product of his new slightly anti-Communist policy, Kassem in the Spring of 1960 commuted the death sentence of Fadhil al Jemali, a former Premier under the old regime, and one of the Middle East's most respected international spokesmen, to ten years in jail. The Communists had demanded the death penalty for him.

Such strange bouleversements must have been bewildering for the local Soviet advisors. Here in one country the Communists had taken over all the key agencies which Moscow's experience suggested should guarantee a stranglehold on any country: press, education, trade, "land reform," communications, censorship. Yet they were not in control. This was partly due to the ineptness of the Iraqi Communists, who had among them no leader of the caliber of Bakdash in Syria. Partly also it was due to the fact that classic Communist methods—at least Russian Communist methods—may have grown too sophisticated for such a primitive country. The highly mechanized Party bureaucracy of Russia, where a Marshal Zhukov could be removed without even a stir, had possibly overlooked the fact that in a country like Iraq it is quite easy for a simple army man to be sole boss.

Nonetheless, Iraq remained the next thing to a Communist client state. And the need for a constant watch on Communist activity had spent most of the new government's energies. In almost two years of existence, Kassem's government had been able to accomplish none of its promises. The land reform was in a shambles. Few if any "peasants" had been given their promised farms. Business was bad, and there had been none of the promised gains in workers' wages, housing or other areas of consumer improvement. Kassem's announced new development scheme was merely an echo of Nuri's old one. Nor had any new political force, including Kassem's favored National Democrats, emerged with anything like an organized following or a national program. By the middle of 1960—for all their divisions—the Communists retained theirs.

Two steps forward, one step back. For the Communists' success in Iraq, and their near-triumph in Syria, they paid in Egypt and the Egyptian-Syrian union of the United Arab Republic. Gamal Abdel Nasser, the supreme dictator of Egypt since 1954, has been known to proclaim his own political sense as negative. "We do not act," was a favorite saying. "We react." His most successful international moves in fact have been reactions, like the closing of the Suez Canal and the 1955 arms deal with the Soviets, after the West refused him. But negative or not, his political helmsmanship is clever. From the beginning of his regime Nasser has shown an acute awareness of the dangers implicit in Communism. Kassem had to learn about these dangers the hard way. As a result, Kassem's country is half-Communized. In Nasser's country Communism is not a present threat, politically or socially, *within* the country.

At the beginning of the Army revolution in Egypt it had some support from Communist and pro-Communist groups, but none of it was decisive or even substantial. Only one leader of the young officers' junta which first seized power in 1952 was a Communist, or nearly one: Khaled Mohieddine. Mohieddine, although he continues to be well-connected socially (his brother Zacchariah Mohieddine, is Nasser's powerful and anti-Communist Minister of the Interior) has had his wings clipped. Like a flower that blooms only in certain years, he is unveiled, as a spokesman for the local Partisans of Peace group, only during times of exceptional Egyptian effort to curry favor with Communist countries.

Barring Mohieddine's ineffectual deviation, and the influence of a few other Communist hangers-on, the attitude of the Nasser regime towards local Communists has been consistently tough. The Party is outlawed and carefully watched. Cairo wits have long contended that in every three-man Communist cell, at least one of the members belongs to Zacchariah Mohieddine's police. From the beginning Nasser has attacked Egyptian Communists as a foreign organization. And his charge is given fuel among nationalist Egyptians by the fact that Communism in Egypt, which began in the early 'twenties, has for most of its existence been directed by non-Egyptians. (The party's founder, Henri Curiel, was a Jewish book-seller; he was deported to Italy in 1950.)

Most Egyptian Communists—by 1952 they had split into three

groups—denounced the Nasser officers' revolt, reciprocating the officers' dislike. But as Nasser's policy turned increasingly anti-Western, the local Communists were ordered to turn the other cheek and do what they could, for the higher political glory of the Soviet Union, to help the regime that was persecuting them. The Democratic Movement of National Liberation (HADITU) in particular, did what it could, for a time, to praise Nasser's growing solidarity with the "Socialist camp."

There have been periodic trials of Communists in Egypt since 1953 in a cyclical process known in Egyptian police circles as "mowing." An estimated thousand of them have been put into prison or detention camps at various times—a heavy blow to a party which has never numbered much more than 15,000 members and sympathizers combined. Only in the universities does Communism have any active strength. There Egypt's friendship with the Communist countries has fostered a more than academic interest in Russia, China and others. But the students are more than carefully watched by the ever-present anti-Communist police force.

The anomaly in this situation is that Egypt is heavily dependent on aid and trade from Communist countries. After Nasser's first arms deal with the Soviets, for which he pledged the Egyptian cotton crop for many years in advance, this dependency hugely increased. Where Egypt exported only 14% of its cotton behind the Iron Curtain in 1954, it was sending fully 34% there in 1956. The figures have risen proportionately since then.

The Russians, Chinese, et al. pounded into Cairo with the same zeal they exihibted in their attempted colonization of Syria, although with more circumspection. Soviet advisors, civilian and military, tended to keep apart from both Egyptians and other foreigners in the country—screened by the bonhommie of the local public relations officers in the Soviet embassy, whose outgoing and obliging manners were in sharp contrast to the normal behavior of Soviet diplomats. They kept their scrupulous distance from the starveling local Communists. It several times happened, e.g., at the Bandung conference of 1955 and the later visit of the then

Soviet Foreign Minister Shepilov, that Nasser would be pledging eternal friendship with the "Socialist camp" after having simultaneously launched a new series of trials for his local Reds. Nowhere did Moscow and—to a lesser degree—Peking more conspicuously exhibit the classic Communist disregard for local parties, if their existence seemed to conflict with a temporary objective of the international center.

For three years Nasser continued his honeymoon with the "Socialist camp." His diatribes against the United States and the rest of the "imperialists" caused serious disruption in the politics of Jordan, Saudi Arabia, Lebanon and Iraq. (They certainly did much to pave the way for the Iraqi revolution.) And they neatly fit the Khrushchev objective, which was simply to move into the Middle East, in line with Russian imperial policy of centuries past, and oust the West from its favored positions there. The aid, loans and promises of more continued to arrive from Moscow. It was a measure of Nasser's political intuition that he realized how valuable he was to the U.S.S.R., and what concessions would be made to keep his friendship. It was a sign of his political naïveté that he failed to realize that the broader aims of Soviet policy did not include him, or any independent nationalists.

The Communists' near conquest of Syria alerted Nasser for the first time to the dangers of his position. It says something for his political cat-footedness that he moved quickly once the danger was apparent. In a speech at Port Said in December 1958 he denounced the Communists in Syria for refusing to disband their party. Shortly thereafter he acted. In the largest roundup ever made in Egypt, police arrested a large spectrum of Communists, Communist sympathizers, leftists and wayward intellectuals. A series of trials of some 64 Party members was begun in August. Before this about 750 had been arrested.

Nasser traded angry words with Khrushchev in early 1959 on the subject of the Iraqi Communists—all the angrier since this second Moscow invasion of the Middle East had alerted Nasser to a hitherto quiescent danger. Witness his speech to some army officers in March 1959 at the height of his anti-Communist campaign:

"When the Communist Party at the beginning of the Revolution tried to curry favor with us and to carry out an invasion from within, we refused to hand over this country to the small Communist minority, so as not to give it a chance to disseminate hate and rancor, or to carry out a campaign of terrorism. . . .

"This, brethren, was our policy: to do away with imperialism and to set up a strong nationalist rule in this country together with a strong nationalist army, so as to restore the motherland to its nationalistic and patriotic sons and so as not to let it be dominated by a minority of reactionary or Communist forces whose aim is to encompass it in spheres of influence.

". . . the Syrian Communists fought the union and the U.A.R. It was at that time that I sent a message to the prime minister of the Soviet Union informing him that Soviet diplomats in Syria were fighting the Union. But he replied that the said diplomats were supporting the union.

". . . we were trying to convince ourselves that the Communist parties in our countries were independent from international Communism. We found that they were not independent, and that is why I always call them Communist stooges;

". . . All the Communists who were in Syria had gone to Iraq to engineer conspiracies against the Syrian region and to begin to plan for a Communist crescent."

Although such forthright utterances left little for the Soviet political analysts to puzzle over, Khrushchev continued his policy of trade-and-aid. In January 1960 the Russians promised financial and technical help to construct the long-imagined High Dam at Aswan, the same place where the denial of aid by Dulles had precipitated Nasser's blustery war with the West. Simultaneously, the United States and the other Western allies were reopening the question of their own aid to Egypt. It almost seemed as if Nasser was in that admired political position of the lady with two suitors and a smile satisfactory to each.

In a sense he was. Khrushchev had gained much by Egypt's break with the West, a political coup well worth the economic aid he offered. That in itself was not too substantial, being geared to the Soviet system of barter and bloc buying. (It was not long after the cotton deals with the Communist bloc, the Egyptians found to their sorrow, that Egyptian cotton was being offered to western European countries at a fraction of its normal price—from warehouses in Hungary and East Germany.) And he could wait out the persecution of the local Egyptian Communists without undue twinges of conscience. What Khrushchev saw ahead was an Egypt without Nasser, an Egypt which had learned to depend on the Soviet Union for much, and which in fact would be hard put to sever the relationships formed.

Against this long-range Soviet scheme Nasser had one advantage which Kassem might well envy. Egypt was politically mobilized on the side of the nationalists. There was discontent, but no significant political divisions. And Nasser slogans like "positive neutrality," "the unity of the Arab people" and "standing between East and West" were repeated with the fervor of Koranic verses.

He had also the advantage of the obvious alternative: If the Russians caused trouble, he could reverse current history and call in the Americans and the British. He presumed that they would come, when summoned.

# CHAPTER IV

# THE NEW FRONTIER

"If help comes too late or too little, the masses may repudiate their democratic leading classes and take leap after leap in the dark . . ."

—ALBERTO LLERAS CAMARGO,
President of Colombia

IN May 1959 an international Communist agent named Jose Fortuny was picked up by Brazilian police, charged with entering the country illegally. He was carrying an Argentine passport, made out to one Pedro Armando Carioli, which had been forged in Moscow. He was returning to Latin America after two years spent in Moscow and Peking, accumulating acquaintances and detailed instructions. His luggage contained interesting lists and plans to establish Brazil as a new bridgehead of Communist infiltration in South America. For carrying out this plan, Fortuny's credentials were impeccable. As Secretary General of the Communist Party of Guatemala, he had pulled the strings behind the gradual Communization of that country under President Jacobo Arbenz in the period 1950–1954.

After holding Fortuny briefly, the police were forced by a court order to release him. The court held that Fortuny could not be deported, since he was a legitimate "political refugee," with right to asylum in Brazil.

On its face, as an exercise in heroic tolerance, the action of the Brazilian court was praiseworthy. But it also underlined the basic problem of contrasts that makes Latin America so curiously vulnerable to Communism. On the one hand the Communist parties in Latin America have long histories, devoted bands of followers and a considerable deposit in the bank of hard experience. Some of the Communist leaders—like Gustavo Machado in Venezuela, Luis Carlos Prestes in Brazil, the officially "pro-Communist" Vicente Lombardo Toledano in Mexico, and the ex-Argentine Ernesto "Che" Guevara in Cuba—are among the most able to have appeared in the history of the movement.

Yet for all the veteran character of these parties and their active connection with the Soviet Union and China, their primary purpose as tools in the general Communist mission has been less heeded in Latin America than elsewhere in the world. There are, officially, no more than 230,000 Party members in the total Latin American population of 180 million. They have been able to play such a large part, in relation to these numbers, thanks to the disorganized character of politics and society in most Latin American countries, at a period when they are almost all being shaken by new currents of nationalism, revolutionary thought and the long suppressed stirrings of the poor and economically maladjusted—part of the world-wide "revolution of expectations." Although Latin American societies are vulnerable to Communist methods and appeals, their danger is little recognized. In a word, the Communists are "remote." As a result, it is easy for many Latin Americans to idealize them as, in the case of Fortuny, "political refugees" instead of political saboteurs.

During the 'fifties in Latin America there has been a notable rise in the movement of Communist parties and their front organizations—here as elsewhere often more important than the parties themselves. This movement has capitalized on local trends or happenings like the Castro revolution in Cuba. But originally its action was artificial, generated by Moscow and, recently, Peking. The new effort in Latin American countries was not visible until after the death of Stalin. Although it began under the post-Stalin collective leadership, it fits in well with Khrushchev's own ideas on Communist expansion, and he has energetically furthered it.

Two handy barometers of Communist activity can chart the rise. In 1954 trade between the Soviet bloc and Latin America suddenly shot up to three times what it had been the year before. It has kept to the higher level ever since. Beginning in 1955, also, there has been an unprecedented series of "incidents" involving Soviet diplomatic or undercover personnel. (See Chapter X.) Soviet emissaries have been implicated in strikes, labor disturbances and riots from Buenos Aires to Mexico City—and not least among them the well-staged anti-Nixon demonstrations in Caracas in 1958. Such activities, and the more skillful ones which do not break to the surface, are part of the new concentration on Latin America by the espionage and subversion apparatus of international Soviet intelligence. It was ordered, as we know from Soviet refugees, by Alexander Panyushkin, then head of the Foreign Intelligence Directorate of the Soviet State Security (K.G.B.), in a meeting with his chief assistants in Moscow in 1953.

Why this sudden interest? The answer lies in the new posture of the Khrushchev Communists. Fought to a stalemate in Europe, embarrassed in Asia by the too obviously aggressive instincts of Red China, well occupied in the Middle East, the Soviet Union has grown enough in resources and experience to try an adventure somewhere else. No longer fearful of their encirclement by the democracies, the Russians are genuinely confident at this moment in history that *they* are the encircling ones. Hence the new interest in areas which once seemed to Moscow remote and unpromising.

To this add the overriding motives of Khrushchev's continual war of "competitive coexistence" on the United States. Angered by the passive but persistent American refusal to recognize the Soviet Union's hegemony over its eastern European satellites, Khrushchev saw the chance to open a real offensive against the Latin American countries, situated in the corresponding back yard of the United States. When you are on the offensive, you move into the enemy's territory as much as possible. A good show of force there has propaganda value in itself.

In November 1957—four years after Panyushkin started his subversion campaign from Moscow—the leaders of the Soviet

Communist Party were ready to communicate their new interests to the loyal noncommissioned officers from Latin America. At a special regional meeting for Latin American delegates, Mikhail A. Sivolobov, acting for the Party Central Committee, outlined the new mission and made promises of increased support. Trading on the invigorated nationalism in many of their countries, local leaders were instructed to stress the Soviet "peace" campaigns and the contrasting warmongering of U. S. "imperialists." They were also to generate support among non-Communists for what Sivolobov called the new "diplomatic" approach.

Most importantly, they were let off the leash as far as the need for stressing strict Marxist doctrine was concerned. As we have seen, Khrushchev himself has never been one to sacrifice a strong Party for stuffy principles. The Latin American leaders confirmed the line at a secret conference among themselves in Cuernavaca, Mexico, in March 1958. And it has since blossomed into a new "policy of flexibility."

Take the recent statement of Luis Carlos Prestes, in Brazil: "We must ally now with the bourgeois and all patriots in the national struggle against Yankee imperialism. Our primary goal is economic emancipation from the foreign trusts. The proletarian revolution can come later." Or, as Venezuela's Gustavo Machado put it: "The goal is state ownership of the means of production. We will not achieve it today, or tomorrow, but when conditions permit. The time can be long or short, depending on events of history. Today we have our immediate tasks. Once we were merely agitators. Today we have responsibility. Some day we will have power."

It is hazardous to generalize upon a "Latin American" situation. Countries are individuals and nowhere more so than in this hemisphere. Between the poles of "European" Argentina and "Indian" Ecuador, there are wide differences in political and social geography. Yet a few Latin American generalizations can be made, which explain Communism's potential in the whole region. They are:

1) *New nationalisms.* The last fifteen years have brought a rush of nationalism to the surface in many of these countries. Dictatorships have toppled. Large masses of people have for the first time in their history been given a sense of real participation in their own governments—an explosive as well as encouraging phenomenon.

2) *The Yanqui complex.* Historically, plucking Uncle Sam's beard is as popular an occupation south of the Rio Grande as twisting the lion's tail used to be with politicians in British colonies. Although relations between the United States and some countries, Mexico for instance, have vastly improved over former times, the memory of American economic exploitation is easily revived. (In some countries, its evidences remain all too clear.) Paradoxically, the same Latin American editors and politicians who blame the North Americans for too much interference, blame them for neglect. They point out, often soundly, that the United States, obsessed by apparently more immediate political problems in Europe and Asia, has ignored Latin America in its aid and development programs. But whatever the causes or justice of the complaints, to be anti-Yanqui is almost always a popular political posture. Conversely, any U.S. pressure on one Latin American country, even such a bad actor as Castro's Cuba, is bound to arouse a certain "family" resentment among the others.

3) *Coalition governments.* In Latin America the splinter party and the coalition cabinet are staples of the political diet. A small Communist Party, therefore, or a Communist "front" party, can often exact a heavy price for swinging its vote to a hard-pressed coalition candidate. This sort of thing has happened, in recent times, in Brazil, Argentina and Chile. At different times, also, the Communists have allied themselves with local dictators—Peron, Batista and Trujillo among them—in similar marriages of convenience.

4) *The intellectual appeal.* In few areas of the earth's surface is the intellectual so canonized as in Latin America. An intelligentsia, recognized as such with more than European deference, is sharply distinguished from the rest of the populace by reason of

its learning and interests. It is traditionally over-educated and underemployed and conditioned to rebel. Even artists are supposed to have political opinions, the wisdom of which is generally in inverse proportion to the quality of their art.

This Latin American intelligentsia, with its weakness for "causes" and doctrinaire solutions of problems, has proved fertile soil for Communism. It is significant that the areas of Communism's greatest spread have been among university students and faculties, journalists and other people engaged in the business of ideas. Even much of what labor support the Communists have they secured through the intellectuals who so often dominate the unions. And, like the progress of a vicious circle, the names of intellectuals or artists in the movement attract others, and confer a kind of immunity against Communism's seamier associations. The poet Pablo Neruda in Chile and the architect Oskar Niemayer in Brazil have made converts by the very fact of their existence. In Mexico, a country with a tough, built-in resistance to Soviet Communism, an artist like David Alfaro Siqueiros was able to direct a flagrant assassination attempt (on Leon Trotsky, as it happened) and escape unpunished purely because of his cultural prestige.

5) *The discontented.* The bulk of the Latin American populations remain ill-housed, ill-fed, ill-educated. Their anger at the inequities of life around them is potentially explosive, and understandably apt to lack discrimination when it does explode. For a century mass discontent was used periodically by lone dictators or the familiar military *juntas* to seize and hold power. Now, with most of the dictators gone, this discontent is easily capable of being canalized by the Communists and their various "allies."

The evolution of the Communist movement in Latin American countries has been sporadic. Its pace is a cautious creep that can, and has, in various countries, broken into a sudden galloping rush. And most importantly, it even seems difficult to isolate what is Communist "proper" and what is merely a "front" used by the Communists. Is the League for the Rights of Man completely Communist? Are the unexceptionably named Fighters Against Famine in Brazil a Communist organization? Were there non-Communists as well as Party members implicated in the 1959 conference of Latin American Women in Santiago? The effort to assess the precise degree of Communist participation in such things is of only scholarly interest. Practically speaking, the purpose served by the fronts is the same as that of the Party itself.

To illuminate the Communist progress, we might consider its background and current situation in six different countries: Brazil, Chile, Argentina, Venezuela, Mexico and Cuba. Four of them have had serious political and social upheavals within the last ten years. A fifth, Chile, has often seemed to hang on the verge of similar crisis. Only one, Mexico, has kept up a stable, steady tradition of government and development through this period. Even there trouble-makers have been active.

There is one other common denominator. In the majority of our examples, the Communist cause has prospered through the devotion of some dramatically capable and single-minded men.

At this moment in history Luis Carlos Prestes, the Secretary General and acknowledged boss of the Communist Party in Brazil, is living high on the hog, politically speaking. His Party is officially outlawed, but through infiltrating other parties, it influences far more members in the Brazilian Congress than it did during its life as a legal organism. In 1958 the long-standing order for his own arrest was quashed. The program of fronts and "alliances" with other "progressive" groups is working splendidly. Prestes himself was able to take sufficient time off from his work at home to journey to Moscow and confer with Nikita Khrushchev. Before returning to Brazil at the end of 1959, he made a further visit to Peking, and attended tenth anniversary ceremonies for the founding of the People's Republic of China.

Now in his early sixties, he has been a member of the Communist Party since 1937; but he was a revolutionary of sorts long before that time. In 1924 as a young captain of army engineers, Prestes led his battalion out of its barracks to join a rebel uprising in Iguaçu. For the next four years he led a fugitive rebel column through the ill-charted back roads of Brazil's western states, before finally fleeing to Bolivia. It was there that he began to study Marx. When he came back to Brazil in 1935 he took charge of his first front group, the Communist-backed *Alianca Nacional Libertadora,* but this "front" career was short-lived. The same year a Soviet agent named Harry Berger engineered a four-day Communist revolt in Natal, Recife and Rio de Janeiro, in which most loyal Party members took part. Prestes was arrested after the revolt's failure and spent the next ten years in jail under the Vargas regime.

He was released in the amnesty of April 18, 1945, and the following December was elected to the Brazilian senate. He and his party turned "legal" with a vengeance. Reacting sharply against the dictatorial Vargas government—and doubtless stimulated by the euphoria of the wartime Soviet alliance, 596,000 Brazilian voters that year voted for the Communist Presidential candidate. Besides Prestes, 16 Communist deputies were elected to the lower house.

As frequently happens, the Communists exploited this advantage too quickly. In 1947, after a series of provocations, the Supreme Electoral Court outlawed the Party as "contrary to the democratic form of government." The government later issued an order for Prestes' arrest, on charges of signing a "subversive manifesto." Wisely, the police never looked very hard for him, on the theory that a fugitive Prestes was less dangerous than a "martyr" reposing inside prison walls. And Party strength continued to make itself felt through endorsements of non-Communist candidates. President Juscelino Kubitschek's margin of victory in the 1955 elections was given to him by Communist supporters, although Kubitschek himself made no deals with Prestes or any of his friends.

The next year, however, the whole edifice of Brazilian Communism was shaken to its foundations by news of the events in Hungary. In the course of a few months, the Communists lost more than half of their friends. One of the principal defectors was

Agildo Barata, an old friend of Prestes who like him had started out as an army officer. Barata was the bag-man of the Party, in charge of dunning contributions out of rich sympathizers and various industrial concerns—who gladly paid it as the price of labor peace with the Communist-run unions in their plants. When he left he took his fund-raising lists with him. As a result, most of the Communist press, among other things, collapsed overnight. Denounced not only as a Communist (by the center and the right) but as a Stalinist (by the left) Prestes seemed to have lost his battle.

Yet in the last two years the tide has been reversed. Party movements are flourishing, capitalizing on discontent and some real financial hardship, among the middle class as well as the hungry, angry farmers of the northeast. But they are not flourishing as "Party" movements. In a volte-face as sweeping as anything seen in the hemisphere, Prestes, the conductor of Communist purges, has transformed himself once more into a reasonable collaborator in nationalist popular fronts. Any popular front that comes along will do.

In March 1958, just before Prestes' arrest order was cancelled, his Party paper published a "political declaration of the Brazilian Communist Party." This document is as succinct an example as one could find of the Khrushchev pattern as interpreted by local communists.

Capitalist development, the manifesto conceded, is going ahead rapidly in Brazil; but it has not "succeeded in eliminating negative factors characterizing Brazil as an under-developed nation." Huge areas continue to depend on North American imperialism. The Brazilian state itself represents the interests of large landowners and capitalists linked to the United States. The Kubitschek government, not wholly bad, was nonetheless a fragile compromise between conservative and "progressive" groups.

But, says Prestes, the proletariat's strength is gaining. "Despite interruptions, the democratic process is a permanent tendency.

This explains why nationalist and democratic (i.e., Communist) forces have supported the Constitution in opposition to the pro-imperialists.

"The Brazilian revolution is no longer socialist, but anti-imperialist, anti-feudal, national and democratic. Hence, the principal target of nationalist, progressive and democratic groups is North American imperialism and the imperialist lackeys . . . proletariat and the middle class are united in the common objective of fighting for independent, progressive development against North American imperialism . . ." Thus Prestes called for radical changes inside his Party, with a view of controlling the government from within, rather than opposing it from without. This program has proved immensely successful. After twenty-four months, working through various "pro-nationalist" alliances, it has elevated the influence of Brazil's 33,000 card-carrying Communists far beyond their expectations. Although the memory of Hungary might have inhibited formal recruitments in the Party, for front organizations it has not seemed to matter.

The major targets of Prestes' new get-acquainted plan are the familiar trio: labor, students and the intelligentsia. There is one added walk of life not normally subject to Communist colonization in Latin American countries: the army. In labor, the Communists have concentrated on regional pockets, notably the Sao Paolo area, to build up their hold on the entire union movement. The *Pacto de Unibade Inter-syndical* in Sao Paolo, largely controlled by Communists, claims to represent over a million workers in various industries there. Two avowed Communists and a veteran Communist collaborator, former Deputy Frota Modiera, are on its board of directors. In September 1957 the Pact brought off a general strike in Sao Paolo which paralyzed industry there for eighteen days.

Other Communist-infiltrated unions—this time in Rio—are the National Maritime Union, the Printers' Union and the National Confederation of Industrial Workers. The last named, whose vice president is a veteran Communist fronter, Ari Campiata, may soon be dropped from the International Confederation of Free Trade Unions for its growing pro-Communist political activity.

The tactics of the labor groups are in the tradition. The Party men find little trouble taking over a union. As the Party's own Office for Economic Studies noted, "Superior Communist discipline is a bulwark which demoralizes non-Communist union directors and government finks (*pelegos*) alike."

Once inside the union, they are quick to divert it to political purposes, often showing a sense of publicity that would do credit to an "imperialist" press agent. Take the recent "bean scandal" in Rio. Stevedores of the leftist Dockworkers' Union "accidentally" spilled open defective samples from a shipment of beans arriving from the United States. Their friends loudly exhibited photos in the press. Shouted Leftist Deputy Benjamin Farah: "These beans are unfit for pigs. It's an American insult to the hungry people of Brazil."

In point of fact, the dockworkers had broken open exactly eight sacks before they "spilled" them and filled them with sweepings from the docks. (Incautiously, they had included a great many castor beans, which are grown in Brazil and could not possibly have come from the United States.)

Nor is Prestes' attention confined to industrial labor. The revived Rural Leagues, first founded on orders from the Party Central Committee in 1948, have been spreading rapidly throughout the northeast, where discontent runs high among sharecroppers and sugar plantation workers. Although the rank and file is hardly Communist, "those at the head of the leagues," as Socialist party president Carlos Luis de Andrade admitted recently, "are Communists." Speaking of the rank-and-file workers, he continued: "These men are entirely unprotected and live in the worst possible conditions. They are easy prey for self-proclaimed Messiahs."

Disturbances in the Pernambuco area have been multiplying— and the leagues have already spread to the agricultural regions around Sao Paolo. Their leader is a deputy named Francisco Juliao, nominally a "Socialist," but a confirmed Communist fellow-traveler. Thus far his agitation has led to repeated invasions of property and a number of killings. The extremes of violence naturally favor even tighter Communist control.

Among Brazil's students the Communists have been even more spectacularly successful. For the last four years a pro-Communist slate has been regularly elected to the directorate of the National Students' Union (U.N.E.), which claims to represent all of Brazil's 130,000 university students. Following the general line, the Students' Union rarely mentions Communism or the Soviet Union, but concentrates on the problems of "nationalism" and "imperialism." Among the recent programs backed by the Union were: expropriation of foreign packing houses, prohibition of Brazilian deposits in foreign banks, passage of laws controlling foreign capital. The Union denounced an agreement between Brazil and Bolivia allowing Brazilian companies to explore for Bolivian oil. Their success might have led people to question the wisdom of Petrobras, the government oil monopoly in Brazil.

Curiously enough, the Students' Union is supported by official government funds, as are its cultural activities. A good deal of the money (for which no accounting is made) is lavished on anti-"imperialist" campaigns and regular liaison is kept up not merely with the Party in Brazil, but with Party headquarters overseas. When Oscar Pellucio, for example, the commander of the Communist cadre "shock troops" among the students, was planning the sanguinary 1956 streetcar riots, he was assisted by two foreign specialists from the International Students' Union, presumably dispatched from Prague for that purpose.

Probably the outstanding Communist success in Brazilian education—not to say government circles—has been the colonization of Brazil's most important graduate school, the Instituto Superior de Estudos Brasileiros. I.S.E.B. is supported by congressional grants and contributions from industry and business. It does a great deal of government economic research and maintains direct contact with many government ministries. Avowedly "nationalist" in mood, the school is heavy with Communists. Nine professors on the staff have been found to keep up Communist affiliations, among them the editor of the official Communist theoretical journal *Estudos Socias*. Their presence is all the more alarming considering the nature of the student body: graduate students, young officers, union leaders, etc.—picked both for scholarly inclinations and their capability for becoming future national leaders.

In the army, finally, the Communizing tendency is also apparent. Officers who helped Barata and Prestes during the 1935 revolution are still prominent on the active list. One lieutenant colonel recently wrote a monograph defending the Communist invasion of Korea. Extremely "nationalist" officers find the Communist line congenial. Soviet and Chinese Communist literature circulates widely.

Linking these outposts of Communist strength together and threading their way through most of Brazil's intellectual circles are the usual front organizations, made more important by the Party's desire for middle-class cooperation. There are branches of the old stand-bys: World Council of Physicians (of which a Brazilian, Dr. Josue de Castro, is President); World Peace Council; Partisans for Peace; International Association of Democratic Lawyers; International Democratic Women's Federation, etc. On a local level the Commission against Famine has been effective in blaming Brazilian economic shortcomings on the United States.

All such efforts, and the continuing infiltration of parliamentary groups, are part of Prestes' new Khrushchevian policy of moderation. The Communists, he has said, no longer seek even radical land reform. He calls for a united front that will include "even landowners." At the moment the actual strength of his front does not pose a direct danger to the country. But Brazil's own position in the world is precarious, thanks to the combined drainage of inflation, the government's ambitious building projects, retarded land reform, and an economy which remains sadly tied to the coffee crop. Against the day when economic stress may bring political crisis, Captain Prestes and his loyal troops are ready.

In Chile the Communists have gone Prestes and his Brazilians one better. Not only do they have a flourishing popular front movement, but they have succeeded in combining with an extraordinarily naïve Socialist party to form a parliamentary Popular Front. This party is no splinter group. The Frente de Acción Popular represents about one-third of the voting electorate of the country. Although the Communists are the weaker of the two major parties in it, their small number of seats in parliament is partly due to the relatively recent lifting of the ban against their legal Communist Party—they have not had time to contest too many districts. But, as usual, numerical inferiority is heavily outweighed by cohesiveness and political skill. As a rule the F.R.A.P. pays compliments to Socialism, but does what Communism wants it to do.

Such popular fronts are not unusual in Chile, nor is the Communist Party itself. In many ways it has deeper roots in Chile than any of the Latin American countries. It was not for nothing Lenin predicted that Chile would be the first Latin American country to go Communist. Communism in Chile was born in a logical cradle, the nitrate desert where Luis Recabarren founded his *Partido Socialista Obrero* during the first World War. The miners, poor, oppressed and discontented, represented the closest thing to an industrial proletariat in the Latin America of that day. Recabarren, a printer, founded the Party's first paper, *El Despertar,* and brought it into the Third International at a congress in 1920.

From that day on, Communism has retained a strong foothold among the copper, nitrate and coal miners—even though the evil conditions which spawned it have largely disappeared. Another place where the Party domiciled itself was on the pitiless plains of Patagonia and Punta Arenas, among the shepherds who tend the vast flocks of the wool companies. There was a Communist uprising there as early as 1922, and pockets of sympathizers have remained to this day.

In the 'thirties, however, the Communists turned to the popular front idea, then in vogue, and began their apostolate among the country's intellectuals. It was the Communist-inspired Popular Front of 1938 which put Pedro Aquirre Cerda in power the following year—the first left-wing government in Chilean history. Ten years later the Communists secured the election of President Gonsalez Videla. In a monumental bit of vote-switching the Party's 50,000 votes were put in Videla's column, thus breaking a deadlocked election in which he had received the highest number of votes, but not a constitutional majority. Grateful for their support, Videla invited three Communists into his cabinet. This was the first time in Latin American history that avowed Party members have held cabinet rank.

Later in the year Gonsalez Videla turned against his new allies. The Defense of Democracy law which followed—the Communists still call it the "cursed law" (*ley maldita*)—deprived the Party of all its representation and ended its legal existence. Yet when the Party was restored to legal status in 1958 its members were readily admitted into "respectable" parliamentary circles.

In constructing a Communist-Socialist alliance things do not always, of course, go the Communists' way. In the December 1959 conference of the Labor Confederation, the Central Unica de Trabajadores, the Communists and Socialists had a violent falling out. The Communists wanted the C.U.T. to affiliate with their old front group, the Latin American Labor Confederation, run by that veteran wheel horse of the front movements, the Mexican Vincente Lombardo Toledano. The Socialists joined with the Communists in rejecting membership in the Inter-American Regional Labor Office (O.R.I.T.) because they regarded it as pro-United States. But they had their way in steering the Congress towards a new "third force" labor movement as yet only in the making. This was in line with the hopes of Salvador Alende, the Socialist who is titular head of the coalition, of fashioning a neutralist position, taking Tito, Nasser and the world's other militant "third-forcers" as his model.

The Communists could wait. They have been steadily winning in their behind-the-scenes struggle with the Socialists for control of individual unions.

How did the Communists slip back so easily into the political life of the country? Mainly because, partly as a legacy of their Popular Front days, they have preserved in Chile a reputation for intellectual interest that has for the most part survived the far-off shocks of Hungary and the Stalinist revelations. The poet Pablo Neruda (his real name is Neftali Reyes Agrella) is one of the best known in Latin America. A winner of a past Stalin prize, he is honored among non-Communists as well as the faithful. His poetry is *The Grapes of Wrath* writ large or, to be more classic about it, Hesiod after Marxist-Leninist indoctrination—full of the stark fate of the down-trodden proletariat toiling in the copper or nitrate mine of the heartless company (American-owned, usually) or the wretched peasant sweating out his life in the rich landowner's fields. Like Portinari and Niemeyer in Brazil and Picasso (when he would allow it) in France, Neruda is dragged into every local Communist movement possible, as warrant of the Party's intellectual respectability.

An equally good warrant, and even more communicative, is the Party daily, *El Siglo,* by all odds the best Communist newspaper in Latin America. While its circulation is thought to be little over 20,000, it is read by numbers of non-Communist or anti-Communist intellectuals and businessmen, apart from Party members. Its political news is excellent and often news that is unobtainable in the other papers. As a Chilean newspaperman noted," *"El Siglo* is 95% highly accurate news. The catch, naturally, is to find out which part of an item you are reading represents the remaining 5% of propaganda or plain and simple lying."

Finally, both China and the Soviet Union have lately had much success in promoting low-cost tours for Chileans. Although the prime targets are fellow-travelers, right-wing and even anti-Communist leaders are often invited to see one or both of the Red Paradises first hand. The tours are either on an "expense paid" basis or at very economical rates. The tourists, when they arrive, are suitably chaperoned.

Quite a few Chileans are taking these cut-rate trips, not including the growing numbers of engineers, medical men and other professionals who are invited to visit Moscow or Peking as delegates to the multitudinous Congresses of the "Socialist camp." Although they hardly become Communist converts en route, they do return with the principal reaction which Khrushchev desires: the favorable image. They see large, powerful and apparently peaceful countries, vocally interested in trade and loudly protesting their desire for disarmament and various types of brotherly love. It makes an impression. So do the Artkino films now pouring in for showing in Chilean theatres. So do the Red Chinese entertainers sent to tour the country gratis—another present from the "Socialist camp." The good feelings thus raised rub off, to a greater or less degree, on the local Communists.

There is another reason, an economic one, that helps fill out the favorable image. Chile's big imports of copper and nitrate have traditionally been dependent on the U.S. market. Because of the U.S. ban on the export of strategic materials to the Soviet Union, the Iron Curtain market is barred. One of the most successful tasks of the Communists inside Chile has been to suggest to local businessmen that, if this barrier could only be raised, Iron Curtain trade in mineral items would bring a wave of unprecedented prosperity. Occasional exports to the U.S.S.R., arranged through third parties, e.g., a $10,000,000 deal in non-strategic copper wire in 1959, are given heavy publicity in the Communist and leftist press.

In 1960 an unofficial delegation of Chilean businessmen and politicians went to Moscow to open informal trade talks. They found, not surprisingly, that the Soviet Union was interested in obtaining copper (a metal in which the "Socialist camp" is generally deficient) and prepared, on paper at least, to send almost anything in return. Shown a list of the commodities which Chile normally imports, the Soviet government traders announced that Moscow could supply every single item, down to passenger cars.

This news was reported, with suitable flourishes, in the country's left-wing press.

In sum we find in Chile a country where Communism has been injected into the parliamentary blood stream. If the normal international front movements do not command such wide attention among Chileans as they do elsewhere on the continent, penetration into intellectual, political and labor circles is far greater.

To a certain extent, it is true, their very familiarity with Communist movements has built up more intelligent resistance in Chile than elsewhere. (The Catholic Church, for example, although generally lax in social work in other Latin American countries, has in the last ten years sponsored a heartening program of land reform, on its own, in Chile.) Nor do Chileans have to look far to find examples of Communist disillusionment. The very founder of the Chilean Party, Luis Recabarren, went off in 1924 on the traditional pilgrimage to Moscow. When he came back to Chile, he kept a strange silence. After months of brooding reflection on what he had seen, he made the silence permanent. With an automatic purchased on his trip, he pumped five bullets into his heart.

In Chile and Brazil the Communists may have forged successful alliances with local Socialists or extreme nationalists. In Argentina they have taken a step beyond this. There the Communists have long had a working agreement with fascism. There is nothing unusual about such a situation—the Soviet Union, after all, once maintained fraternal relations with Hitler's Germany. But in the light of the current situation in Latin America, when one comes automatically to associate "leftist" or "Communist" at least with anti-dictator, it is worth remembering that Communists have as often as not found it more useful to throw in with the local generalissimo than to oppose him. This was so for a considerable time in Batista's Cuba, in Trujillo's Dominican Republic and, notably, in Peron's Argentina.

In January 1959, while Communist leaders elsewhere in the hemisphere were busy denouncing "fascism," Communist and

Peronista unions, working through an organization called the
United Workers' Movement, literally paralyzed Argentina in a ruthless general strike, while the newly elected President, Arturo Frondizi was on a visit to the United States. On April 9, the combined
groups struck again. The occasion, handily thought up by the Communists, was the raising of rates by a Swiss-owned power company.
With the usual cries of "foreign imperialists" and "bloodsucking
of the proletariat," the organizers went into action. Hundreds of
militant Communists and Peronistas rampaged through the streets
of Buenos Aires. They looted stores, smashed cars and buses.
Shots were fired. For a matter of hours, before the police brought
them under control, they managed to stage a pocket-sized reign of
terror in the capital.

The result was that President Frondizi, himself a liberal, was
forced to declare a state of siege. On September 2, 1959, he called
for state attorneys throughout the country to seek legal abolition
of the Communist Party.

The march of the Communist Party into the Peron alliance was
only the culmination of the usual policy of alliances for expediency.
In the 1945 elections, Communists joined the Conservatives and
the Liberals in an anti-Peron coalition. But after Peron was elected,
the Communists made a sort of informal non-aggression pact, at
least until 1950. Peron persecuted the local party from time to time
thereafter. But, in a manner analagous to Nasser's, he served the
interests of the cause so well with his anti-American policy that
once again, "turn the other cheek" became an approved tactic.*

After Peron was overthrown in 1955, the Communists hoped
to fill *El Lider's* shoes. But their efforts to take over the Peronista
trade unions were only partly successful. Typically, they then made
common cause with the Peronistas against the successor governments. In 1957, when six of Peron's former lieutenants fled from
Argentina, they were sheltered by the Communist Party in Chile.

* One of the famous Peron edicts, part of his 1949 Constitution, was
the classic "There shall be no freedom to attack liberty." This was con-
strued as anti-Communist.

(Only one of them, Guillermo Kelly, former head of Peron's police militia, was denied this asylum because he had in his day persecuted Communists with overmuch rigor.) Having supported Frondizi, along with the Peronistas, in his electoral campaign, the Communists turned against him when it became very evident that he was no leftist stooge.

The rioting they provoked in Buenos Aires in 1959 did not particularly help the Party's reputation in the country. Worse still was the succession of Soviet spy incidents and the discovery at the end of 1958 of a school of Communist subversion, for candidates all over Latin America. The electorate in Argentina, more sophisticated politically than in other Latin American countries, has long been aware of Communism's unpleasant international associations. This awareness the incidents only served to confirm.

Most of the normal front organizations are scantily supported in Argentina, droning along with the same names, generally, on different letterheads, but there are two important exceptions to the public indifference on this score. The first reflects public concern over the American A-bomb tests, notably Operation Argonaut, the nuclear testing in the South Atlantic in September 1958. It has been quite easy to whip up popular denunciations of Washington for its policies with regard to nuclear weapons and tests.

The second involves housewives. Curiously, the most successful front activity in all Argentina is the innocently-named Argentine Women's Union. Founded in 1947 as a sort of Ladies' Auxiliary to the Party, it met with steady success in its recruiting efforts through the years, picking up militant non-Communist feminists with the ease of a smooth-running vacuum cleaner. In 1958, when President Frondizi started Argentina's long-needed, but admittedly painful, austerity campaign to rationalize the economy, the Women's Union really hit its stride. With Argentine housewives feeling the pinch of a suddenly doubled cost of living, the Communist ladies suddenly found wide popular support for their anti-government programs. As they proved time and again, a sprinkling of efficient militants from the Women's Union can raise a howling mob of housewives, brandishing their shopping baskets in front of government offices, as fast as the Peronistas used to turn out their unionists. The Women's Union is a meeting place of strange bedfellows. Its Communist control is comparable, in American terms, to a crooked political machine taking over the combined forces of the League of Women Voters and the Women's Christian Temperance Union. But it can have a powerful effect. Women's Union delegates make the circuit of international Communist "front" congresses with unfailing regularity. At home they continue to direct a stream of telegrams to congressmen, with the advocacy of various Communist causes neatly sandwiched in between protests about the rising cost of bread and meat. Typically, some of its most zealous Communist proprietors are themselves too rich ever to be honestly bothered by rising living costs. Mathilde Aleman, for example, editor of the Union's monthly magazine *Nuestras Mujeres* is the owner of enormous estates in the Chaco province.

The Argentine Communists joined forces with the exiled dictator, Peron, after having been denied a chance to infiltrate the revolution of 1955. In Venezuela, where the five-year-old dictatorship of Marcos Pérez Jiménez was toppled in 1957, they were alert enough to be in on the kill. It is only due to the comparable alertness of President Rómulo Betancourt that they have not swallowed up more of the revolution's gains. Betancourt's success is all the more admirable in view of the fact that the Venezuelan Communists, unlike those in Argentina, are favored with distinguished leadership.

Film fans fond of type-casting would nominate Gustavo Machado as the Adolphe Menjou of Latin American Communism. Now in his early sixties, Machado has lived the life of a dedicated—and persecuted—Communist with the distinctive overtones of wealth, good birth and breeding to relieve his sufferings. Few secretaries of Communist parties anywhere have access to so many drawing rooms in polite society. Machado, now that his party is legal, lives openly and quite handsomely in an $80,000 town house in the

Altamira section of Caracas. He is generally accessible to foreign correspondents and other visitors—the type of approachable Communist equally well exemplified by his contemporaries on other continents, Palmiro Togliatti in Italy and Sanzo Nozaka in Japan. He uses the soft-sell approach in discussing Communism and, as his statements suggest, has long ago learned the virtue of patience. Even now, with his party commanding far more influence than it has ever before in its history, Machado prefers to speak softly, but firmly, about the future.

His biography is in great measure the history of Communism in Venezuela—which as in Brazil and most Latin American countries, was imported and nurtured there by a small group of determined, patient men. In 1920, two years after he began his studies at the Central University of Venezuela, Machado was expelled for his advanced political views by the dictatorship of Juan Vincente Gómez. He then went overseas to Paris for the formal part of his education, a doctorate in political and social sciences at the Sorbonne and the more important ideological portion, the study of Communist theory with such past masters as the veteran French Party leader, Maurice Thorez. In 1922 he went to Moscow for a year's further training and thereafter returned to Paris. He did not return to Venezuela, barring brief visits, until 1936, when he arrived as Secretary General of the fugitive local Communist Party. It was only three years after the Party's founding.

Needless to say the Communists were repressed—along with other Venezuelans—during the twenty-seven-year-long Gómez dictatorship; and they fared little better under Pérez Jiménez. Yet persecution gave them a kind of glamour and the sort of nationalist cachet that they could not normally have purchased. In the 1957 revolution their success at making noise was more impressive than their actual work in overturning the P.J. dictatorship—a charge which cannot infrequently be made against the Party. In the election of December 7, 1958 they polled a total of 150,000 votes. But their candidate, Rear Admiral Wolfgang Larrazabal, one of the revolutionary junta (and a non-Communist himself), came in second to Betancourt.

Before the election Machado had predicted that none of the candidates (Larrazabal included) would try to seek Communist cooperation—and he was correct. It would be in any case difficult, he conceded with his usual charm, to have even one Communist minister in the government, due to the need for relations with the United States. But he pledged his party to defense of Venezuelan "democracy" come what may. He asked only that "independent" men be appointed to the ministries (so traditionally beloved by Communists) of education, labor and the interior.

As things worked out, the three ministers in the Betancourt cabinet proved to be no friends of the Communists, although not particularly strongly anti-Communist in their views. They could legitimately be regarded as "independent." But Machado's Communists, whose numbers have tripled in the last thirteen years, speedily proved how scant was *their* devotion to the national independence. At the beginning of the revolution they were honored collaborators. Larrazabal himself had said that Venezuelan Communists were "different." But before the end of Betancourt's first year in office they had shown themselves in quite a different light.

The most obvious surfacing of Communist agitation was the riot surrounding Vice President Nixon's visit to Caracas in 1959. Well-organized by Party-controlled student and union groups, it was in a sense an international prototype of similar demonstrations which occurred later in Japan.

But such agitation of the streets was secondary to the major injection of Party members and fellow-travelers into three key areas of Venezuelan life: journalism, radio and the universities. With rare exceptions, Communists occupy high positions in Venezuelan newspapers. In the most recent Venezuelan university elections 33% of the students voted Communist. Six out of seven professors in the School of Journalism at the University of Caracas are probably fellow-travelers. The entire Venezuelan Association of Journalists is Communist-tainted. A Communist, Servando Garcia Ponce, serves as its Secretary General. Another Communist, Eleazar Dias, presides over the Caracas chapter. The Press Union is also under Communist control.

As with other of the Latin American Party groups, the Communists in Venezuela are strong for land reform and justice for the workers, against "imperialism" and, of course, the United States. They have the disadvantage of attempting to undermine a demonstrably democratic government, energetic as well as good-intentioned, which is itself sponsoring land reform and a large program of social and economic welfare. All the Communists can do is demand that everything be speeded up—or suggest that they could do it better. Nor do they yet have any strong popular foothold among the masses, as for example, Prestes does in parts of Brazil. They remain a party of the intelligentsia.

But Machado and his Party retain the priceless advantage of having identified themselves with a revolutionary cause. And they can note gratifying signs of growth. Their new Ezequiel Zamora Institute in Caracas, acknowledging itself to be the "university of Marxism in Venezuela," has been unable to accommodate all the students and white-collar workers clamoring for admission to its day and evening classes. There are new ties with the Communist-run International Organization of Journalists—and a heightened traffic in visiting "delegates" from the Socialist camp.

For all his apparent softness, Machado is playing a ruthless game. The Caracas riots over the Nixon trip gave only a sample of his Party's potential. He has been ruthless enough thus far to justify this comment of President Betancourt—hardly a rightist himself— in his inaugural speech: "The Communist political philosophy does not agree with the democratic structure of the Venezuelan state, nor does the judgment of that party with respect to the international policy which Venezuela ought to follow coincide with the country's best interests."

It was a quiet comment, but an encouraging one from the head of a still-revolutionary government. Communists, it must be remembered, capture revolutions more often than they start them. In the next chapter, comparing the cases of Cuba and Mexico, we shall see the contrast between a new revolution threatened by Communists and an old one which shook them off.

# CHAPTER V

# TWO REVOLUTIONS
# VERY FAR APART

"Why is it considered that the only democratic governments are those elected by votes?"

—FIDEL CASTRO

IN late 1959 the Mexican painter and long-time Communist
leader, David Alfaro Siqueiros, visited Fidel Castro's Cuba, on
the sort of worshipful pilgrimage that has become *de rigueur* for
the Party faithful in Latin America. Issuing a statement on his
return to Mexico, he exclaimed over Fidel's progress, noting how
far the Cuban revolution was ahead of the Mexican. His comparison was not surprising, considering its source. For the "revolution"
of Fidel Castro in Cuba represents the most promising development
for Communism in Latin America since the Arevalho and Arbenz
governments instituted their abortive imitation of a Soviet satellite
in the early 'fifties. On the other hand, the Mexican Revolution
and its achievements—like the later Betancourt government in
Venezuela—represent one of Communism's toughest and sorest
stumbling blocks.

The true comparison between the Cuba of Fidel Castro and the
Mexico of President Adolfo Lopez Mateos is politically illuminat-
ing, because it throws light both on the ease with which a national
revolution can be captured by Communists and the only way a
national revolution can successfully resist them. There are many
surface ironies in the two countries' respective situations. In Cuba,
where criticism of Communists is now taken as the mark of an

86

"anti-revolutionary" and is physically dangerous for the critic, there has never been much knowledge of Communism or Marxist thought—and even less discussion. In Mexico, where Communist leaders have lately received rough official treatment, there is a long history of Marxist and openly Communist thought and discussion, and rather wide familiarity with it. Mexicans applauded the 1960 visit of Anastas Mikoyan and his Soviet trade exposition, but equally applauded their government's expulsion of Soviet diplomats not long before for fomenting unrest among Mexican students. Students in Cuba rioted in protest against Mikoyan's appearance there, but their government shortly afterward signed the first of a series of trade and "aid" pacts with the U.S.S.R. that will make their country into a postulant member of the Soviet bloc. The bulk of the Communists in both countries are intellectuals, artists, students or journalists. In Mexico they are respected, but not politically powerful. In Cuba they are politically powerful, but they have won no respect at all.

The Mexican revolution dates itself from the overthrow of Porfirio Díaz in 1910; but it has been a containing process which extended through the decades succeeding. Inside Mexico it has emphasized land reform, some aspects of Socialism and anti-clericalism—although the force of the last is now rather spent. Facing the world, it has been strongly nationalist. But the violent nationalism at home, which climaxed in the expropriation of American and other foreign oil properties in the thirties, has gradually abated. It has given way to a responsible, liberal concern which has made Mexico's voice highly respected in international discussions.

As Mexicans are well aware, their revolution antedated Russia's. They have consistently resisted foreign expropriation of their own revolutionary ideology. In the late 'twenties Communist agitation reached the point of exasperation. The Mexican government declared the Party illegal, banished scores of its leaders and, in 1929, broke off diplomatic relations with the Soviet Union. In the 'thirties, they were legalized once more and ingratiated themselves with President Lázaro Cárdenas, at a time during his struggle with the foreign oil companies when he needed every friend he could get.

The growing Communist prestige in Mexico crumpled at the time of the Trotsky assassination in 1940. Leon Trotsky, who had been granted asylum in Mexico by President Cárdenas, was killed by a Soviet agent named Raymond Mercader, alias Jacques Mornard, who had been trained and sent from Moscow for this purpose. His boss, temporarily on the scene in Mexico, was Lieutenant General Leonid Eitingon, who at the time headed "terror" operations for the Soviet State Security (see Chapter X), and a horde of Mexican Communists were implicated in the attempt. Not the least of them was the painter Siqueiros, who left his easel long enough to lead a band of machine-gun-carrying Communists in an earlier unsuccessful attempt to take the Trotsky residence by storm.

A storm of indignation swept Mexico after Trotsky's murder. Cárdenas himself correctly evaluated the Communist Party as an instrument of a foreign power, in a statement denouncing the assassination as a criminal act. The Communists have never been able to live down this crass use of the local Party by the Soviet Union. Succeeding shifts by the local Communists to reflect the Party line have only confirmed further the popular realization that they are agents of a foreign power. For the last twenty years the political strength of the Communist Party has steadily ebbed.

At the same time local Marxists remain socially respectable and this includes the Communists. Communist painters like Siqueiros and Diego Rivera have been mixing Marx and the U.S.S.R. with their paints as long as anyone can remember. Their influence and "revolutionary content" of their style have passed on to succeeding generations of younger artists.

The respect for local Marxists is complemented by an interest— no less real for being critical—in the current situation of the Soviet Union. The interest is actively returned. The Soviet Embassy in Mexico City, with its swollen complement of personnel, is a center for espionage and infiltration activities throughout Latin America.

In fact, it is constantly used by the Russians as a training ground, where agents destined for other countries are indoctrinated in Latin American problems and customs.

In this situation the role of the Communist Party is a negative one, far less important than it was in the palmier days of the 'thirties. A recent analysis done by the executive committee of the Party of Workers and Peasants, noting the failure of a campaign of labor unrest, tells in Communist terms the reasons for its difficulties:

"New negative elements have arisen which have been revealed through greater pressure of imperialism, a process of development of the big bourgeoisie, as well as extraordinary activity of the political clergy, which explain the repression of the railway movement and the anti-Soviet provocations. On the other hand, there are seen characteristics of greater pressures from different sectors of the nationalist bourgeoisie which compel the government to adopt measures favorable to the nation, concretely in the diversification of foreign trade . . .

"These facts are proof of the existence in the bosom of the bourgeoisie, and therefore within the government, of contradictions that lead to a ratification of the characterization of the present government of President Adolfo Lopez Mateos as one of compromise between the reactionary and the progressive bourgeoisie, with the former predominating . . ."

In other words, there may be conflicts between left and right inside the Mexican body politic; there may be correct relations with the Soviet Union and even closer economic ties; but it all benefits the Communist parties very little.

The word "parties" is used advisedly. In Mexico, as in a great many other countries, there are two Communist Parties, one the official Communist Party of Mexico (PCM) and the other the aforementioned Party of Mexican Workers and Peasants (POCM). The POCM was founded by dissident members of the official Party and is headed at present by Valentin Campa, a former leader of the railway unions, who was expelled for his Communist activity in 1949. The two parties cooperate, however, and it is suspected that both feed at the same trough, i.e., the disbursing office of the local Soviet embassy.

There is a third pro-Communist political organization, the *Partido Popular* of Vincente Lombardo Toledano, the veteran labor leader who founded the once-powerful Confederation of Trade Unions of Latin America (CTAL), the western hemisphere affiliate of the World Federation of Trade Unions. Lombardo Toledano, although widely regarded as the most prominent agent of Moscow in Latin America, has never admitted to being a Communist. In fact, he has on occasion ostentatiously criticized the Party's activities, as with the strikes of 1958 and 1959. This was doubtless done at Soviet direction; for it will be seen that the fronts and pro-Communist groups in Mexico are far more valuable to the U.S.S.R. than the regular Communist parties.

The working organization of the Soviet movement in Mexico can, broadly speaking, be broken down into four levels. At the top is the pro-Communist network of Lombardo Toledano, who retains full legality for his party and takes care not to oppose the government frontally. He is a frequent commuter to Moscow and other Communist capitals, on W.F.T.U. and other business. In January, 1960, back from a W.F.T.U. conference in Romania, he said that he was planning a series of "interchanges" between European and Latin American labor leaders, a program surely aimed to counter the success of the Inter-American Regional Workers Organization (O.R.I.T.), the Western hemisphere branch of the International Confederation of Free Trade Unions.

For O.R.I.T., which has its headquarters in Mexico, has made heavy inroads into the old strength of Lombardo Toledano among the workers. Over the last twenty years the Mexican Labor Federation (C.T.M.) has made several house-cleanings of Communists in its ranks, and now they are not a decisive force inside the union. As Lombardo Toledano (again expressing it in Communist language) recently noted: "The formerly glorious C.T.M., which was born as a militant and anti-imperialist force, is now under domination of the O.R.I.T., an instrument of the State Department of Washington for the control of the labor movement in Latin America."

Several far-left strongholds remain, however, with innumerable cells and individuals who fellow the Communist line. There is also a considerable residue of Marxist "class struggle" thinking among the union membership—a latent advantage which can easily be exploited. Communist influences of varying sorts are especially strong in the teachers' union, the oil and railway workers' unions and certain others.

*El Popular,* the organ of Lombardo Toledano's Popular Party, is the only Mexican daily paper that steadily toes the Communist line (the official Party newspaper, *The Voices of the People,* is published clandestinely and has a very small circulation). But like the official pronouncements of its boss, the paper takes pains never to season its Party line with any revolutionary propaganda directly attacking the national government.

At the moment, the personal prestige of Lombardo Toledano is far greater than the actual strength of the unions and the political movement he influences. This is true of certain other prominent Mexicans, who are constantly being exploited to Communist advantage. General Heriberto Jara, the head of the Communist-sponsored "peace" group in Mexico, is also a recipient of the Stalin prize. In the tradition, his Movement for Peace devotes most of its energy to anti-United States propaganda. Not long ago on the occasion of a government medal, given him on the floor of the Mexican Senate, Jara criticized the government for its "tolerance of monopolies, profiteers and attackers of freedom" and thanked the Senators for having given him the award without taking into consideration the imputations of Redling (*rojillo*) or Communistoid (*communistoida*) often made against him.

An offshoot of Jara's movement is the newly founded Committee for the Promotion and Coordination of Peace and International Cooperation, headed by Jorge Tamayo, the artist. Its treasurer is

Cuauntemoc Cárdenas, a civil engineer and son of former President Cárdenas. Young Cárdenas has been active since his student days in various pro-Communist causes.

Which brings us to the question of Cuauntemoc's father. Although Cárdenas broke with his Communist allies of the 'thirties on the issue of Trotsky's assassination, he has continued to keep up his personal contacts with Communist leaders. He is a wealthy man with considerable national following and the Communists try hard to hang on to his coattails.

He has only rarely tried to brush them off and, whether to please his Party-lining son or from other motives, Cárdenas acts as if he were indeed a Communist supporter. He has accepted a Stalin "Peace" prize, made highly publicized trips to the Soviet Union and Red China and lent his prestige to a variety of Communist front movements. Outside of Rivera and the artist groups, Cárdenas is the principal aid to respectability which the Mexican Communists have.

The second level of Communist penetration in Mexico includes the intellectual fellow-traveler and the various front organizations to which he belongs. There is, for example, the Circle of Mexican Studies, formed under the leadership of the late Narciso Bassols, who at different times held cabinet posts in the Mexican government and was considered the real mastermind of the Soviet movement in Mexico. The Circle, which includes various economists and social scientists in its membership, harps on the danger of foreign (i.e. principally United States) investments in Mexico and asserts a vigorous economic nationalism. Not long ago one of its members, José Domingo Lavin, resigned from the Circle, after issuing a statement that the group was "covering other objectives with its patriotic rhetoric."

On the third level of Communist activity in Mexico are various expatriate foreigners with extensive Communist connections who live there more or less permanently. Many of these people, including Americans, come to Mexico to escape the attentions of investigating committees in their own countries. They are useful in many ways—as cultural ambassadors for Communism, as actual couriers or message centers, or as propagandists who may have considerable influence on young intellectuals in Mexico. A typical illustration was the case of Alfred Stern and his wife Martha Dodd Stern, Americans who fled to Mexico City from the United States, where they were wanted for questioning in connection with Soviet espionage activity. In 1957, when Mexican authorities in turn began to ask questions, the Sterns managed to escape to safety behind the Iron Curtain.

The final level of Communist action in Mexico is occupied by the two Communist Parties themselves. Neither has been strong enough to elect any representative to the Mexican Congress. (The PCM is estimated to have an absolute maximum of 5,000 members.) The only hope for successful "action" has been to capitalize: 1) on the influence of the more prominent fellow-travelers; and 2) on the existence of continuing discontent among trade unionists and agricultural workers.

In early 1958 the Mexican Communists and their allies attempted to mount a series of planned disorders, mainly strikes and work stoppages, designed to coincide with the change between the administrations of Lopez Mateos and the outgoing President Ruiz Cortines. There were recurrent wildcat strikes, sitdowns and work-stoppages involving principally government workers—in the telegraph system, public schools, Petroleos Mexicanos (the nationalized oil operation) and the National Railways of Mexico, under the direction of its pro-Communist general secretary, Demetrio Vallejo.

The movement failed, only causing trouble for the luckless workers who had been exploited for political purposes in the demonstrations. Hundreds of railway workers were imprisoned in the final stages of the strike campaign, during March and April, 1959. It provoked the Mexican government to institute the most severe crackdown on Mexican Communists since the late 'twenties. Party offices were raided, leaders imprisoned and tons of printed propaganda confiscated by the federal police. By late 1959, after the arrest of Dionisio Encinas, general secretary of the Communist Party, the party had been for practical purposes driven underground, although it was not declared illegal.

In the preliminary hearing for Encinas, the government set forth the pattern of the Communist agitation program, based on the discoveries of its investigators. It covered five points:

1. Inciting students and Mexico City labor groups to demand that the city take over all transport facilities.

2. Street meetings demanding release of "political prisoners" and appeal of the "social dissolution" law.

3. Agitation for the nationalization of electric power firms and credit institutions.

4. Demands for less subjection to "imperialist capitalism," which "prevents Mexico from achieving economic independence."

5. Agitation in rural areas, organized through the General Union of Workers and Peasants (UGOCM) the only Mexican union remaining under the control of Lombardo Toledano's parent organization.

It is an index of the political sophistication of Mexicans that all five of these focal points for agitation were economic—even the anti-American slogans had to be decked out in economic terms. For the only hope of present-day Communism in Mexico is to hook on to real or fancied economic problems of the electorate. As a political force standing on its own, Communism or political Popular Frontism has little or no appeal. The same people who admire Diego Rivera's paintings have long since learned to leave his politics alone.

If there was any doubt about the inner political motivation of Mexico's Communists, it was dispelled by the implication of two Soviet Embassy officials, Capitain Nikolai M. Remisov and Second Secretary Nikolai V. Aksenov, in the 1958 demonstrations. The government found conclusive evidence that they were directly connected with centers of the agitation; and they were withdrawn to

Moscow. Rarely had a country been given such clear-cut evidence of its adversary's true intentions.

"I think Cubans will remember," said Major Ernesto (Che) Guevara, "that while the North American government was giving military assistance to Batista, many members of the Communist Party were losing their lives fighting with us against Batista. I think the Communists have earned the right to be one more party in Cuba."

With this modest beginning, Fidel Castro and his publicity-hungry *barbudos* began their march to Communism. Guevara said it in January, 1959, three days after Castro and the bearded guerrillas had completed their physical progress from the hills of the Sierra Maestra to Havana. Given the temper of the times, the statement sounded naïve, perhaps, but understandable—just as understandable as the declarations of friendship with Communists which so many trusting European statesmen made in the false glow of Resistance cooperation. There was nothing naïve, however, about Guevara's making it. Since arriving in Havana with the idealistic, but addle-pated Fidel (whom Americans have called with justice the only beatnik ever to find himself in charge of a whole government) Guevara has maneuvered his hastily adopted country (he is an Argentine) into a position where the Communist Party is the only political party in Cuba which one can join.

On May Day, 1960, Castro, Guevara and their friends staged a huge "workers and peasants" rally, of the type familiar in the Communist-bloc countries. The rally was complete with the fraternal delegations from the "Socialist camp," tagged and numbered according to their country of origin. The speeches turned the air blue with denunciations of "North American imperialism," alternating with constant praise of the "Socialist" countries, and they faithfully reflected the foreign policy of the Castro government.

After the visit of Anastas Mikoyan and his traveling trade fair early in 1960, the Castro government had begun a series of trade "deals" with the Soviet Union and its allies, the while continuing its expropriation of American and other foreign business interests. It was not healthy for anti-Communist Cubans to point out the differences between this expropriation and the nationalist expropriation of foreign-owned business by Mexico in the 'thirties. There no other foreign nation was waiting to replace the ousted interests.*

By 1960 the international good will first generated by Castro's overthrow of Batista's dictatorship had been almost wholly expended, except for the official friendliness of the Communist countries. In the last year most of the Latin American governments drew the fire of Castro's professionally angry press propagandists. These targets included people like Luiz Munoz Marin of Puerto Rico, one of the first champions of the anti-Batista movement, and the former President of Costa Rica, Jose Figueros Ferrer, who helped Castro find arms for his rebellion—to say nothing of Presidents Frondizi of Argentina, Lleras Camargo of Colombia and Alessandri Rodriguez of Chile. In April 1960 the Castro press turned against Rómulo Betancourt, the liberal President of Venezuela, with its usual accusation that he was a "puppet" of the United States, a "traitor to democracy." (Finally, in pursuit of alliances through Latin America, Castro did find one dependable bedfellow: Juan Peron. By July 1960 Castro's emissaries had opened friendly talks with Peronista representatives and Jose Pardo Llada, Fidel's official radio voice, had started praising Peron on the air.)

What turned Castro against Betancourt was probably Betancourt's proposal, made at the Inter-American Congress for Democracy and Freedom, that the Organization of American States should bar from membership governments which have not been freely elected. For Castro since taking power has been no more sympathetic to elections than was Batista. He prefers to rely on what he calls the "revolutionary process," a round of enforced popular mass meetings which are summoned to give a kind of mob approval to the government's fiats.

---

* In addition, Mexico paid for the sequestered property.

The Castro regime could hardly stand electoral criticism or parliamentary opposition. Its sweeping land reforms, showy expropriations, and spectacular housing developments are unable to hide an economic incompetence that is speedily wrecking the prosperity of a naturally well-endowed country. Yet whether "incompetence" is exactly the word is debatable. Since the economic changes in Cuba are inevitably bringing Castro into dependence on the Soviet bloc, it is fair to examine the competence and the motives of the men behind them. A check-off list of the men running Cuba (and Castro) offers the most vivid illustration of how far Communism has gone in that island.

*Raul Castro:* Fidel's brother and the heir apparent to leadership of the July 26th Movement. Raul belonged to a Communist-front group at the University of Havana and later received some indoctrination in Prague. His wife, Vilma Espin, is a Party member. As supreme chief of the armed forces, Raul controls national security. His chief advisor is one Carlos Rodriguez, a Communist intellectual who is managing editor of the Communist daily *Hoy,* the newspaper which with increasing authority mirrors the views of the Castro leadership. Raul's private secretary is Joaquim Ordoqui, a well-known Communist who recently took a refresher trip to Moscow himself. Raul recently created in the army a new branch of "culture and publicity," run by Alfredo Guevara, a trained Communist.

*Captain Nunez Jiminez:* Director of the National Institute for Agrarian Reform, in charge of the national program of confiscating and redistributing holdings to the peasants. A useful assistant to Raul Castro, he recommended the Sierra Maestra mountains as the best spot for launching the revolution. In pre-revolutionary days, his book, *Geography of Cuba,* was banned as Communist literature.

*Carlos Franqui:* Editor of *Revolucion* (circulation: 80,000), the official newspaper of the July 26th Movement. He was connected with the Communist Party before 1953, when he worked as a proofreader on the Communist daily, *Hoy*. He later published a clandestine newsletter, *Carta Semanal,* for the Communists.

*David Salvador:* Head of the Cuban Confederation of Labor. He was backed by the Communists in the 1954 election, running for Councilman in Las Villas province. His two chief assistants, Miguel Quintero Ruano and Victor Miranda, received their training in Moscow. Between them, they control the executive board of the Confederation, which in turn is riveting a tight hold on all Cuban workers. Salvador's other close associates—although they are not formally affiliated with the labor movement—are Blas Roca, Secretary General of the Party, and Lazaro Pena, one-time Communist labor leader in Havana.

*Alfredo Guevara:* Director of the new Culture branch of the arm and head of the Cinema Institute. Formerly president of the Communist Youth Movement in Cuba, he visited Prague and Moscow in the late 'forties, winning the title of Latin American Secretary of the International Students' Union, a venerable Communist-front organization. He is regarded as one of the most faithful Communists in Cuba.

*Carlos Rafael Rodriguez:* Fidel's Communist theoretician. He directs the Communist monthly magazine, *Fundamentos,* which was published in secret before the Party was restored to legality by Castro last year. (It had been banned in 1952.)

*Juan Marinello:* President of the *Partido Socialista Popular,* the official name for Cuba's Communist Party. He recently returned from Moscow, where he was the correspondent for *Hoy*. His wife, a teacher, is also an active Party member.

*Major Juan Almeida:* Currently Chief of Staff of the rebel army, he was formerly a Communist leader in Guantánamo City.

*Blas Roca:* Secretary General of the Communist Party in Cuba since 1933, he was friendly with Batista, despite the latter's surface demonstrations of anti-Communism, until his regime fell. A Party member since 1928, he helped organize Communism in Venezuela. His real name is Juan Calderio.

*Major Ernesto (Che) Guevara:* At present commander of La

Cabana Fortress and President of the National Bank of Cuba. Born in Argentina, he has become a Cuban citizen, eligible for the presidency by special decree of the revolutionary government. His background has been almost unreservedly Communist. (His mother, a card-carrying Communist in Argentina, has received promotion in Party circles since her son's prominence in Cuba.) Bitterly anti-American, Guevara helped run the Communist-line government of Jacob Arbenz Guzman in Guatemala, being specifically interested in its "land reform" aspects. He then took shelter with Vincente Lombardo Toledano in Mexico after the anti-Communist Guatemala revolution. His first official appearance in Havana after the revolution ended was to make a speech before a Communist cultural organization.

Of these men, Raul Castro and Guevara are unquestionably the most powerful and quite possibly the most competent, albeit in a negative direction. Castro has organized the deep Communist penetration of the Revolutionary Army. As of February 1960 at least twenty well-placed officers are outright Communists. Classes in Communist theory have long been regularly held at La Cabana Fortress in Havana. Similar instruction has spread to army posts in the provinces.

The two Castros and Guevara have organized a government of cells and circles, in the approved Communist tradition. With them at the top are Nunez Jiminez, Franqui, and Education Minister Armando Hart Davalo, a man of far leftist views who was one of Fidel's first revolutionary associates. Next come Rodriguez and Marinello, a frequent participant—as official Party leader—in the innumerable round tables, discussions and oratory gatherings sponsored by the regime. From this group power runs to a trusted cadre of army officers, majors and captains, who not only control the armed forces, but who preside over the civilian government, through key jobs in the various ministries and important outside organizations. One of them, for instance, Major Rolando Cubela, was put in charge of the Students' Union at Havana University. By

July 1960 Cubela and his strong-arm squads had forced the resig-
nation of most of Havana's independent professors, regimented the
students and reduced the various faculties to rubber stamp propaganda centers, with new professors apparently on route fror the
U.S.S.R. or its satellites to complete the process.

Of the civilian agencies, the Institute for Agrarian Reform, in
direct charge of the land reform program, is the most solidly controlled by the Castro clique. As a brand-new agency, its founders
had no problems with hold-over bureaucratic personnel from the
preceding regime. The Institute has a larger ratio of Communists
than any other government agency. Six Communist economists have
been imported from Chile alone.

Guevara has been in charge of the industrial department of the
Institute. Since Castro named him president of the National Bank,
in November 1959, he has been in a position to dictate the course
of the national economy. First Guevara "intervened" hundreds of
thousands of acres of able and grazing land—"intervention" is the
preliminary to formal expropriation proceedings. Then he pre-
sided over the expropriation of American oil and sugar companies.

New production cooperatives have sprung up, equipped with
"people's stores" and the familiar devices, as well as the circumlo-
cutions, of the modern Marxist economy. Fishermen's cooperatives
have been organized, and (again as of February, 1960) some 440
consumers' cooperatives. All of these new activities are run
by the Institute, which has set itself up as a sort of giant holding
company controlling the country's economy. Needless to say,
nothing has been done about actually giving the Cuban small
farmers title to the confiscated land. They will instead have to
discover for themselves the purgatorial existence of life on a Communist "cooperative," a hair's breadth removed from the notorious
model of the Soviet or Chinese collective.

Guevara also runs the Institute for Sugar Stabilization, now in
charge of nationalizing the mills that process the country's big
money crop. Gradually the Institute has taken over the bloc export
of this commodity, also on the analogy of Communist practice.

While completing their economic capture of Cuba—and continuing to delight the multitude with a well-planned campaign of bread and circuses, Castro and his pro-Communist associates have acted swiftly against dissidents. The number of defectors who have deserted the regime is huge. By the spring of 1960 Latin American experts in Washington had lost count of them. By the middle of 1960 a good proportion of the diplomatic service had publicly defected.

Almost all of the defectors were long-time enemies of Batista and originally followers of the Revolution. All of them broke with Castro on the issue of Communism. The first major break in the regime was the protest of Major Hubert Matos, an important army commander in Camaguey province who opposed the drastic Guevara version of economics and asked for some moderation in the wholesale proscription both of land and of people. Major Camilo Cienfuegos, then chief of staff, was sent to Camaguey province at Fidel Castro's personal request to bring Matos back to Havana, on charges of treason.

Officers who were present said later that Cienfuegos, himself an anti-Communist, was shaken by this experience. Matos was taken into custody, and received twenty years in prison merely for having voiced his discontent (he had not been actively conspiring against the regime). Cienfuegos took off from Camaguey the next week in a light plane. He has not been heard from since.

It is natural that defections were heaviest, as in the Batista regime, among persons in a position to escape the country, e.g., diplomats and airline pilots. Editors and commentators have also fled, when they were able, as the Castro censorship tightened to a degree where freedom of press has become a mockery. In April, Jose Conte Aguero, Cuba's most popular TV commentator and a long-time participant in the July 26th Movement, fled the country after he had been forced off the air for making a statement critical of the Communists. A few months before Jorge Zayas, editor and published of the Cuban daily *Avance,* had his paper taken over by the government lock, stock and barrel when he refused to append the prescribed "explanatory notes" to news agency dispatches he printed.

These notes incidentally, were added to any stories thought derogatory to the government or disrespectful of "freedom of the press" (the use of the phrase shows how readily the Cubans have mastered Communist double-think). Inserted by the local branch of the newspaper union, they disclaimed responsibility for the story, suggesting that it is wholly or in part a fabrication. By mid-1960, with the free press virtually extinct, the "note" system was no longer needed.

The mention of the newspaper union suggests another classic Communist device for getting leverage on a non-Communist country. Under the aggressive leadership of Salvador, the unions have been taken over by Castro and the pro-Communists to form another control arm of this emergent totalitarian state. This was accomplished all the more smoothly since the Cuban unions had previously been run by a solid slate of Batista supporters. The new dictatorship had only to exploit a tradition of subservience already long established. There was a partial revolt against this domination of the Communists, when independent union leaders tried to vote down a pro-Communist "unity" slate within the Cuban Federation of Labor in November 1959. With difficulty, it was subdued and Salvador was given a mandate to enforce discipline within the unions. As things now stand, a worker in Havana cannot get a work card unless his political outlook is approved by the Federation's Communist-run committee.

A more serious sign of unrest was the giant Catholic demonstration in the same month when 500,000 Cubans gathered in the rain to honor the Virgin of Charity, Cuba's patron saint. The tone of this demonstration was anti-Communist, and Catholic slogans were also seen among the students who tried to break up Mikoyan's reception at the Soviet trade fair in Havana several months later. By August, 1960, the Catholic hierarchy in Cuba had been forced to issue plain warnings about the country's swing towards Communism.

The most active opposition to Fidel's dictatorship comes from Cuba's middle class, the business and professional people who did the most to bring Castro to power. These are the people who believed Castro's promise to hold early elections, hoping that this would mean the beginning of a stable, democratic government. Now they are suffering most from the economic mistakes of the Castro officers, as well as their incipient collectivism. It must hardly inspire confidence in the future of Cuba among them to view manifestations like the May Day 1960 parade in Havana, a militant and military demonstration that attracted a crowd of 250,000. There they could hear Fidel harangue the crowd with this type of monologue: "Why is it considered that the only democratic governments are those elected by votes? A revolutionary government is brought to power not by a pencil but by the blood of the people." To which the mob responded: "We have already voted for Fidel." At which the fraternal delegates from the U.S.S.R., Communist China, East Germany and elsewhere in the bloc applauded.

What is the assessment of the Castro government, at this point in its evolution? It has already passed the point where the camouflage of its Communist front movements is necessary. As Salvador Diaz-Verson, president of the Inter-American Organization of anti-Communist Journalists (and himself a refugee from Castro Cuba), has said: "To be an anti-Communist in Cuba today is to be branded a counter-revolutionary and to be labeled a counter-revolutionary now means a quick trip to La Cabana fortress and certain execution." One might quarrel with his adjective "certain," but the rest of the statement is true. The number of prisoners held at La Cabana, the Isle of Pines and elsewhere is now well up into the thousands. (The best current estimate is 6,000.) And for an accused in Cuba today democratic rights have little meaning.

On the international level, Cuba is passing into alignment with the Communists as fast as Fidel's Communist friends can carry it. In another age, Fidel's anti-Americanism would be a normal sign of a partly suppressed nationalism. In 1960 the anti-American campaign in Cuba is inescapably tied in with world Communist objectives—a fact of which the Cuban regime is well aware. Possibly on the theory that a loud offensive, everywhere, will preclude a successful attack, the Castro regime has been making itself useful to the Communist movement throughout Latin America. In his continuing threats against the United States, which he carried to the U.N. in July 1960, Castro has been hoping for that successful martyr's crown which has helped similar regimes to solidify their popular appeal in Latin America: counter-threats and "aggressive" gestures from the U.S.

The most dubious front international meeting can count on a heavy Cuban delegation. Castro's private news agency, the newly founded Prensa Latina, is run from its shiny Havana headquarters by a professional anti-American from Argentina, Jorge Masetti. Its dispatches, widely circulated in Latin America, are a combination of anti-Americanism and a "popular front" nationalism. Castro's agents have dubious connections. Early in 1960 a Cuban diplomat in Guatemala was expelled for distributing Communist propaganda.

It is perhaps untrue to accuse the Castro regime, *en bloc,* of being Communist. The fact remains that the non-Communist members of the Revolutionary Movement, whether fanatic ultra-nationalists, self-seekers or disillusioned but timid patriots, have found it comfortable to maintain common cause with the Communists. It could be uncomfortable and embarrassing for the Soviet bloc, in any case, to have an outright Communist satellite in the Caribbean—with the constant threat of overt United States action against it. It is far more satisfactory to have in Castro a kind of willing "watermelon" ally—green on the outside, as the Havana wits say,* and red within.

The contrast with the Mexican situation stands out with depressing clarity. The Mexican people know a good deal about Communism and its international connections. And they have sub-

---

* Green is the official color of the July 26th Movement.

stantially rejected it.* In Cuba the masses of people know nothing about Communism, or the Soviet Union. Nor can they understand the sort of economic emasculation which the Castro regime is practicing, with its headlong "reforms" and badly administered new collectives. All they do recognize at the moment is the concrete improvements in their lot—food allowances, new parks, housing— which Castro has been shrewd enough to brandish before them. There is no question but that Fidel has tapped a deep well of discontent in Cuba—economic, social and patriotic. Unfortunately Cuba did not have reform and revolution early, as did Mexico.

What is happening to Cuba is a harbinger of what could easily happen elsewhere. The Communists joined a struggling revolutionary movement that had much courage but few plans. The Communists supplied the plans, the rationale and, ultimately, most of the direction. As usual, they won by default. But their victory was impressive.

---

* Which is not to say that Mexican popular sentiment does not enjoy the spectacle of a Latin-American country, Red or not, causing pain or inconvenience to Washington.

# CHAPTER VI

# MAO AND THE GENERALS

"I feel like a piece of wood in the fire. . . ."
—PRESIDENT SUKARNO of Indonesia,
addressing the 1959 Congress of the
Indonesian Communist Party

THE Communist movements of Asia were born in Moscow; they were nurtured by Tokyo; they are most vigorously exploited by Peking. That is to say that in the beginning the Communist leaders of the Asian countries either went to the Soviet Union for their training and indoctrination, or made contact with others who had. The Tokyo nutriment was quite unintended; nonetheless it was the advance of the Japanese armies through Asia which exploded the revolt against the colonial powers and brought forth the sleeping nationalism of so many countries, which the Communists have so well maneuvered. Since the Communist conquest of China in 1949, the Peking government has adopted a policy of violent expansion, ideological as much as territorial, in which the Communist parties and their friends have played a leading role, the useful idiots of the front groups not least among them.

This tortuous triangle of Marxism, anti-colonialism and the forceful personality of Mao Tse-tung must be visualized when considering the march of the Communists and their allies in Asia. Nowhere else in the world has the Communist movement made such a swift advance; yet the speed of Communist conquests have been in some ways deceptive. They have raised undercurrents of opposition and confusion that can only be understood in an Asian context. In the orthodox Marxist sense of the word, most of the Communist parties of Asia, apart from the Chinese, have critical

106

defects. They are too "nationalist," because of their penchant for associating with "bourgeois" elements in broadly based agrarian or anti-colonial movements. This tendency stemmed from the Chinese Communist experience; it has in past years made Moscow highly suspicious.

As anti-colonialists, the Communists have been puissant allies to the non-Communist nationalists; but their tendency to sacrifice national interests to those of Moscow or Peking has been noticed, and in some cases it has led to violence and bloodshed. As servants of Peking, the local Communists—particularly in southeast Asia—have their drawbacks. For as Peking grows stronger and historical enmities reassert themselves, the gap grows wider between the interests of an expansionist China and its neighbors. Often the strains of the Chinese connection prove almost too much to bear, the more so as the Chinese tend to grow more and more doctrinaire in their views of ideology. So in the last few years, we have the curious situation of many Asian Communists becoming more attracted by the friendly and non-Asian new Communist image of Nikita Khrushchev.

First let us put the Asian Communist movement in its historical setting. Its great opportunity came in 1945, when the Japanese retreated from Asia, leaving destruction and confusion in their wake. Although the colonial powers moved swiftly to reclaim their captured territories, no amount of force was able to restore the *status quo ante*. The Japanese army and navy had forever lifted the white man's burden from him by smashing the myth of white supremacy.

Nor should the propaganda of the Japanese be discounted. The Greater East Asia Co-Prosperity Sphere was a million-dollar slogan. It degenerated into a mockery only because the Japanese made it so. Unwilling to share the spoils of their victory with the other Asian peoples, they reduced them to the same state of subjugation which they had suffered under the rule of the British, Dutch or French. (It was much the same mistake that the Nazis made when they antagonized the anti-Soviet millions of their oc-

cupied zone in the Soviet Union. Both mistakes were probably endemic to their makers.) Yet in their first moments of conquest, at
least, the Japanese allowed local nationalist movements to come
into the open and encouraged collaboration. This was true in India
and in Burma. In Indonesia, the Japanese finally played a bitter
trick on their conquerors, when they evacuated large areas in favor
of the Indonesian nationalist forces and supplied them with arms.

As a result of the upheavals caused by the Japanese, the late
'forties witnessed a startling growth of national liberation movements. In these the Communists, as the most aggressive and best
organized of the "nationalist" parties, played a large part—and
the only one, as usual, with any idea where it was going. Goaded
by the aggressive instructions of Moscow, specifically those of
Andrei Zhdanov in 1948,* the Communists turned as quickly as
possible to open revolt. In Malaya they fought a skillful jungle
war for years against the British, in which for long periods, and
over large areas of that rich country, the Communist guerrilla army
was the law of the land. In Indonesia the Communists mounted
a full-scale revolution in 1948, even before the independence of
the country was complete. In the Philippines, the Hukbalahap
revolt, led by the enigmatic and aggressive Luis Taruc, managed
to make enough capital of agrarian discontent, mainly on the island
of Luzon, to keep part of the country in a form of chaos throughout the 'forties. It was not until the advent of the late President
Ramon Magsaysay that they were finally crushed.

Communists even gained a foothold of sorts in Pakistan; the disclosure of the Rawalpindi conspiracy in 1951—aimed at taking
over the country—resulted in the outlawing of the Party. In South
Korea, as a forerunner of the later Communist invasion, the South
Korean Labor Party (the local circumlocution for Communists) fomented armed revolts in Taegu and Cheju-do. In October, 1948,
Communists succeeded in engineering the mutiny of an R.O.K.
infantry regiment at the south-coast port of Yosu; its survivors con-

* Which signalized a general tightening of "revolutionary" discipline
throughout the Communist world.

tinued guerrilla warfare until the moment of the North Korean invasion.

The model for all such armed insurrection was of course the remarkable military success of the Communist Chinese. This, too, was a by-product of World War II. The burden of the struggle against the Japanese fell on the government of Chiang Kai-shek, while the Communists, concentrated in agrarian areas in the west and north of China, were able to fight the Japanese—or the Nationalists—at will, while consolidating their system and husbanding their resources. When Chiang returned to Nanking in 1945, he was a popular hero, but the strain of six years of bare subsistence struggle against the Japanese had undermined both the capacity and the morale of his government. Corruption bred inefficiency, which in turn bred more corruption. To the wearied Chinese people, the appeal of the disciplined, Spartan and loudly incorruptible Communists was considerable by contrast. In 1949 the Chinese Communists took effective control of the country, ending a persistent struggle they had waged since 1931.

Surprisingly, the forward momentum of Mao Tse-tung and his huge Party continued to increase, even after he obtained power. As a result, to quote the American Chinese expert, A. Doak Barnett, writing ten years after the Communist take-over: "During the past decade one of the most far-reaching political revolutions in history has taken place in China. In a few short years the Chinese Communists have established a strong, monolithic, totalitarian regime which has brought the most populous nation in the world under tight political, social, and psychological control. They have demonstrated with frightening efficiency how the dynamism of a totalitarian state and the power of its 'organizational weapon' can be applied even in a nation of roughly 650,000,000 people with deep-rooted traditions which clash with totalitarian discipline. Today Communist China is a huge mass in motion under strict control. Virtually the entire population of the country has been organized, regimented, and mobilized in support of the revolutionary goals set by Peking's new leaders."

Not surprisingly, the success of the Chinese stimulated the revolutionary urges of the weaker Communist parties. In the guerrilla hide-outs in the Philippine hills and the zealous Communist study groups in East Pakistan, local Red luminaries turned more and more to Mao, rather than Stalin and the Russians, for their evidence of Holy Writ. Solemnly they quoted the Peking theoreticians to the effect that the successful Chinese revolution represented a new type of revolt, its strength based on the peasant rather than the urban proletariat, its hopes dependent on guerrilla armies in the countryside rather than workers' militia in the cities. Knowingly the Chinese noted the contrasts between their revolution and the Russian. As one Party functionary put it: "The classic type of revolution in imperialist countries is the October revolution. The classic type of revolution in colonial or semi-colonial countries is the Chinese revolution."

In Indo-China Ho Chi-minh, a Communist whose seniority was second only to that of Mao himself in the national parties of Asia, worked out a brilliant pocket-sized edition of Mao's peasant army theories. His final victory in 1955, although admittedly impossible without aid of the incredibly near-sighted military and political policies of the French, boosted the prestige of Mao's Communism to a new high. It complemented the claims made for the stand-off in Korea, which Communist propagandists were skillful in interpreting as a victory of the Chinese "people's volunteers" over the United States. And beyond question, the fact that the Chinese armies resisted the United Nations forces so doggedly drove home again the lesson which the Japanese began: the West is no longer invincible.

At the same time, at the apparent crest of Mao's particular wave-of-the-future, the Communists felt the effects of a disturbing undertow. If the agrarian rebellion, Yenan style, was successful in northern Indo-China, it had back-fired in Indonesia and India, it had been crushed in Malaya and the Philippines, it had disintegrated in Burma. If Mao's government was the leading light at

the Bandung conference of the Afro-Asian peoples, it had also
begun to offend with its own Chinese nationalism. Even more
sharply than the peoples of eastern Europe in the early Soviet days,
the young nations of Asia were conscious of a steady Chinese pressure southward and eastward. The Chinese pressure on India cul-
minated, after the Tibetan rebellion of 1959, in serious border in-
cursions. Burma had already experienced the same sort of thing.
The savagery with which the Chinese put down the Tibetan rebellion in itself opened the eyes of many to the true nature of Mao's
"agrarian democrats."

The overseas Chinese in southeast Asia had by this time become
an important political factor in themselves. In Indonesia, the Communist Chinese embassy tried by the most blatant means to further
the fortunes of the pro-Communist overseas Chinese resident there
—to the abiding discomfort of the local Communist party. As it
was, the overseas Chinese merchant because of his most diligent
prosperity—and ubiquity—tended to be an object of suspicion
throughout Southeast Asia. Add the factor of an ambitious, aggressive government supporting him and the suspicion deepened
into real fear.

The net result of these conflicting currents was that many of
the Asian Communists and their sympathizers turned the more
readily toward Khrushchev's new ideas of a modern popular
front. Nothing could have been more pleasant to the groups
of rebuffed violent revolutionaries than Khrushchev's striking
deviation from the classic Leninist dogma that there must be a
violent showdown with capitalism, when he said at the Twentieth
Party Congress in 1956 that the proletariat, "by rallying around
itself a toiling peasantry, the intelligentsia and all patriotic forces
. . . has the possibility of inflicting a defeat on the reactionary anti-
popular forces and gaining a firm majority in parliament, converting it from an organ of bourgeois democracy into an instrument of
genuine popular will." And just as easily they could cite the stress
laid by the Chinese Communists on incorporating all elements and

all classes into the "anti-colonial," "anti-imperialist" struggle that must precede the establishment of Communism.

Heading into the *sputnik* era, also, the Communists could bask in the general admiration for Soviet achievements in science and technology, as well as the ponderous but remarkable strides made by Communist China. A government might deal harshly with its local Communists, but what leader would fail to turn up at the airport for a flower-decked reception to Nikita Sergeyevich Khrushchev or Chou En-lai making the grand tour?

There was no sharper symptom of the change to the new approach than the Communists' behavior in the new country of Malaya and the virtually independent city of Singapore. In 1957, shortly after Tungku Abdul Rahman became Chief Minister of Malaya, the veteran Communist leader Chin Peng came out of the jungle to meet him. The Tungku had agreed to explain his amnesty terms to Chin, who had been fighting a bitter guerrilla war against first the British, then the new Malay state, since his open Communist revolt failed in the cities and towns in 1948. Just before the meeting, the Malayan Communist Party announced a new program, broadcast in full over the Peking radio. The program called for an end to the fighting and the realization of Malayan independence as soon as possible. A new constitution was needed, but it should "have respect for the position of the sultans." Malay, not Chinese (the majority of the Communists in Malaya are overseas Chinese), should be the national language. Under the new constitution, the Party would continue its peaceful struggle for a people's democracy and socialism.

The talks in Malaya were inconclusive and Chin Peng went back to his few remaining guerrillas—estimated at less than five hundred —hiding out in the jungles along the frontier with Thailand. But, significantly, he broadcast an additional communique stating his willingness to discontinue violent action. The Malayan Communists reverted to their immediate post-war role of attempting to infiltrate and subvert labor organizations and leftist political parties throughout the country.

A similar switch could be observed in Singapore, where the Communists and their allies were infinitely stronger. There, for ten years, Party activity had run to assassination, bomb throwing, the organization of strikes and fomenting various social disturbances. The city's overwhelmingly Chinese population, well colonized by emissaries of the Peking government, had drifted steadily leftward, as Communist China flexed its muscles. Under the limited home rule government begun in 1955, the Communists, heavily represented within the large People's Action Party, at times brought life in Singapore to a virtual standstill. But after 1957, when a more complete form of self-government was announced, the Communists turned off their open agitation. This was partly due to the intelligence of a non-Communist left-wing government, the self-same People's Action Party purged of many of its obviously Communist associates. But the justification was furnished by the new image of "peaceful" Communism.

The P.A.P. government, anxious to spread socialism throughout the area, wants a merger with the country of Malaya. The Communists heartily second this project, although they have other ideas about the type of "socialism" to be adopted. They do not want to stir up trouble, lest the Malays be unduly alarmed about their influence. (If Singapore were taken into Malaya, the combined populations of both places would result in a heavy ethnic majority of Chinese—a prospect the Malayans dread.) So they have kept quiet, very happy to let the useful idiots do their work for them—up to a point.

The new "parliamentary" Communism—just the sort of thing that Sanzo Nozaka has so long advocated in Japan (Chapter VII)—has already run up heavy gains in Laos and Indonesia. It stands to make capital out of the new party alignments in Burma. With isolated exceptions it has no serious party rivals in the welter of hastily organized democracies—at least those in east Asia. The one strong force that has at times thwarted it is not a political movement at all, but the emergence of various men and groups in various countries who go by the name of: the Army. This Army activity is not so puzzling as it seems. It might have been expected that some of the ablest and most idealistic of the newly educated, newly liberated Asians would go into military life. All the national revolutions, barring India's, were to some extent military ones. As in the Middle East, the young Asian officer has assumed a political importance that he has not known in the West for a long time.

The leaders of the Army are in many cases the closest thing to genuine patriots found in the public life of these countries. They are almost universally anti-colonialist, but also anti-Communist. They share a military love of order; but, as in the two cases we cite below, they have thus far not let the urge to orderliness stampede them into any form of fascism. On the contrary, they have exerted a powerful stabilizing force on a most unstable set of political elements. The best of them is probably Ayub Khan in Pakistan. The least idealistic—which is one way of putting it—is Marshal Sarit Thanarat of Thailand. In neither of these countries, however, has Communism or Communist front parties been lately much of a factor. For instances of a real struggle between Communists and the new military men, we had better look at Indonesia and Burma. For each of them represents an excellent opportunity for the new image of Communism to flourish.

President Sukarno of Indonesia stood beneath huge pictures of himself, Lenin and Mao Tse-tung and beamed at the crowd in the big, barn-like structure that stood across the street from his Instana Merkeka Palace—and an equal distance away from Army headquarters. He tapped the microphones on the dais, motioned for the whistling and handclapping to cease, then began the final speech of the Sixth National Congress of the Indonesian Communist Party.

"In the beginning," he said, "Aidit [the Party chairman] came to me in my palace and asked me, 'Bung [Brother] Karno, there's a ban on political activities, but could the P.K.I. within a short time hold a Congress?'

"I said, 'Yes, have your Congress. But after August first.' . . . And now that Congress has taken place and Aidit has asked me to attend this reception. And here I am in your midst, welcomed with love as a comrade for which I express my gratitude."

With these words Sukarno set off a chorus of ringing cheers and more rhythmic handclapping. The massed crowd of delegates began chanting one of his favorite phrases *"gotong royong"* [mutual consent]—a big talking point in Sukarno's hazy new theory of "guided democracy."

Bung Karno smiled his best company smile again. "I may be the only President in the world, the only President of a non-Socialist state attending a Communist Congress."

While the President was smiling his best at the delegates, a number of stony-faced Indonesian Army officers, representatives of the President's loyal Army, sat silently in the front row center of the hall. Outside, armed, helmeted military police sentries saw to it that no one not approved by the Army could enter. As part of the Army's "precautionary measures" leading up to the Congress, virtually every placard the Party put up had been torn down, by military order, and all outdoor gatherings of Communists or sympathizers prohibited. The Army Chief of Staff, General Abdul Haris Nasution, had banned several dates for the meeting, and it was only on the President's personal representations that it was finally held, in September, 1959. As it was, the Party was required to submit a written report on each session to Army authorities, giving details of all the speeches and comments made.

This strange juxtaposition of Sukarno, the still popular boss of Indonesia, and the two most powerful elements in his state was only one chapter in their continuing, heightening conflict. On their side the Communists have, to begin with, the strongest party in the country. The 1955 elections were the only ones held before Bung Karno superseded the beginnings of representative government with "guided democracy." In them the Communists won close to a majority of the votes cast. This made them the biggest vote-getters among the world's Communist parties outside the Iron Curtain—the Italian Party, as previously noted, has the largest actual Party membership. The Communists control the huge

Indonesian Labor Federation S.O.B.S.I. (for Sentral Organisasi Buruh Seleru Indonesia) and a barnacles' convention of subsidiary and generally successful "front" groups.

The Army is an Army. That is to say, it possesses the only military power to speak of in Indonesia. It is composed of diverse and often quarreling personalities. Many officers went into revolt in 1958, taking part in a military and political rebellion against Sukarno's authority, which continues to exist and hold Indonesian territory. Most Army officers remember more vividly the armed Communist rebellion in central Java in 1948, which was crushed by the crack Siliwangi Division, the best-trained and officered units in Indonesia. Instrumental in putting down the revolt was Nasution, then a colonel. The one thing uniting the diverse individuals and factions in the Indonesian Army is a universal hatred of Communism.

Already the Army and the Communists have had tests of strength, few of them very polite. When the Communists, working through S.O.B.S.I., instigated a mass and unruly seizure of Dutch properties, the Army repossessed them from the S.O.B.S.I. labor squads. After noting the ease with which Communists could instigate mob violence of almost any sort, the Army banned all public demonstrations—a ban that remains in effect. The Party for its part continually propagandizes against the Army, attacking alleged "corruption."

In early 1959 hundreds of laborers walked off a large rubber estate in northern Sumatra, directly violating a martial law decree prohibiting strikes. Hundreds of strikers and union officials were arrested and tried. Some time later the Army arrested a number of local Party officials in a small village in central Java, where Communist influence is greatest, for possessing arms illegally. What were the Communists doing? Infiltrating the local village guard, the one militia organization in Indonesia that the Communists might hope to exploit, in the event of an armed showdown.

Yet all such conflicts, or most of them, are deliberately muffled by both Communist and Army spokesmen, who vie with each other in their praises of Sukarno. Aidit, the Party secretary general, has even gone so far as to deny reports of any friction. "Reports of a duel between the P.K.I. and the army by the imperialist press represent just another move to conceal the real duel—between the Indonesian people and the imperialists. . . ."

This soft-sell approach, a beautiful illustration of the Khrushchev line at work, is the creation of a bright Sumatran, Dipa Nusantara Aidit, who is only thirty-six years old. When Aidit took over the Party in 1953 as secretary general, it had fallen on evil days. The early generation of Indonesian Communists, many of them trained in Moscow, had come back from exile after World War II, made their bid for power and lost it. The old secretary, Musso, had been killed in the 1948 rebellion, an obviously subversive activity that in itself alienated most of the popular following the Communists were seeking.

Aidit and a younger group had learned their applied Marx and Lenin under more accessible masters. Aidit spent at least a year in China and north Vietnam before taking over his new job. They began a series of radical changes in party policies as early as 1952. First among them, on the Chinese theory, was the transformation of the Party from a tight elite group to a mass-membership party. Membership soared from eight thousand in 1952 to more than one million by 1957—or so the Party claimed. The Party inaugurated a "national unity front" policy, looked for a larger constitutional role and sent out feelers for cooperating with the other Indonesian political organisms—as long as they were "anti-imperialist."

Most important of all, Aidit swung his Party from a position of opposition to Sukarno to one of utter support. Whatever Bung did, the Communists were only too happy to cheer for. The Moslem Masjumi Party Aidit saw as his greatest enemy, and the Communists set out to isolate it. (As it happened, the Masjumi party was also critical of Sukarno.) Communist parliamentarians worked up alliances with other parties against the Masjumi—although always for Sukarno.

By 1955 Aidit had maneuvered his party into a position where the coalition government could not exist without its support. In the ensuing elections, the Communists polled about 17 per cent of the total vote, doubling their number of seats.

Not only did the Party get control of the S.O.B.S.I. labor federation, but it virtually took over almost equally important farmers' and veterans' groups. Aidit was able to pyramid its strength by virtue of heavy financial assistance, partly directly from Communist embassies, partly in the form of a virtual tax levied on Chinese businessmen in Indonesia through the good offices of the Peking embassy there.

But with all this power, Aidit is painstaking in his desire to allay any fears of revolution. "The course of *coup d'état*," he has said, "is a course taken by people out of their minds. . . . We are not afraid of any election and we do not need a *coup* to bring us victory. The P.K.I. is prepared for an election any time." This was not an idle boast.

The great and as yet unfailing popular weapon that the Indonesian Communists wield is the "anti-imperialist" issue, in the form of attacks on the Dutch for their retention of what the Indonesians call Irian and the Dutch, West New Guinea. Any move by any group, including the Army, to suggest moderation on this issue brings immediate charges of "pro-Dutch" from the Communists and their fronts, charges that produce a predictable response in the volatile Indonesian public, still upset from its three-century overdose of Dutch colonialism.

In Indonesia perhaps more than in any country the Communists have been able to harp on issues involving the Afro-Asian nations. Phrases like "the Bandung spirit," "Afro-Asian solidarity," "Asian brotherhood," have a great appeal to Indonesians. Communists use them more steadily than anyone else. As with other national parties, they turn their heaviest fire on the United States. The existence of Western-owned oil companies in Indonesia—Shell, Standard-Vacuum and Caltex—offers a made-to-order occasion for strikes and other "anti-imperialist" agitation.

Here again, however, Aidit uses the perfect "front" technique. The Communists often start the hue and cry, but they leave it to the organizations they control to finish it and bring matters to the crisis point. Similarly, in a sense, with criticism of the government. It is always this or that minister they attack, never Sukarno himself.

The P.K.I., Aidit hastens to say, is the foremost champion of Sukarno's "guided democracy." And with its innumerable "labor squads," hard at work doing voluntary labor projects, its tight Party organizations down to the village level, its penetration of the local militia, Aidit's Party has become the one big political bloc in Sukarno's state. In 1960 Sukarno suppressed the Masjumi and remaining major independent parties. Now only the Army stands in its way. And the Army, with no political program of its own (except for Sukarno's), can use only two arguments: rule by fiat or rule by force.

At the moment, in mid-1960 the Army has been successful in curbing the Communists on several points, even down to asserting strict central government control over the appointment of all local officials. And popular sympathy has been alienated somewhat from the Communists not only by the native Indonesian outcry against the Chinese merchants—most of whom are sympathetic to the Peking government—but also by the published details of Chinese Communist aggression against Tibet and the Indian border clashes.

Yet the skillful "new image" tactics of Aidit have for the time being stifled most of his purely political opposition. If opposition raises its head, it can often be quelled by the simple expedient of enhanced support for Sukarno, the greatest "useful idiot" of them all. "Mountains may be big," said Aidit at his last Party Congress, "but our hearts are bigger tonight because in our midst is Sukarno, the greatest Indonesian patriot and uniter."

In Burma the shoe is on the other foot. There it is the Communists who have been disorganized. By their disunity they have already lost several golden opportunities to take over the country. Not that the other political parties have been smooth-running by contrast. But order has been kept—or, to put it more exactly, restored—by another Army chief of staff, but one whose leadership qualities can be compared on an equal footing with talented Communist leaders like the redoubtable Aidit. His name is General Ne Win.

Ne Win assumed control of the country reluctantly, on October 28, 1958—after it became apparent that the alternatives to his doing so were civil war or virtual capitulation to the Communists. He and the Army, working solidly behind him, produced an astonishing spectacle of a nation suddenly pulling itself up by its bootstraps. In a year he reformed the police force, brought down the prices of consumer goods (by fixing arbitrary maximum profit margins) and reorganized the machinery of export trade. A record rice harvest was produced and marketed. National industries that had been steadily losing money began to make profits. The demoralized civil service rediscovered the idea of efficiency. The trains ran on time, for the first time since before the war. Trade unions were divorced from their political affiliations—an obvious blow at Communist infiltrators. Political influences were drastically reduced in schools and colleges.

As a highly visible sign of reform, Rangoon was forcibly deprived of its long-standing reputation as one of the filthiest cities in the East. (Among other civic improvements, 100,000 diseased or stray dogs were poisoned, and thousands of crows and rats.) Squatters were resettled. Pavements were repaired, drains unclogged, markets and stalls relocated. In a year Rangoon's death rate dropped sensationally.

Having done all this Ne Win confidently announced another election on February 9, 1960. A firm believer in democracy, the general stepped down as soon as his work was done. Before turning the administration back to the politicians, he could safely say that the Communist menace was effectively checked.

That he was able to roll back Communist influence so decisively is in part a testimonial to the efficiency of Ne Win and his colonels. It is also a commentary on the centrifugal character imparted even to Communism in a country whose Buddhist population is excessively fond of theological hair-splitting. The mores of Communism in Burma are so complicated that, one suspects, even Peking and Moscow have long since expressed their bewilderment. Yet it is a commentary, again, on the weakness of the new non-Communist political organizations in Burma as in most of Asia that, divided as they were, the Communists were ultimately able to hold something like a political balance of power before Ne Win took over.

Burma regained its independence of British rule, which had begun 124 years earlier, on January 4, 1948, at 4:20 A.M., the time thought most auspicious by the astrologers. Within three months the Burma Communist Party was at war with the government in yet another reflection of the "tough" mood dictated by Moscow in the late 'forties. The Communist revolt was serious—the more so since the ruling political coalition, the Anti-Fascist People's Freedom League, had been led by a group of intellectuals, many of whom had Communist or at least Marxist leanings.

But scarcely one month after the Burma Communists began their revolt, a rival Communist group took the field, which had splintered off from the other under the name of the Communist Party of Burma. Known as "White Flag" and "Red Flag" Communists respectively, the two warring groups were soon joined by a third, the avowedly Marxist People's Volunteer Organization—otherwise known as the "White Band PVO." Since the Burmese government was bedeviled at the same time by rebellion of the Karen peoples, fighting for autonomy, and a mutiny of Army troops, the situation was—to put it mildly—grave. There was a time when the central government could be said to have control of Rangoon and little else.

As this polygonal revolution went its way, regional Communist headquarters began to attempt a braking action. After one Communist leader had attempted to set up an autonomous state on the Chinese border. Liu Shau-chi, the Communist Chinese theoretician, criticized the Burmese Communists for having adopted an ultra-left line, instead of cooperating with the A.F.P.F.L. government. The Party or Parties, he urged, should drop this warlike behavior and attempt to form a single united front of all revolutionary forces. This was of course in line with Mao's approved tactic of using the "bourgeoisie" in the first stages of Communization.

While the avowed Communists were arguing among themselves about ceasing their guerrilla activities, Marxist elements within the A.F.P.F.L. itself broke away to found the Burma Workers and Peasants Party, intending to set up the People's Democratic Front. This was evidently in accord with Peking's wishes. They were later joined by another People's Peace Front and a People's Unity Party. All of them professed standard Communist objectives, with varying nuances.

By 1957 almost 29,000 rebels had surrendered, and the government had long since regained control of its territory. Most of the surviving Communists or semi-Communists had combined by then into something called the National United Front, although some still remained in open rebellion. To complicate matters still further, the Burma Workers and Peasants Party had some hard second thoughts about the Peasants, and shortened its name to the Burma Workers Party. This party, combining many of the Communist remnants, formed the bulk of the National United Front.

By this time, the ruling coalition had itself split, into two factions picturesquely known as the Stable A.F.P.F.L. and the Clean A.F.P.F.L. In the 1956 elections the Communists—or more precisely their front group—received one-third of the votes cast, purely because of popular protest against the government's lassitude and corruption. Until General Ne Win intervened in 1958, this group held a virtual balance of power position in Burmese parliamentary politics.

During slightly more than one year as an emergency Prime Minister, Ne Win clipped the wings of the Communists in as thorough an operation as has been seen in recent history. He demanded and got the surrender of all unlicensed arms in the country (a by-product of this rule was a 30 per cent decrease in the crime rate) and his troops killed or captured some 2,000 unregenerate Communists, almost all the guerrillas remaining in the field. Ne Win went after both the Burma Workers Party and the National United Front, arresting all officials suspected of having contacts with the Communists still fighting in the jungle. Although propagating Communist ideology is no offense in Burma, it is an offense to consort with rebels fighting the government; on this basis a substantial number of legal Communists, mainstays of the front organizations, peace committees, captive trade unions, were put behind bars. Thakin Chit Maung, head of the Burma Workers Party, complained bitterly: "Ne Win has cut away the pillars of our movement and carefully left a few leaders out in the open to deceive the world into believing the Army supports democracy. We are still free to advocate Communism, but they have destroyed our means of doing so."

The General's Psychological Warfare Department was lucky enough to come upon a notebook used by a Communist cadre member, containing a violent, contemptuous attack on Buddhism by Thakin Soe, one of Burma's leading Communists. Publication of the notebook shocked this most Buddhist of countries (more than a million and a half copies were marketed). Public reaction to this book, called *Buddhism in Danger,* and other similar information efforts of the government aroused the entire population against Communism.

In the face of such efforts, the legal Communists lost much of the sympathy they had gained through the usual propaganda. Nor could they accuse Ne Win of being pro-West, since he scrupulously kept up good relations with the Communist countries. Like Nasser in the Middle East, although less dangerously, he saw how careless the Communist headquarters are of local parties—especially if the local parties are not doing so well—and exploited this to his and Burma's advantage. Nor was the cause of Communism materially assisted by Chinese occupation of areas inside the Burmese border.

Having left his country politically disinfected, Ne Win stood aside for the politicians, but he and the army remain watchful. He had reversed the power balance of the situation in Indonesia. It was perhaps fortunate for him that he did not face a clever "gradualist" Communist like Aidit in Burma. Then again, Aidit is doubtless fortunate that in Indonesia he ran into no such resolute, shrewd and democratic soldier as Ne Win.

In countries other than these two, a fight in Asia will continue to be waged between Mao's junior partners and the patriotic generals. At the moment, except for Japan, India, the Philippines, Ceylon and, let us hope, Malaya, there is no middle ground. It would be expecting too much, possibly, to wish for a more stable democratic tradition in Asia. Fifteen years is not very long in which to build one.

# CHAPTER VII

# VIOLENT OR "LOVABLE"?

"India has been playing a great role in the world-wide battle for the preservation of peace. . . . The Communist Party, which has been fighting for a consistent policy of peace, welcomes and supports this orientation. . . ."

—Central Committee,
Communist Party of India, 1955

"SHOULD I order a bombing incident at the Prime Minister's reception, or should I accept my own invitation and try to do some recruiting there?" This dilemma, if rarely put in such a poignant form, has occurred time and time again in the life of almost every local Communist leader. Moscow resolved it on an international level by the new image which Nikita Khrushchev constructed for the Party in the late 'fifties. His advice would probably be, "By all means go to the reception, but let them know there may be a bombing later." Khrushchev, however, has had the advantage of power and a stabilized Communist nation behind him. What happens to the Party leader in a critical area, trying to face this question and come up with something like Khrushchev's answer? What happens when his problem is complicated by the fact that he lives in a large nation in Asia, whose Asian traditions are tempered by a considerable history of modern, Western, industrial experience, whose capture is of vital importance to the Communist world, but is complicated not only by local nationalist suspicion, but by the problem of which Communist motherland—Russia or China—should be its goal and exemplar?

The questions above have accurately described the problem of the Communist Party leadership in the pivotal Asian countries of India and Japan. Their countries represent unique amalgams of the East and the West, the underdeveloped and the over-industrialized and over-educated. At various times since World War II both parties have tried to solve the problems by force. In 1948, in Telengana, Indian Communists staged a full-dress war against the central government, supplementing it by riots and acts of violence elsewhere in India. Jawaharlal Nehru himself, although in international policy quick to make allowances wherever possible for Communists, declared that the Communists in India had been responsible for a program of "murder, arson and looting, as well as acts of sabotage."

In Japan the Communists used a gradualist approach to what their leaders called "democratic revolution" until January 1950. Then Moscow through the Cominform journal formally rebuked the party leader Sanzo Nozaka for his "anti-democratic and anti-Socialist" tendencies, and darkly hinted at Titoism. Responding smartly to this public direction, Nozaka led his party into a brief campaign of open violence and sabotage. This resulted in the Party's Central Committee (although not the Party itself) being outlawed several months later, after its activities had shocked and estranged the great bulk of the Japanese people.

Their respective explosions in 1948 and 1950 came as part of a constant pendulum swing in both the Indian and Japanese parties between the extremes of violent action and the gradualist, parliamentary tactics of what the Japanese Party leaders once characterized as a "lovable Communist Party." Khrushchev's 1956 renunciation of Lenin's doctrine of inevitable class warfare came as a godsend to both parties. As the Japanese Party noted in April of that year, in a tidy brochure explaining "peaceful revolution": "The path from capitalism to socialism is certainly not the same everywhere. It is calumny and contrary to facts to assert that we believe in violence and civil war as the only way of socialist revolution."

The peaceful policy of the 'fifties met with great success. The Indian Communists gained control of the entire state of Kerala by parliamentary methods—the first time this happened in a large area of Asia. The Japanese Communists, although they remained weak as a Party, managed to infiltrate the large Japanese Socialist Party so effectively that its left-wing majority became little more than a mouthpiece for Communist foreign and domestic policies. Yet even these considerable gains have been periodically erased by the parties' revolutionary excesses. It was long ago, during the ruthless and headlong rush to collectivize Soviet agriculture, that Stalin censured Soviet Communists for becoming "dizzy with success." In fact, "dizziness with success" is a malady which is endemic in any Communist movement. It is inescapable by reason of the movement's goals and the type of recruit it attracts.

Fortunately for the rest of the world, to say nothing of India and Japan, this recurrent switch of tactics has prevented both parties from taking full advantage of their circumstances. India, with its 300 million people, its universities, its growing industry and its experienced political leadership is the one large rival of Communist China in Asia. Yet the great numbers of the poorly employed, the uneducated and, quite literally, the starving among its population offer a fertile row for the Communists to hoe in their fashion. Japan's 92 million people, crowded on their rocky islands, present a challenge for Communism that is equally tempting. Here is the one large modern industrial base in Asia. The Japanese, unique in Asia, possess many characteristics of industrialized Western societies, including almost universal literacy, a huge press and publishing business and, in the bargain, something approximating an urban proletariat.

At different times during the past fifteen years the Communist movement could have made far greater gains in both these countries than it has. Generally, the gains were precluded by the use of overmuch violence or the tendency to move too quickly. There was another factor, also, which has reared its head elsewhere in Asia: confusion over the international chain of command. Historically the Communist Party of India has depended on the Soviet Party in Moscow, and it still does. But the entry on the scene of a huge neighboring Communist state, whose interests even Indians now concede run sharply counter to their own, has complicated this relationship. Although Peking has not attempted to interfere with Moscow's hold on the Indian Party, it exerts its influence nonetheless.

With the Japanese Communists the situation is different. Here Moscow and Peking exercise a joint dominion—and their directives have often clashed. The early gradualist policy of Sanzo Nozaka, for instance, was the direct outgrowth of his wartime experience with the Chinese Communists in Yenan. His rebuke by the Cominform in 1950 was an implied rebuke by Moscow to Peking as well. Now Peking has the primacy of influence. And, even more than the Indians, the Japanese Party faithful have the long-term handicap of being tied to a rapidly industrializing country whose interests are at root hostile to its own.

History will probably hear more from the Communist movement both in India and Japan. The smaller Parties in other Asian countries will certainly base much of their conduct on this big-power experience. So their successes and their failures are instructive. As we shall see, they were directly related to the question of tactics. Where the Communists courted the "useful idiots" with front groups, Socialist alliances and reliance on parliamentary procedures, their gains were great. When they began relying on strong-arm tactics or outright sabotage, they lost ground. Perhaps this was inevitable. For, as the Communists seem to think themselves, a party that for long periods eschews violent tactics loses its "militancy"— that is to say, with apologies to Marxist-Leninist conviction, its soul.

In 1922 the man who did most to found and organize the Communist Party of India, Manbendra Nath Roy, wrote what seemed to be a simple directive: "The government maintained by violence and brute force cannot be overthrown without violence and brute force." Facing the single challenge of British rule, the small, but growing group of Indian Communists would seem to have little trouble acting out this thesis. But, especially as independence drew near, their problems multiplied. For there were other and more vigorous forces working for independence which were distinctly non-Communist, Gandhi and the Indian Congress Party. Should the Communists unite with the larger "bourgeois" forces in the common struggle? Or should the Communists regard the "bourgeoisie" as menaces equal or even worse than the British and fight them, as the German Communists later fought the anti-Nazi Social Democrats?

As a recent study of Indian Communism put it:* "The history of the Communist Party of India may be summed up as a series of alternations between 'left' and 'right' policies—that is, anti-capitalist and anti-imperialist strategies. . . . The 'left' strategy, aimed against capitalism *in toto,* regards bourgeois nationalism as an enemy. The 'right' strategy, aimed against imperialism, feudalism and monopoly capitalism, regards bourgeois nationalism as an ally. As the CPI followed one or another of these strategies, it found itself alternately locked in battle with the Indian National Congress—the primary agent of bourgeois nationalism in India—or joined with the Congress (with its leader or only with its membership) in battle against British imperialism."

Through the years Indian Communists staggered along the tightrope between these two policies. Left to themselves the Communists generally preferred to fight both the Congress and the British. But Moscow constantly intervened in favor of a broad anti-British front of all parties, due to its own national objectives.

In the World War II years, however, thanks to the temporary Soviet alliance with the West, the Party was ordered to support the British it had always attacked. This brought it in direct conflict with Mahatma Gandhi's "quit India" movement. When India gained its independence, the Communists found themselves very definitely outside of a nationalist movement which was by then far too strong and solidly based for sudden infiltration or capture.

As a result the activists took Roy's old injunction literally and began to fight a small war of revolution. They chose the area of

* Gene D. Overstreet and Marshall Windmiller, *Communism in India* (Berkeley: University of California Press, 1959).

Telengana, in the eastern half of Hyderabad, at the time the Nizam of Hyderabad was still resisting Indian efforts to absorb his state into the new republic. By the middle of 1946, taking advantage of the wretched condition of the Telengana peasantry, the Communists had gained strength heavily. Armed village brigades were posted through the area, and the peasants encouraged to seize land and kill or drive out landlords and local government officials. In September 1948 when the Indian Army marched into Hyderabad to take over the Nizam's principality, Communist guerrillas began a long campaign of terrorism against the Nehru government. In 1952, Gopalaswamy Ayyangar, then Minister of Defence, noted that 1,026 persons had been murdered in a "most brutal manner" by the Telengana Communists.

In the neighboring state of Andhra similar action was tried, although less successfully. "The people did not join us," the Party spokesmen reported later. "Our activities proved to be like a battle in the air . . . On the whole there were no struggles or strikes in the entire province." Yet the violence and the coercion attempted were enough to drive two-thirds of Andrha's 21,000 Party members out of the movement.

The result of these actions was the outlawing of the Party in half of the Indian states. Even then the thought of revolution died hard. In August 1948 the General Secretary of the Party, Balchandra T. Ranadive, announced from an underground headquarters that there would be a general strike and large-scale peasant uprisings throughout India within six months. He failed in both objectives.

In the next few years the Party strategy changed. It was decided to concentrate in certain areas of Communist strength, like Andhra and Calcutta and other places in West Bengal, in an effort to gain loci of power peaceably, which could then be used for ultimate revolutionary activity. The new strategy bore considerable fruit, and nowhere more than in the new state of Kerala.

Kerala was created as a political entity in 1957, out of the old states of Malabar and Travancore-Cochin, a narrow strip of hot, flat, overpopulated coastland on India's southwest shore. It was a problem child from the beginning. Its population combined some of the best-educated groups in India with the highest percentage of Christians in the country. But factional feelings ran high. The Congress Party government in Travancore-Cochin had become notorious for corruption and ineffectiveness, in the face of the constant feuding among a hodgepodge of different sects and races— Hindus and both Catholic and Protestant Christians, Malayalis and Tamils. Kerala was ripe for Communist penetration.

In the first elections held in Kerala in 1957, it was not surprising, therefore, that the local Communists capitalized grandly on the general disgust with the former Congress Party government. The Communists received 60 out of 120 seats in the Kerala State Parliament. This, added to the votes of six independents, gave them an absolute majority and the right to form a government.

As premier of the state, the Party selected a wealthy Brahmin lawyer named Elamkulam Mana Sankaran Namboodiripad. In his early years Namboodiripad had fought with the Congress Party in the civil disobedience movement. For this he was jailed by the British. Although he remained in the movement, as a founder of the Congress Socialist Party, he drifted steadily leftward. He joined the Communist Party in 1937, but he did not announce the fact until three years later. In Kerala his conversion to the Party had a powerful effect among leftist Congress members, and many of them followed him. An urbane, well-spoken man and a great admirer of Mao Tse-Tung, he stood for the parliamentary method, the "climb to power by capturing seat by seat and state by state." (Non-Communist Indians referred to this as the "baloney system—Communism slice by slice.")

For the greater part of a year, Namboodiripad and his government trod very softly. They made a point of emphasizing both Communist legality and efficiency. To bolster the latter reputation, the Communists set about several obvious reforms, including a measure of land redistribution. Graft and corruption were ostentatiously denounced. Proclamations were drawn up asserting the rights of the "untouchables" and other "oppressed" classes to justice. On the whole, popular reaction was good. The go-slow method served to lull the suspicions of anti-Communists and steered a great deal of local "undecided" voters towards the Communist affiliation.

By the summer of 1958, however, it was clear that the drive for legality and efficiency was merely a brief honeymoon. Once the Communists had inserted their own people or fellow-travelers into positions of authority in the state bureaucracy, notably in the judiciary and the police, the pace began to quicken. On July 26, 1958 five members of the Congress Party were killed in a fight with Communists. Soon outbreaks of violence had become commonplace. Throughout the state the Communists incited groups of factory workers to take over their employers' plants, or otherwise intimidate them. Namboodiripad's government ordered the police to offer no protection, in case violence should occur in this process. The incidents multiplied, although the workers received scant gain for their trouble.

Early in 1959 the Communists put through a new Education Act. On its face it was unexceptionable. It provided only that teachers in the private schools of the state—most of them actually public schools operated by separate religious communities—be selected from a list compiled by a state commission. This act, following on the domination of the public schools by Communists, amounted to a complete take-over of the state's educational facilities.

The religious communities, representing a great many of Kerala's citizens, were outraged. Most of the private schools were closed. In Roman Catholic areas, in particular, they remained closed through the summer. Meanwhile the labor disturbances were increasing, carefully fomented by the government itself. It was clear that all private—or cooperative—industry would be in time forced out, in favor of a rigid statism. General amnesties had been given indiscriminately to criminals as well as pro-Communist political prisoners. Their places were taken in the jails by non-Communists and the police power was slowly being turned into an instrument of Party coercion.

In June 1959 the other political parties in Kerala—Congress, Muslim League and Praja Socialist—combined to form a joint league to fight for removal of the government. They charged, among other things, that: fundamental rights had been denied, with no security for life and property; corruption was increasing "like a flood"; Communist "cooperatives" received state funds, while non-Communist cooperatives were denied registration and encouragement; government officers and police were made servants of the Communist Party; unemployment had reached record proportions; school textbooks had been converted into Communist propaganda.

The Opposition parties called a general strike throughout the state and began mass picketing of local government offices. Arrests multiplied. Police fired on non-Communist demonstrators. Opposition supporters were jailed by the hundreds—in the first week of the campaign several thousand people were arrested.

After Nehru himself made a visit to Trivandrum to discuss the situation, Namboodiripad backtracked. He agreed to suspend the Education Act, and "discuss" it. But he had gone too far to allay public indignation. On July 1, 1959 it was officially stated in Trivandrum that 24,961 people had either been "arrested or removed" by the police between June 10 and June 30 in connection with the demonstrations. In a report to the central government the Governor of Kerala, Dr. Ramakrishna Rao, confirmed the Opposition's charges. ". . . a feeling was created among industrial and other workers," he said, "that a government representing the workers or the 'proletariat' had come into power in Kerala and that any excesses committed by labor in their dealings with employers would be condoned. . . . The police became powerless to take preventive action under the Criminal Procedure Code, with the result that in plantations alone 120 incidents of a violent nature occurred during the few months that followed. . . . There is no doubt that the government has used the administrative machinery for consolidating its own party at the expense of others. It has given reasonable ground for the allegation that under cover of democratic garb and the technical majority that the government enjoys, the content of democracy had been crushed."

On July 29 the Central Government's Cabinet met to consider the Governor's report. Acting under article 356 of the Constitution, it dismissed Kerala's state government and assumed its functions. In the elections subsequently held, in February 1960, the Communists and their allies lost 36 of their 65 seats. Kerala returned to democratic government.

By overplaying their hand the Communists had united the opposition parties, which insured their defeat. But they had by no means alienated the electorate. For their popular vote jumped by 1,200,000 to a total of 3,500,000—over 50% higher than they had originally received in 1957. Which raises the question of whether the Kerala Communist interregnum was a total failure from the Communist point of view. Admittedly, had Namboodiripad and his government not grown "dizzy from success" so quickly, their rule might have been followed by other parliamentary victories in the states where the Party is strong, in a political chain reaction. Yet the large vote in 1960 showed that their reckless preachments of pie-in-the-sky for all "workers" had touched a nerve among the poor and downtrodden. Most of these people were too ignorant to see the trap that lay behind the glossy façade of "land for everybody" and "workers' solidarity." What they did remember, even after the law-breaking of the Communists, was that the Communists had paid some attention to them, where other parties had apparently not.

For Namboodiripad and his friends, the dilemma remains: would it have been better to have used peaceful methods a little longer, before resorting to violence?

For the time being, the Party officially holds to the former. In its 1958 constitution the Indian Communists pledged their party to "achieve full democracy and socialism by peaceful means," even dispensing with such old-fashioned Communist words as "politburo" and "cell." (The Russians had abandoned them long since.)

The gains from this tactic have been in one sense gratifying. Party membership almost doubled between 1957 and 1960; the membership at present numbers 300,000.

On the other hand, the Party lost heavily in its united front activities, both because of the Kerala crisis and the embarrassments handed it by Mao Tse-Tung's aggression on the Indian border. Communist defense of Mao caused a revulsion against this foreign-dominated organism, which will be hard to shake. Although Party membership may have increased, the number of "useful idiots" in India has sharply dropped. Party apologists try to concentrate on their ties with the Soviet Union, which receives a far better press in India than its Chinese ally. But the lure of cooperating with the "Socialist camp" is not so powerful as it once was.

For the immediate future, the Communists can hope for little more than protest votes, from people oppressed by economic want and gullible enough to believe that Communism can cure it. In modern India, that protest vote can be quite heavy.

Mr. Sanzo Nozaka could have given Mr. Namboodiripad some helpful advice. Nozaka, a mild-spoken man of scholarly pretensions, now 69 years old, has been leading the Japanese Communist Party since he returned from wartime exile at Yenan with Mao Tse-tung. He has had his own disastrous experience with "dizziness from success," with the added irony that the dizziness in this case was dictated by Moscow. Nozaka gives the impression of a medium-sized gray cat, as he sits, calm and heavy-lidded, inside his stronghold, the Yoyogi headquarters of the Communist Party in Tokyo; and he demonstrates cat-like political reflexes. But his well-laid preparations seem destined to be scotched by rough interference, whether from the ruling leadership in Moscow or Peking, or the agitators inside his own party.

Nozaka today is one of the few survivors of that once abundant species, the well-traveled international Communist. He joined the Party—or at least was deeply influenced by it—in London, as a student there in the 'twenties. After one earlier visit, he went to

Moscow in 1931 and stayed there for almost a decade, working himself up to the status of a member of the old Comintern's Praesidium. In 1940 he went to Yenan and spent the next five years with the Chinese Communists. Despite his long Russian training, the Chinese experience appears to have been more important to him. Consistently, in his speeches and pronouncements, he refers to the "Asian" character of his Party and its struggle. The "Maoist" tactic of a united front for "independence" against foreigners has been his big stock in trade.

When he was flown back from Yenan to Tokyo in 1945, courtesy of the U.S. Air Force, Nozaka reestablished control of the Japanese Communist Party and took stock of the situation. Although the Party had been outlawed until the American occupation, it had picked up a great many sympathizers through the years. More than any other major Communist group in the world the Party in Japan is one of intellectuals. To the Japanese student, whose plate has traditionally been heaped high with Hegel and seasoned with Marx, the theories of Communism have always had their fascination. On a practical level this bent has been reinforced here, as elsewhere, by the fondness of reactionary or militarist standard-bearers for labeling *all* decent liberal elements as "Communist."

Nozaka's plan was simple. Taking advantage of the Marxist sympathies among many intellectuals, he would rebuild a cadre, reinforcing it with workers (most of them turned out to be intellectuals, too). He could hang on the coattails of the reformers in the Occupation, trying hard to build up a democracy in Japan overnight, and profit by the hostility of the conservative post-war Japanese governments, which were often notably unenthusiastic for Occupation reforms.

From the beginning Nozaka emphasized the constitutional processes by which his "lovable" party would work. Violence was not to be used, except in case of rare necessity. The Communists were to group themselves with all parties on the left and center, in an effort to solidify the reforms of the Occupation, and go them one better. The sweeping nature of the Occupation's edicts, like that enforcing an unprecedented land reform in Japan, took much of the wind out of Nozaka's sails. But he correctly counted the conservatives in the caretaker governments to resist them as much as they could. By pushing for bigger and better reforms, the Communists could mobilize, ultimately, the wave of democratic sentiment which the American Occupation was exciting.

On the whole this tactic worked. From a strength of almost zero, the Communists pushed their way up to 10% of the vote in the 1949 elections. A popular front was aborning. The Socialists, outflanked by Nozaka and his competent assistants, often made common cause with the Communists, as did one or two other smaller parties in the Diet. Unlike Communists elsewhere in the world, Nozaka and his men were friendly and approachable. The Communist views were interesting and—always—expressed on a lofty level. "Revolution" was almost a word to joke about.

Then in early 1950 the Cominform struck Nozaka down. He made an abject self-criticism, of the Communist variety, and acknowledged that he had been lax in pursuing the revolutionary struggle. The party forthwith became more militant—which is to say Nozaka's younger followers took out their banners and their blackjacks. A succession of strikes, riots and other labor disturbances severely provoked most non-Communist Japanese, and there were few regrets when the Central Committee of the Party was outlawed. Anti-Communist feeling was increased by the violent demonstrations in front of the Imperial Palace on May Day 1952.

The upshot of this re-direction was the loss of whatever voting pull the Communists possessed. As in India, the wave of violence was blown back on its instigators, and without even the consolation of added votes. In the next elections, the Communists were able to seat only one representative in the lower house of the Diet. Thanks to Moscow's interference, Nozaka had lost his chance to forge a parliamentary popular front. He was probably saved from dismissal as party head only through the intervention of the Chinese Communists, whose early united front tactics he had been borrowing so faithfully.

The Soviet motive in ordering Nozaka to act like a "revolutionary" was no doubt partly inspired by a fear that Nozaka's nationalism would end up in some form of heresy. There was also the faint possibility of using Japan's Communists for behind-the-lines sabotage against Japan-based troops in the forthcoming Korean war, which Stalin was just then planning.

In 1955, when Nozaka and the Party officially came out of hiding, Soviet policy had changed. The Khrushchev plan for a popular front and united multi-party "peace" campaigns was in fact just what Nozaka had once preached himself. The Party officially denounced its "ultraleftist adventurism" and set out to find whatever partners it could—on a sound parliamentary basis.

Unfortunately for him, however, Nozaka had to pay off the accrued interest of five years of Korea, the cold war, and the aggressions, soon-to-happen, in Hungary and Tibet. In a prosperous and notably stable Japan the Party had lost its hopes of becoming a mass movement. Accordingly, Nozaka had only a few scattered strongholds on which to base his policy. Unlike the Indians, he had no pieces of geography—depressed areas or the like—where Communists were locally entrenched. But he did have one political party, his old friends, the Socialists, and several negotiable hunks of popular-front property, including a noisy students' union, a sprawling labor federation, and one serviceable "peace" committee.

Of them all the students' union is most definitely scarred with the Communist trademark, and Nozaka's peaceful popular-front policy scarred in turn by the students. The young leaders of the National Federation of Student Self-Government Associations, known generally by its Japanese abbreviated name of *Zengakuren,* claim a strength of 300,000. The claim is exaggerated, along with their concurrent claim to speak for all Japanese students. But it would be hard to exaggerate the intensity of the students' views, or their lack of any strong opposition. On November 27, 1959, they staged the loudest, most violent and at that time the most disgraceful riot in recent Japanese history. The riot grew out of a front mass-meeting, "The People's Congress Against Revision of the Security Treaty," organized to protest the negotiations for a mutual security treaty between Japan and the United States then going on in Tokyo. Participating were the Socialist party, leftist and Communist-run labor unions, and other front groups. Representatives of these groups paraded in 200 cities throughout Japan. They were about 200,000 strong according to National Police estimates. Of these 30,000 turned out to wave their slogan-painted banners before the iron gates of the white Diet building in Tokyo, within sight of the Imperial Palace grounds.

The crowd at first was good-humored, in the sort of "strike-holiday" mood that features so many of these demonstrations. There were 5,000 police along, mindful of the May 1952 demonstrations, to see that the crowd's humor stayed that way. As the banners clustered outside the gates, a flying squad of 200 students scaled the walls of the Diet compound and opened the gate from the inside. All of them were trusted activists from *Zengakuren*. The mob rushed inside the gates in a mood of exhilaration, Nozaka and Inejiro Asanuma, secretary general of the Socialist Party, at its head. Then, as police tried to push it back, the mood of the mob turned ugly. Another flying squad of 600 more "students" forced its way inside the Diet buildings. People were getting badly hurt.

It was clear by this time to Nozaka and the other leaders that the "peaceful demonstration" was getting out of hand. But this was what *Zengakuren* wanted. Union leaders called through loudspeakers that the "meeting" was a success and they should go home. The students shouted them down as "traitors to the working class." The mob raged through the Diet grounds as uncontrollable as a lynching party. Finally, in a last orgy of defiance, hundreds of the students urinated en masse on the Diet steps.

The violence of the attack shocked even the Communists. The Socialists barred *Zengakuren* from any demonstrations in the future. The Communists let it be known that the students' federation had been read out of the party. For, however effective as a temporary display of mob power, the demonstration—like other destructive jobs of *Zengakuren*—had disgusted the bulk of the Japanese people, who quite justly blamed it on "Communist plotting."

Nozaka has already dismissed large numbers of *Zengakuren* members from the Party. Many of the students themselves have walked out to form splinter "hard-line" or so-called Trotskyist Communist groups, who denounce Nozaka and Khrushchev both as "rightist opportunists." They have hardly been an asset to Nozaka's "peaceful democratic revolutionary" tactics. Yet to most of the Japanese people, these student extremists—many of whom have only tangential relationships to classes at universities—are purely and simply Communists. Another illustration of the Nozaka dilemma.

The major trade-union federation Nozaka finds more docile and, naturally, more serviceable. Sohyo—the abbreviation for the Japanese Federation of Labor—has an estimated membership of 3,597,000. Led by a far left-wing boss named Kaoru Ota, who ironically began life as a trade unionist when he was ordered by his bosses at the Ube Nitrogen Company to form a company union, Sohyo was originally anti-Communist. Sohyo was founded in 1950 as a protest against the Communist-line policies of Sambetsu, the Japanese League of Industrial Organizations, and it still retains a membership in the International Federation of Trade Unions. But, again, hard-working leftists gradually captured most of the key jobs. In recent years, Sohyo has parroted the Communist line on every question of foreign and domestic policy, leaning most heavily on its demand to abolish the U.S. alliance and initiate friendly relations with Communist China.

Sohyo is the kind of front organization which fits in with Nozaka's gradualist policy. Probably no more than 10% of its high command are card-holding Communists and only a tiny percentage of the rank-and-file. The party-liners comprise an additional 15% of the membership. The useful idiots make up the docile majority. At its recent convention in 1959 Sohyo abandoned its traditional support of the Socialist Party, to permit members to support the Communists, if they so chose. The newspapers of its member unions frequently sound more inflammatory than Nozaka's own Party paper, *Akahata,* in hawking the Party line. (They are supplied by a dummy outfit called the Japan Press Association, which exists principally to disseminate pro-Communist W.F.T.U. propaganda.) Some of its member unions, like the Japan Teachers' Union, have been strongholds of Communist activity for years.

The Teachers' Union could also be used as an object lesson of what happens when a union is exploited wholly for political purposes. It is the largest union in Sohyo, with 500,000 members. It was once the richest. Its treasury is now almost empty and its influence has been slackening. For the Teachers' Union throughout the late 'forties and the 'fifties has diverted most of the energies and the funds which should have been used for its members' welfare to furthering the left-wing indoctrination of its students.

Posing as a bulwark against the return of rightist influence in the Ministry of Education and the prefectural school systems, the Teachers' Union wrote its own textbooks, mobilized students in constant "anti-atomic" rallies, which speedily became anti-American rallies, and often imprisoned principals and prefectural officials in their own offices to enforce its demands. Finally, supported by a slightly aroused public opinion, the conservative Tokyo government was able to push back the Union on a number of fronts. Because the Communists and their allies in the Union captured most of the local school boards, school boards are now appointive. An efficiency "rating" system for teachers is now in force in all but three prefectures—as a weapon against teachers who spent most of their time organizing strikes. Thus the Ministry of Education has regained some control of the schools.

This new trend to centralization is by no means an unmixed blessing. What it may mean, ultimately, is that the Teachers' Union, by exploiting for political purposes the new freedom of the Japanese local schools, has in the end destroyed them. The honestly liberal Japanese schoolteacher is ground between two pressures. On one side are the Communists subverting the school system. On the other there are diehard conservatives who wish to return Japanese schools to the dictatorial standard in vogue before war and the U.S. occupation replaced it.

There are other front organizations which prosper in Japan. One of the most prominent is the Japanese Council Against Atomic and Hydrogen Bombs—Gensuiko for short—which has staged annual "conventions" in Hiroshima, featuring horribly maimed victims of the Hiroshima A-Bomb, real or fancied, as props for their arguments. Three of the eleven members of Gensuiko's board of directors have been exposed as Communists, and the degree of anti-American, anti-government, and pro-Communist propaganda featured at its annual mass-meetings have forced the Hiroshima government, finally, to refuse to sponsor its peace rally in 1960. Like front organizations everywhere, the most successful of these in Japan have innocuous names, and frequently innocuous sponsors —there are not many ladies in the All-Japan Federation of Women's Organizations who realize the extent to which they are being used.

The Socialist Party of Japan is probably the most useful of all to Nozaka. Here, through the years, he and other Communists have been able to take advantage of a chronic Socialist split between left and right wings to link hands with the left and by far the larger wing of the Party in a virtual popular-front alliance. Here is the one real success of the popular-front policy, which makes up for a number of excesses and failures. For the Socialists are a major party. They polled roughly one-third of the popular vote in the last Japanese elections.

The Communist strategy in close electoral districts has been to put up a candidate of their own, then withdraw in favor of the Socialist at the last minute, after due conferences between Party representatives. A great many Socialist members of the Diet owe their seats to this stratagem, and they are not allowed to forget it. But beyond this tactical alliance, the Socialists' major policy planks —friendship with Communist China and abolition of the U.S. alliance—are so dear to the Communists' hearts that constant cooperation has become inevitable. At the end of 1959 the veteran Socialist Suehiro Nishio found this hardening alliance so objectionable that he bolted the party. He took 54 of the 250-man Socialist Diet membership with him.

This Socialist collaboration with Communism is a curiously old-fashioned survival which experience long ago proved disastrous to so many Socialists in Europe. It is, in fact, symptomatic of the stagnant nature of Japanese intellectual life, on which Nozaka has so patiently fed. The Japanese intellectuals remain for the most part high-buttoned-shoe types who tend to feel that Marxism must be a sound philosophy, principally since it was banned by the pre-war militarists. They profited greatly by the reforms of the U.S. occupation, but resented them because they were imposed from without. So they affect anti-Americanism. In Japan, anti-Americanism, to borrow the American aphorism, is the anti-Semitism of the intellectuals. Obsessed by the horrors of nuclear war, as seen by them at close quarters, they tend to forget its clear cause. Japanese egghead publications, even reputable organs like *Bungei-Shunju,* have already started hinting that Syngman Rhee and the Americans really started the Korean war, and it is doubtless only a matter of time before they allege that the Japanese fist was hit by the American chin in an unprovoked attack at Pearl Harbor.

Because the Russians are remote, even the furor over a Hungary dies down after a time. It is hard for the Tokyo eggheadery to believe that Communists can be aggressive (especially since U.S. protection has made such aggression against Japan academic). In April 1960, for instance, Nobel Prize winner Hideki Yukawa, the scientist, demanded that the seven-man Committee for World Peace be disbanded, after its Secretary General had had the temerity to invite the Dalai Lama to visit Japan.

The leader of the Japanese left-wing Socialists, Inejiro Asanuma, had originally been strongly against collaboration with the Communists. After a visit to Peking and assurances from Nozaka that peaceful parliamentarianism was all the Communists wanted, Asanuma buried the hatchet with the Communists and became, ostensibly, a neutralist. In fact, he ended up playing the Communist game. With the same logic used by other Japanese intellectuals, he reasoned that if conservative groups, e.g., the former Premier Kishi, were pro-American, then the only patriotic course was to insist on a rapprochement with the Communist Chinese and the Russians. Since his about-face, his policies have grown almost indistinguishable from those of the Communists. The Japanese Socialists still affect a belief in Marxist theories of the class struggle and capitalist decline so doctrinaire that Khrushchev himself has discarded them. They have no body of basic principles which might prevent them from being used by Nozaka.

In contrast to the militancy of the students, the Communists and their useful idiot friends, the bulk of the Japanese public has been passive about politics since 1945, content to vote overwhelmingly conservative inside the voting booth, but unwilling to speak out against the loud leftist minority among them. There was no more striking illustration of this popular unconcern than the events of June 1960.

In a series of riots, ostensibly directed against Premier Kishi and the revised security pact with the United States, fighting students—assisted by trade unionists and militants from Nozaka's Communists and the Asanuma Socialists—caused such violent commotion in Tokyo that the Japanese government withdrew its invitation to President Eisenhower for an official visit. The police, it was said, were not sure of their ability to protect him.

If the riots were allegedly directed against the security pact, it was quite clear that the Eisenhower visit was their principal target. In the wake of the new Soviet hard line after the Summit failure and the U-2 incident, Moscow and particularly Peking wanted no demonstration of American-Japanese solidarity. The riots had no effect on the security pact (which actually involved a restoration of military sovereignty to Japan and a sharp curtailment of the use by American forces of Japanese bases). Kishi and his majority party ratified it despite them. But in keeping off the Eisenhower visit, they scored a propaganda victory for the Russians and the Chinese.

Their scope and fury was appalling, if impersonal. (The same people shouting anti-American slogans would politely greet American passers-by.) It brought this statement from the long-time Socialist Diet member, Mrs. Shizue Kato (the former Baroness Ishimoto of birth-control fame): "Watching the battle of the Diet on television my heart sank. It was an attempt to throw out the government by force, planned by a small group run by a subversive ideology. As a Socialist, I wish to apologize to the nation for having been too cowardly those past weeks to say what I knew was right."

The sentiment of this statement would doubtless be echoed by the Japanese electorate, as farmers and workers went to the polls clucking with disapproval about Communist excesses—but doing nothing to counter them outside. It would quite probably bring tougher police controls. Some observers suspected that Japanese right-wing politicians had not overworked themselves in ordering the riots checked, so that they could get a new and more stringent set of police regulations from the aroused voters.

Sanzo Nozaka's Communists would find it a mixed victory. Once again, they had sacrificed the new campaign to sell their "lovable" Communist party for the sake of Moscow and Peking policy. They stood exposed as a subversive group.

At the same time, they had shown the world how well a crowd of not overly bright intellectuals, trade unionists and Socialist leaders could be manipulated. For want of any opposition from an apathetic electorate and a press which still seems to think the world's principal worry is pre-war Japanese militarism, the Communists had twisted a complex issue into a simple equation of "security pact means war" and "no pact means peace." The "useful idiots" believed it. Nozaka's words in a 1956 speech were borne out, when he said: "These mass movements and organizations are like transmission belts for our Party in establishing its links with the multi-millioned masses and are, simultaneously, a school of the national liberation democratic revolution. As these transmission belts gain in strength, the Party's links with the masses will become stronger and stronger."

# CHAPTER VIII

# NO EUROPEANS NEED APPLY

"We do not need Communism to obtain social justice in
our country . . ."

—ABDULLAH IBRAHIM,
former Premier of Morocco

AFRICA is not called the Dark Continent for nothing. This thought
has doubtless occurred to the Soviet (and, to a lesser extent, the
Chinese) proprietors of the international Communist movement
as they go about their daily round. For the problem of colonizing
the institutions of the new emerging African countries for Communism is no less difficult than the more constructive task of the
Western democracies in trying to make these countries into stable
members of the free world community.

To cite an example: by September 1960 Communists of the
Soviet order had infiltrated the independence movement in the
newly freed Congo after its shaky governmental structure had virtually fallen in pieces following the mutiny of the small Congolese
army. The mutineers, who understandably confused independence
with pie-in-the-sky after listening to their new leaders, had swarmed
over the former Belgian Congo's cities and settlements, looting,
raping and killing. Their new leader, an unscrupulous young dema-
gogue named Lumumba, had defied the U.N., accepted Soviet
advisors, and attempted to set up a Communist-line state. Yet the
target of the Congolese rage was not "capitalists" or "colonialists"
but whites. There were no lists of demands, no party programs,
nothing but the expression of a chaotic discontent. In fact, outside
of the fiercely held tribal loyalties, there was no politics in the
Congo at all.

Although the chaos of the Congo was an extreme, nationalist revolution all over Africa has flared up in similar fits and starts, kindled among peoples who only yesterday had been thought poor soil for any political activity. Its direction is unpredictable, because it moves by no known set of political ground rules or precedents. It would hardly have seemed probable that an American-educated anti-Communist democrat, Tom Mboya, could suddenly crystallize a Kenya independence movement, based on a swelling trade unionism, scarcely two years after the Mau Mau rebellion—with its strange mixture of tribalism and home-grown Marx—had been destroyed. There is no reference chapter in the Marxist textbooks to the Universal Socialism of Kwame Nkrumah, who likes to refer to his party as "Christian Marxist." It was gratifying to the Soviet Union when President Sekou Touré, of Guinea, formally visited Moscow and lined himself up with his hosts in the fight against "reaction." But the Russians, after giving Guinea a handsome Moscow embassy, are still attempting to discover what Touré means by "African Socialism."

In Asia as well as in Europe, the Communist movement had the advantage of traditions or at least guide-lines for future action. In Africa it has all happened too fast. The original Communists in that continent, as we have seen in the case of Egypt, were mostly foreign to the countries they represented—and the ideal of "Socialist" fraternity diminished accordingly. Moroccan Party members grew notably unenthusiastic about taking orders from Frenchmen or Italians; and there was little to attract thinking black Africans in the origins of something like the Communist Party of South Africa, whose first workers' "revolution" in 1922 was predicated on the slogan: "Workers of the world, unite—and fight for a white South Africa."

The old Marxist dogma, so capable of torsion and tension to suit the varying needs of Europeans or, in its Maoist dispensation, of Asians, seems just that to most Africans—old, jaded, hardly applicable to their circumstance. Africans find little of the murky romance or idealism in the canons of Communism that so stirred the intellectuals of other continents. They see it in the drab daylight. One of Accra's brightest young newspapermen, educated in Prague, recalls that his principal impressions during his stay were of the low standard of living and the oppression prevalent under Communism. Similarly, a man like Jomo Kenyatta could spend eighteen months studying in Soviet universities, yet show not a trace of Marxist influence or sympathy in his classic work of anthropology, "Facing Mount Kenya."

The new leaders *do* admire the discipline of the Communist states, or other totalitarian models. Witness the structure of Sekou Touré's *Parti Démocratique de Guinée,* which swept the first elections there after Guinea demanded and received its independence from the French. The supreme governing body—under Touré—is a sort of pocket Politburo; the National Assembly exists principally to carry out the Politburo's decisions. In the villages, district political committees are the supreme authority. Other trappings of Communism include youth labor brigades, professedly voluntary, and weekly criticism sessions before the village committees, at which citizens publicly examine each other's faults and loyalties.

Private schools are being abolished, as are all opposition groups. In September 1959 M. Touré explained the principle of rule in his new country in this fashion: "The *Parti Démocratique de Guinée* is identical with Guinea. The Party's decisions must be respected by everyone." Yet there is no evidence that this strong central government owed any direct debt, originally, to Soviet instructors. It is merely another dictatorship.

The principal card which can be safely played with such a country by the Soviet Union and its lesser tentmates in the Socialist camp is of course their offers of economic aid. The new nations of Africa are greedy for self-sufficiency and they do not relish being beholden to foreigners. As a result, they are quick to appreciate the joys of playing both sides of the street. If their normal trade relations in the past have been with the West, that is no reason why the traffic should be closed to the East. In fact they are all the more eager to get their supplies from countries without past colonial connections. Hence the situation of the new country of Guinea, which turned towards the Soviet bloc for arms and other desired produce the moment the Touré government seemed cooly dealt with by the West. The fact that Guinea had itself rejected a stop-gap tie with the French Union, and dealt very summarily with Western businesses was of course not accepted as a valid reason for Western caution—in Guinea.

There is an odd mixture of cynicism and naïveté in such attitudes. The young African leaders (most of them are in their twenties or thirties) are wise enough to realize the bargaining power they gain by playing the Soviet bloc against the West and vice versa. They are naïve enough to believe that they can accept aid from all quarters without giving economic-political concessions (in the case of the Communist bloc) or at least guarantees of responsibility (to the Western allies) in return. In short, they feel the world owes them a living. They are particularly vulnerable to the Soviet promises of rapid industrialization, which the Khrushchev regime makes with such an appearance of faithfulness.

Every emergent nation wants a steel mill in its back yard. Smoke from the new factory has become something of a heraldic symbol among the world's underdeveloped countries. The new countries of Africa are naturally suspicious of Western advisors and missions who advocate caution and patience in aid-for-industrialization programs. The Soviet bloc experts who visit them are generally refreshingly free of such cautions—an understandable position since the aid or credits they administer need be justified only incidentally on an economic basis. The new nations of Asia, older at this business than they, might be able to impart some cautions of their own, like the Burmese statesmen who finally acknowledged the folly of building a steel mill in a country without either coal or iron with the wistful words, "We dreamed too much." Unfortunately, everyone has to learn for himself.

The showcase for the Soviet Union's campaign in Africa is the United Arab Republic. Russian and satellite diplomats can point to their continuing aid to Nasser, despite his domestic anti-Communist policies, as simon-pure evidence of their disinterestedness in the politics of persuasion. As the Moscow radio set forth the doctrine a few years ago: "Peoples freeing themselves from the foreign yoke could make use of the achievements of the world Socialist camp without any military or political obligations. Their most active friend and defender is, as always, the Soviet Union, which is helping countries hampered in their development by the colonial regime. The Soviet Union actively contributes to the aspirations of all peoples who are freeing themselves from the foreign yoke."

There is of course no mention of the fine print that is appended to most such contributions, to be found after the recipient is past the bright red ribbons of the wrapping. The objective is to keep the credits running for as long a period as possible, to inject as many Soviet advisers and technical experts as possible into the country—in general, to build up a long-term dependence on the Soviet bloc. If this underlying premise is accepted, then the terms are often very reasonable (the interest rarely exceeds three percent). Undoubtedly, good value can often be had in accepting Soviet assistance, at least if one is interested only in the immediate material object of the credit.

The United Arab Republic can point to much useful assistance from the Soviet Union and the "Socialist camp." Yet the bulk of it has been in the form of arms and munitions, articles where the need for spare parts and fresh supplies constitutes a self-perpetuating element. As previously noted, the payment which Egypt and Syria each made for such Soviet aid was to pledge their cotton crop for a period of years—exactly how long a time has not been revealed. The Soviet Union, it is true, has contracted to build Nasser's favorite long-term project, the High Dam at Aswan. But it should be remembered that the loans and technical help for this activity are being doled out piece by piece, so that continuation of the project becomes a constant threat which can be held over Nasser's head.

The Communist approach to the new African countries was enunciated by the Moscow radio, celebrating the independence of Ghana in March 1957: "Special importance should be attached to the birth of Ghana. Following in the footsteps of Asia, Black Africa, too, is beginning to cast off the yoke of slavery. Though the new state may be very small compared with the rest of this enormous continent, still smarting under the imperialist yoke, its emergence marks a fresh blow to colonialism."

For a time attempts were made to build up front groups in Ghana, but they made little progress. A typical failure was that of the Communist-led International Union of Students. As early as February 1957 the Ghana National Union of Students seceded from IUS, banning all further contact with it. Its reason was simple: "IUS subordinated the welfare of students to the dictates of political regimes, which was contrary to student interests." Accordingly the movement broke off its serious efforts to work from inside the country. There is no Communist Party in Ghana, in any case, to form a nucleus for such activity. There is little prospect of one being created; if it were, there is even less prospect that Nkrumah's People's Convention Party, already working hard to kill off its legal opposition the United Party, would permit the existence of another contender.

This is not to say that the new Soviet image does not project itself with vigor. The Soviet diplomatic mission in Ghana already numbers a total staff of seventy and the ambassador is one of the most active, accessible diplomats in Africa. Pravda and the New China News Agency station correspondents in Accra who spend their days writing long articles about the "Afro-Asian struggle against imperialism." There is not much room for rapid expansion of trade between Ghana and the bloc—Nkrumah's pet dam on the Volta River, a $150 million project, is being built by the West. But cultural embassies, missions and the ubiquitous delegations appear with frequency. About 100 students from Ghana are studying in Soviet bloc universities at the moment; 50 more scholarships are offered this year, 150 for 1961.

So far this is the best that the "Socialist camp" can do. Although Nkrumah himself had many leftist associations when he studied in London—at the time it was the sad fact that Communists and Socialists were almost the only people who would associate with young African students—he has disavowed with fervor any Communist connection. Among the practical African politicians of his area, the matter of being pro-Communist or anti-Communist rarely comes up. And by imperialism, the politically vocal in Ghana include what they regard as both the Russian and the Western variety, indiscriminately. Africa is the one continent in the world where Soviet Russians are often regarded as merely another variety of European.

Nigeria, whose 35,000,000 people make it the largest of the new African countries, is also the most stable. The Communist connection appears equally remote. The emergent Nigerian government has cooperated with the British Colonial Office, until October 1, 1960, still technically responsible for the country, in keeping a rigid ban even on Communist literature. Recently a minor civil servant in Lagos was dismissed, when two copies of the English edition of the Soviet "New Times" were found in his desk. A few intellectuals proclaim themselves Marxist, but resist the thought of any Communist affiliation. A handful of trade unionists boast of their Marxist principles, but again insist that they are not Communists. The Nigerian Trade Union Congress itself is firmly tied to the ICFTU. Union officials accused of Marxist leanings resist the imputation. As the Secretary of the Public Utility Technical and General Workers Union, M.O. Essiet said recently: "I am half as formidable as the government folks say I am. I am a Democrat."

Wherever one, goes, except for a few small pockets in some former French colonies, the supply of Communists is almost nil, the reservoir of potential fellow-travelers extremely shallow. The brother of Sekou Touré, the president of Guinea, is probably a

Communist. Some student groups at Khartoum University did found an "Anti-Imperialist Front." A young civil servant from the Belgian Congo, by name Pierre Leopold Elengesa, after rapid promotion, did go to the 1958 World's Fair at Brussels, was visited by prominent Belgian Communists and went off to pursue his studies in Moscow, awaiting the Congo's independence. But such cases are few and far between. In attempting to colonize Africa, Khrushchev has no Mao to blaze the trail for him. Nor has Mao, for that matter. On the whole, African society is primitive enough either not to understand the Communist message at all, or be bored by it, or see it with the clarity of a child as simply another manifestation of European influence which shrewd Africans might be able to exploit.

To see how imperfectly Communism is able to capitalize on crisis in this area, we have only to look at the Communist role in two explosions which began in the recent past, which continue as a chain reaction at present, and which will continue until Africa achieves its complete independence. They are the crises in Kenya and South Africa.

The original explosion in Kenya was the Mau Mau revolt, a brutish exercise in terrorism which curiously enough had its origins in a worthy education movement. The Kikuyu Independent Schools movement was founded by Peter Mbiu Koinange, a son of a Kikuyu chief, who received an education in the United States (B.A. Ohio State, M.A. Columbia). Koinange started the Independent Schools for three reasons: 1) the educational facilities open to Africans were woefully inadequate; 2) most of those available were conducted by missionaries, who Koinange felt undermined Kikuyu traditions to the detriment of tribal unity; 3) Koinange regarded the existing schools as vehicles of British propaganda, which were indoctrinating their students with a spirit of subservience.

Koinange started the schools movement in the early 'thirties. By the 'fifties they had become a dominant force in the life of the Kikuyu. They were in effect training grounds for African nationalists. When Jomo Kenyatta came back from his overseas education in London and Moscow, he used the schools and their graduates as the groundwork for a spectacular campaign of agitation and political activity. Thousands were swept into his Kenya African Union. Even deep in the bush, where politics could not be imagined apart from the tribe and the village, entire populations would gather to hear Kenyatta speak.

The machine blew up in Kenyatta's face with the Mau Mau revolt, which he became powerless to control—so primitive were the passions it unleashed. The Independent Schools movement was banned, the teachers' training college closed. Kenyatta was sentenced to a seven-year jail term on the charge of managing Mau Mau; Koinange remained in exile. But although Kenyatta, thanks to his Moscow stay, had long been accused of Communist leanings, the Mau Mau revolt and his actions in inciting it, in effect, scared the Communists stiff.

In the first place, Kenyatta's appeal was openly racialist and anti-white. The official Communist line in Africa (since Russians find it inexpedient to change their skins) stoutly preaches racial co-operation. This generally runs head-on into the gospel of the African nationalists, who understandably advocate equality first and cooperation second. Orthodox Communists, ever ready with a phrase, condemn this viewpoint as "black chauvinism."

Secondly, the Communists objected that Kenyatta was organizing much too quickly among the Kikuyu, not enough among the other tribes. They feared that he was emphasizing tribal divisions instead of creating a united movement of the African people. To organize by tribes (outside of the Soviet Union, at least) was not according to the book.

Finally, the Communists looked with utter suspicion on the mystical and semi-religious nature of some of Kenyatta's propaganda. They felt this was not only reactionary but dangerous, because so hard to control. The Mau Mau uprising that resulted confirmed their fears. The suppression of Mau Mau seemed to set back the anti-colonial movement in Kenya by years. The brutalities of the Mau Mau fanatics, also, took much of the sting from the Africa-wide Communist propaganda about Britain's "ruthless suppression of colonial peoples."

Yet Mau Mau and the aftermath did not destroy the independence movement in Kenya. On the contrary, the Kenya nationalists very shortly afterward began building up their forces peaceably, based on a nascent trade union tradition, and wrung concessions out of the British, where the Mau Mau terrorism had only justifiably enraged them. The founder of this political nationalist movement, as it happens, is an Indian Communist, Makhan Singh, son of a respected member of Kenya's Sikh community, who was exiled ten years ago to the remote wilderness in the far north of the colony. There were no Communists, however, to take his place, and the movement which succeeded both Singh and Mau Mau has been led by Tom Mboya, a strong anti-Communist nationalist.

Mboya strengthened his trade union movement with other politically conscious people of the Africa community, forging the beginnings of real self-government. There are no front groups sharing the limelight with him and his nationalists. None, apparently, are desired. For the Kenya independence movement is regarded as a purely African struggle.

In the Union of South Africa there are Communists included in the African National Congress and other organizations fighting the white apartheid of the South African government. Two of the most prominent of the African leaders, Moses Kotane and Dr. Yusuf Dadoo, an Indian, are Communists. But here again the efficiency of the Communist effort was sorely diluted by racial differences, which the Party was never quite capable of solving.

The first trade unions in South Africa arose in the mines, over the fight for protective measures against silicosis. One of the leaders in this fight was a Lincolnshireman named William Andrews. "Comrade Bill," as he was known to Communists over most of the world, who began by organizing the mining unions, became the first General Secretary of the South African Trades and Labor

Council. In 1916, after Comrade Bill's left-wing views had estranged other factions in the Council and the new Labor Party, he bolted to form the International Socialist League and after that, in 1921, the Communist Party of South Africa.

The South African Communists aimed at establishing a pure white Soviet and they found their opportunity in the great mine strike of 1922. Field Marshal Smuts, then Premier, smashed the uprising with troops, but his action lost him the next election. In the succeeding Labor-Nationalist coalition the one-time strikers worked out a compromise with the government and the mine-owners— which amounted to cutting the cake, at the expense of the unskilled Negro labor. With this the Communists lost forever their once strong base in the white trade unions.

For the next three decades the Communist Party faithful groped through a succession of party lines, and acquired a scattering of non-white recruits. In 1929 Zinoviev laid down the doctrine from Moscow that they should fight for "an independent native republic of South Africa." As a corollary of this policy Kotane, then a young Tswana tribesman, was smuggled out of South Africa and sent to study at the University of the Toilers of the East in Moscow. He later became South Africa's permanent delegate to the Comintern and, ironically, was chosen to announce the next sharp turn in the line: according to the popular-front theory of the 'thirties, Party members were ordered to push for a democratic republic of all the races.

After several inner convulsions, the membership accepted the change. Until the Party's suppression in 1951, it remained the official objective. It still does, in the Party's clandestine councils. Ironically, in the state of race war now existing in South Africa, this makes the Communists the moderates of the African National Congress movement. The extremists, called "Africanists," believe there will be no place for whites in a "free" South Africa. The few Communists in the movement have worked consistently to moderate and mediate, at one point heading off a planned armed revolt which the Africanists had long been hatching.

There are other ironies. Because of rigid segregation laws, the white Communists and the black and colored Communists have had to separate. The former predominate in the all-white Congress of Democrats. The latter have their own informal organizations inside the African National Congress. There, contrary to precedents set elsewhere, they continue to exercise a somewhat confused moderating role. Neither underground Party organization nor a corps of front groups exists.

All this was too confusing for Comrade Bill. Before he died recently, the man who held Party card No. 1 of the South African Communist Party washed his hands of his old friends in protest against the Party's "cowardly suicide." He asked for membership in the British Communist Party.

Meanwhile the struggles go on in Kenya and South Africa, the one organized and fought on a democratic parliamentary basis, the other a seething, illegal rebellion-in-being against a ruthless police state. By all the canons of European and Asian experience Communists should be parading in the front ranks of both, infiltrating, ingratiating, leading on occasion. Nothing could be further from the fact.

On its face the fighting for independence in North Africa would seem to be as much a gift to the Communists as the struggle of the Arabs against Israel in the Middle East. In Algeria the Communist movement was well rooted, with local Communist cells present since 1920, when the Communists broke off with the Socialists in France. Later an autonomous Algerian Communist Party was constituted. A number of Algerian towns had Communist mayors and municipal councillors. Until 1956 Communist deputies from Algerian departments sat in the National Assembly in Paris.

Yet there has been little or no direct Communist influence on the Algerian F.L.N. or other movements for a free Algeria, if for no other reason than that most of Algeria's leading Communists have always been French. There were very few Moslems among the Party faithful there and the orders from the top always came from

French Party headquarters. Older Algerian Nationalists could remember that back in the 'twenties, at the congress of the Third Internationale, Leon Trotsky was once moved to denounce the Algerian Communists (i.e. the French Algerian Communists) for opposing an early emancipation of the Moslem populations.

During the course of the Algerian war Communists have been of considerable assistance to the Algerian rebels; but in most cases the Communists involved have been Frenchmen from France, whose interest in the rebel cause was directly related to its potential for disrupting the orderly processes of the government in Paris. When it has dealt with the Algerian rebels, the Communist movement has been constrained to move through its governments in the Soviet bloc.

In Morocco, an independent Arab government has been no friendlier to the Communist movement than the struggling Algerians. On February 9, 1960 the Moroccan Court of Appeals upheld a ruling of a lower court banning the Moroccan Communist Party. The Party was ordered to cease operations and close down its offices. The lower court's decision had originally been taken on the basis of a decree permitting the suspension of any association whose aims threatened the monarchical basis of the state. The events leading up to it—the Algerian Communist experience writ large—only underlined the difficulties in the way of Africa's few local Communists.

The Moroccan Party began operations in 1936 as an offshoot of the mother church in Paris. Although a few Party cards were handed out to Arabs, even the Arab nationalist parties were then in an embryonic stage; and, as in Algeria, almost all the original membership was either French or Spanish. In 1943 a French lawyer of Algerian origin, Leon Sultan, officially founded the Communist Party of Morocco. At the same period the left-dominated unions of the French C.G.T. formed a Moroccan subsidiary, which began to attract many Arab members.

Because of the unions, rather than the Communists among them, the leaders of the Moroccan independence movement, which had taken shape by World War II, had to make an important decision. As Abderrahim Bouabid, then the Istiqlal (independence) Party's expert on union questions, later recalled their problem: "Were we to let Moroccan workers join and C.G.T. defend their most vital interests—their wages and social conditions? The risk was great [but] we took a negative attitude and [in 1946] we ordered all workers not to enter the C.G.T." Thus the leftist unionists of France were hoisted on their own petard. Long accustomed to exploiting their hold on trade unionists for political purposes, they found themselves rejected—at a time when their union could offer its membership in Morocco definite advantages—because the canny Arabs did not want to be politically compromised by a French-led organization.

It was some time before this that the Communist Party proper made its major and, for a long time, decisive blunder in Morocco. As part of the world-wide Communist line, it had endorsed the Allied war effort, calling for "unity of the French nation" in the process. When the Istiqlal leaders made their first call for independence, in January 1944, the Communists refused to associate themselves with it.

As Istiqlal grew stronger, the Communists tried desperately to horn in. The Frenchman, Sultan, who died in 1945, was succeeded as Secretary General of the Party by a young teacher named Ali Yata, who was on good terms with some of the Istiqlal leaders. The older French, Spanish or Italian Communists removed themselves to the background as mere "advisors," while a small group of Communist Arabs went out to win support among the rural population.

In the early 1950's the independence struggle passed from the level of manifestoes and appeals to one of riots, police raids and arrests. King Mohammed V was first deposed by the French in 1953, then exiled in March 1955 to Madagascar—a date which begins what Moroccans call their "revolutionary era." The local

French *colons* were unable to prove Istiqlal's collaboration with the Communists before this period. On the contrary, the nationalist leaders had been on the point of moving *against* Communist influence in the trade unions. But the later underground struggle against the French gave the Communists some chance to regain favor with the nationalists.

This "liberation" role never quite materialized. Most of the effective action against the French was taken by the rural Army of Liberation, dominated by Istiqlal and smaller non-Communist groups like the Democratic Independence Party (PDI) which pinned down three divisions of the French Army in the Riff and the far south in 1955-56. After independence and the King's recall, bitter gang warfare broke out between partisans of Istiqlal and the Communists. The Istiqlal governments had little more sympathy with the Communists than their followers—and until the summer of 1958 the French banishment of Ali Yata from Morocco was upheld by the Moroccans. Not until 1959—a bare year before its official suppression—was the Party able to get permission for its own Arabic newspaper.

There were a few points in the Party's favor, however. The increasingly friendly policy of the Soviet bloc towards Nasser and the Arab Middle Eastern countries cast a faint reflected glow over the local Communists. Not only the French, but other members of the Western alliance, on the other hand, shared unpopularity because of the French efforts in Algeria. On Moscow's initiative, external liaison responsibilities for the Moroccan Party were removed from the French Communists and given to the Italians. Palmiro Togliatti had already had years of experience "guiding" Party work in Tunisia.

Later, however, the Arabs in Morocco as well as the Middle East began to realize that Moscow's friendliness to the Arabs was only part of a cynical policy combining pressure and favors, according to the situation. The Communist infiltration of the Iraqi government after the revolution there caused understandable nervousness—to say nothing of the actual Communist outbreaks of disorder. When Crown Prince Moulay Hassan visited Cairo in 1959, President Nasser issued his hardly coincidental statement denouncing Communism. When Premier Abdullah Ibrahim banned the Party later in that year, he was impelled partly by a motive not unknown in many countries of the West, the hope of placating growing numbers of people who accused him of being "soft on Communism."

In the years before its banning, after the initial disturbance of the independence era, the Party had walked softly. No one had tried more conscientiously to present the new image of the Khrushchev Communists. The Party had announced itself pro-monarchist. Following one of his periodic trips to Moscow and the "People's Democracies," Ali Yata told a French journalist in Geneva that "in the present phase of Moroccan society, as a new nation is being moulded," he considered that the country's unity and independence came first; the prestige of the king was the best guaranty of both.

Again in October 1959, after a Casablanca court had temporarily reversed the ban on the Party, Yata declared: "We work within the framework of a constitutional monarchy . . . We also work for union with other national parties and strive to support the king in his struggle to liberate our country completely."

One of the most valuable executors of this broad "national front" policy was a capable and cultured medical man named Messaouak, whose enthusiasm for philosophic Marxism led him to break with Istiqlal and join the Party in 1949. Dr. Messaouak, a surgeon who has attended the king on occasion, was always quick to point out the identity of nationalist and Communist hopes. ("We don't want to be branded as a foreign movement.") This professed identity was of course in the tradition of Communist work in most of the underdeveloped countries. In 1946 the bulletin *Hayat ech Chaab,* published by the emerging Arab section of the Moroccan Party, had set down the principle: "A Communist organization based exclusively on the working class results in the formation of a sect, not a party." Khrushchev himself could not have said it better.

There was little mourning among the Soviet bloc diplomats dealing with the Moroccan question, when the ban on the local Party was reasserted. "Ban the Communist Party?" a member of the Soviet embassy had said, discussing the matter with a French newspaperman. "Yes, perhaps the palace will succeed in doing just that. And this would not make us unhappy at all." For the Soviet diplomats could see for themselves how fresh and thin were the roots of Communism in this country. It was not a Cuba or an Iraq or even an Italy. No one denied the weakness of the local Communists; the ban against them had been on ideological grounds, not because of their own provocations. There was not yet a fertile soil in Morocco even for "front" groups. And there was little attraction in a Communist Party that could keep in the public eye only by repeating "me-too," behind the large nationalist blocs.

Moscow and Peking were handling the Moroccan situation by themselves. They were handling most relationships with African countries the same way. In North Africa they had all but missed the boat. In the countries to the south the roots of Communism almost everywhere were too shallow, the urges of nationalism or racial self-expression too complicated for quick colonization by the Communists or their domestic allies.

The markets of these countries, however, were open to them. The trade fairs had begun to sprout. To new nations eager for self-improvement, offers of visits to China, the Soviet Union or the other satellites were not to be spurned. In the early summer of 1956, just after Morocco had won its independence, Moscow and Peking had begun inviting delegations of students, professional people, etc., to come and see the "peaceful achievements of Socialism." In these exchanges, notably those involving trade or hard cash, the Moroccans had shown themselves wary. Already, after beginning talks with the Russians in 1959, they had held off from concluding an agreement because the Soviet terms were too stiff and politically slanted.

But more talks would be coming. The Communist politicians who run Soviet international trade were confident in any case that other nations in Africa would not prove so hard to sell. There was, also, the growing political troubles of the new nations south of the Sahara, their welter of tribal loyalties, their lack of experience or direction, other than the urge to "freedom." All this offered an excellent long-term prospect for the chaos from which Communism generally prospers. The disorders in the Congo were only a beginning.

# CHAPTER IX

# OLD EUROPE
# AND THE LOST CHANCES

"We owe an unswerving obedience to the U.S.S.R."

—MAURICE THOREZ

WHEN the Soviet tank gunners trained their weapons on the people of Budapest in those grim days of November 1956, they were shooting down more than a city. Their guns tore down an image of a cooperative, peaceful Communist society which had been built up over the decades, an image which had been exposed, disproved and rebuked time and time again, but never before faced such a rude conflict with reality. Europe knows Communism. Communism was born there. It is not illogical, therefore, that Europe— thanks to Hungary and certain other happenings of the last decade—is comparatively well informed about the discrepancies between Communism's message and its true identity.

Not that Europeans were unaware of Communism's deceptions before Hungary. The 1939 partition of Poland with the Nazis, the painful series of Soviet aggressions after World War II, the Berlin blockade, the destruction of freedom in Eastern Europe, the backstabbing tactics of local Communist parties—these occurrences had all been duly noted. But there were always apologists handy to explain them away. In particular, there were the battalions of Communist or party-line or "neutralist" *literati,* who if they could not explain away every Soviet political indiscretion, were at the least skilled in pointing out that other countries were no better, that *Machtpolitik* was not a Soviet invention—". . . and what about the Negroes in the South?"

When the smoke cleared after Hungary, there were few "useful idiots" left to carry on with apologies in behalf of the Soviets. Defection within the various national parties in Western Europe came immediately and in volume. In Italy, an estimated 500,000 Communists left the Party in protest. (The Communists themselves admitted to a loss of 300,000.) The tiny Communist Party of Switzerland lost one-third of its 6,000 members. Proportionate defections occurred in other countries and slippages have continued in the four years since then. The Belgian Communist Party, 200,000 strong in 1947, is down to a bare 20,000 today. In the levelheaded country of Denmark, what was left of the Party in 1959 splintered into two quarreling sub-parties (in this instance largely because the veteran Communist, Aksel Larsen, with a wit rare among his fellows, had posed with his neck in a noose for a local theatrical page). The few who remained in the Communist Party of Sweden after Hungary became even fewer after the Soviet denunciation of Boris Pasternak and his Nobel Prize in 1958. Virtually all that is left of Communism there now is one literary fellow-traveler—and occasional newspaper disclosures of Soviet espionage.

Probably the most revealing thing about the ebb of Communist influence in Western Europe was the utter failure of the Communist-planned general strike in Spain in 1959. The Spain of the Franco dictatorship, one might suppose, would be ripe for a thriving Communist underground or some form of popular-front action. But apparently modern Spaniards remember not only Hungary but their own sad experiences with popular fronts as well. The various opposition parties, inside and outside Spain, explicitly disclaimed any connection with the Communist anti-Franco movement. "One does not have to be either a Franco supporter or a Communist," one Spanish unionist said. "There *is* a third way."

All this is not to say that western European populations are immune to the massive, if spurious appeals for nuclear disarmament or the continual boasts (and threats) of Sputnik technology which are beamed at them directly from the Kremlin. Certainly the Khru-

shchev regime's vaunted achievements in missilery have made
their impression; and there are many in Europe, as in the United
States, who believe in the Soviet protestations against war. But
such a belief is founded on nuclear realities and comes from
practical appraisals of Soviet risks and goals. It no longer stems
from the hope that the Soviet Union has a fundamental peace-
loving nature. For the most part the people of Western Europe—to
say nothing of their unfortunate cultural brethren in the East—
have realized the predatory nature of Soviet Communism and
the direct control which Moscow exercises both on its satellite
governments and on the Communist Parties of the West. The
groaning board is still set for the spurious Communist fellowship
agape, but most of the guests have long since left their chairs.

Behind this resistance to old Communist appeals lies Western
Europe's new economic confidence, and the gestures for political—
or at least social—union which have accompanied it. With all its
bumbling, hesitancy and missed opportunities, the American Marshall Plan worked. The early transfusions of gold and goods
given the European nations founded the prosperity which has now
followed. As a recent study for the Foreign Relations Committee
of the U.S. Senate noted: "The rapid economic growth and tech-
nological progress of Western Europe has been one of the most
remarkable phenomena of the post-war era. During the last
decade, Europe's overall rate of economic expansion has been
greater than that of either the United States or the Soviet Union,
and its rate of growth in the next decade will probably compare
favorably with those of the latter."

This prosperity owes nothing to Communism or Communism
methods and precious little, in fact, even to Socialism. It has been
distributed over a wide area of the populations involved. Although
depressed areas remain, the general standard of living in Europe
has bounded upwards.

Another factor in western Europe's hardening against Communism has been its growing consciousness of something known
and felt as a "European community." This consciousness arose

out of a sense of common danger—which was Communist. The days of the 1948 Berlin blockade seem far-off, although they may return in another form; but this and other power strokes of the Russians gave a sense of danger, and a concurrent unity in danger, to the nations of the West. The Italian elections of 1948 first brought the crisis to a head. It was an uneasy spring in Europe that year, for after a post-war time of confusion and misunderstanding the realness of the Communist danger had shown itself. The issue at last appeared simple: if Togliatti and his Communists won the 1948 elections, Italy would go off the map of Europe as an independent nation—or else suffer the miseries of a civil war. In the effort of many parties and many nations to see that this brink was never again reached in a Western country, this continental unity had its beginning.

The final reason for Europe's rejection of Communism lies in the very nature of Khrushchev's new image. Having cast itself as the professional "friend" of the underdeveloped nations, the loyal fellow fighter in the struggle against "colonialism," the Communist movement can hardly expect to find much aid and comfort among the well-developed countries which are being constantly attacked as "monopolistic" and "colonialist." The message is now pitched at the "have-nots" of the world. But the countries of Western Europe are "haves"—as are indeed, in an emergent way, the people of the U.S.S.R. itself.

If a Communist mob in Iraq shoots a visiting German businessman as a "white imperialist," the reaction in Germany will be predictable. Both in its economic competition and its inflammatory social propaganda, the Communist movement is a threat to the new power and prosperity of the European community.

Similar conflicts between Soviet objectives around the world have arisen in the past, and there have always been enough "useful idiots" among the European intelligentsia to think up artful reasons why their countries should turn the other cheek. But this has not been the case after the Hungarian brutality, followed over the years by Chinese aggression against Tibet and India and Khrushchev's saber-rattling over Berlin and the 1960 Summit. It is hard for the Communists to find "useful idiots" in Europe these days. Many of the people on whom they could once rely for popular-front appeals are preparing new translations of Boris Pasternak, visiting the United States on Ford Foundation grants, or writing press releases for President De Gaulle.

In the circumstances, what do the Communist Parties in Western Europe have left? Their strength remains not inconsiderable. The Party in Italy retains 1,787,338 card-carrying followers—the largest in the world, after the Soviet Union and China—and can muster one-third of the votes in Italian elections. The French Party still has 425,000 cards in circulation. But in the old Europe the great hope for even such large organisms was to combine with the misguided and/or the well-meaning into popular fronts or "working-class" alliances. Now this hope is not visible.

For the time at least, the Communists of Western Europe have been driven into a ghetto of their own making. Exposed as agents of the common enemy, their only value to the Communist movement is as guerrillas, who may still make severe attacks on the flanks of their respective polities, taking advantage of economic or political stresses, whenever they occur. They have slipped far from the old days, when the hope of revolution in the West lingered. As a good example of how they are exploited by the Soviet Union, one has only to look at the career of Maurice Thorez and his Party in France. For newer Communist leaders elsewhere in the world, the extent of his abasement may be instructive.

On October 29, 1959, the guests who crowded the left-bank residence of the President of the French National Assembly, Jacques Chaban-Delmas, were appropriately surprised when the members of the *Garde Republicaine* at the doors ushered in a Communist Party delegation, led by its Secretary General, Maurice Thorez. For twelve years, the Communists had boycotted all official receptions, as a sign of their implacable opposition to the bourgeois governments of France. Now they stood nervously alongside a table laden with expensive food and champagne (delicacies rarely handed out to non-Russian Communists), waiting for the President of the Republic to make an appearance.

When De Gaulle appeared, he made a leisurely progress through the room, shaking hands and exchanging greetings with the guests, until he spotted the Communists. Calmly, the general veered aside and walked away, deliberately snubbing them.

The publication of this incident in the "bourgeois" press the next day, related with the embellishment characteristic of French journalism, caused an understandable stir among the militants of the French Party. It was a bitter pill to swallow for people who had been denouncing De Gaulle as an authoritarian "uncrowned monarch" the more vehemently since he came back to political life. But Thorez went before the Central Committee without hesitation to explain the necessity for his attendance. "Yes," he said, "we went to this reception. The Political Bureau decided that such an attitude was in line with the orientation of the Party in the present circumstances and that it did not befit the Party to stay away from the reception, though we have only twenty-four senators and deputies. Times have changed."

Thorez went further than a mere defense of his own action. He criticized Communist municipal councillors and other elected officials for boycotting the September 4 reception given by the Paris Municipal Council for President Eisenhower during his visit to France. The boycott, he noted, was "an error."

The attitude of Thorez was of course the result of Moscow's current political honeymoon with De Gaulle. It also reflected the friendliness towards President Eisenhower (before the U-2 incident) —all part of the genial Khrushchev image. It told in microcosm the story of the modern French Communists, who wriggle hot or cold, like prisoners held under a giant faucet.

Thorez had in fact been visiting the Soviet Union on September 16, when De Gaulle made his famous avowal of self-determination for Algeria as a means of clearing the political future. But the Party's Politburo in Paris was quick to denounce the De Gaulle

policy in Thorez' absence. ("It is a policy of protracted war, of
an all-out war ... a political maneuver to try to win by cunning,
confusion and corruption what cannot be imposed by force.")
When Thorez himself returned to France on September 23, he
spoke in the same coin at ceremonies in the southern department of
Gard, celebrating the forty-year tenure of office of Communist
municipal councils in two villages. "The promise of self-determination," he said, "constitutes nothing more than a political maneuver."

On the very day that Thorez was speaking, however, the rebel
Provisional Government of the Algerian Republic announced in
Tunis its acceptance of De Gaulle's principle of self-determination.
Concurrently, De Gaulle was preparing his own invitation for
Khrushchev to visit France. So the line changed. On October 26,
three days after the announcement of Khrushchev's Paris trip,
Thorez wrote in *L'Humanité:* "To put an end to the Algerian war,
immediate negotiations are needed on the basis of self-determina-
tion. ... Realizing in fact the failure of pacification, General De
Gaulle has recognized the right of the Algerian people to self-
determination." This was only a prefiguring of the ensuing address
by Khrushchev on November 1, just after Thorez had led his
deputies into the official reception for Khrushchev's host, De
Gaulle. Said the Soviet First Secretary: "The recent proposals of
President De Gaulle to solve the Algerian problem on a principle
of self-determination, by general elections in Algeria, can play an
important role in the settlement of the Algerian question. ...

"One knows that between France and Algeria exist close ties
which have been created over the course of history. Naturally, if
the future links were established on a new mutually acceptable
basis, if the principle of the free choice and equality of rights was
truly observed, then all this would contribute to re-establish peace
in this region."

At a meeting of the Central Committee, Thorez again chalked
out the new Soviet line on the blackboard with a few words of
explanation. Criticizing the first French Communist reaction against
De Gaulle's plans for Algeria, he said: "Right after my return from

Russia, I made observations about the declaration of the Political Bureau dated September 17. I found it to be over-hasty and therefore incomplete." On November 3, the Central Committee announced that the Politburo had "completed and modified its first analysis" of the Algerian situation. The French Party militants brushed themselves off and adjusted to a new world where they would be temporarily supporting the policies of General De Gaulle.

Thorez has spent his life making similar readjustments. Their record is worth repeating since he exemplifies the one overriding virtue which Moscow prizes in a local Communist leader: loyalty to the Soviet Union. He was born in Noyelles-Godault in the mining country of northern France on April 28, 1900. He can legitimately claim to be a son of the working classes—he went to work in a colliery at the age of twelve. At nineteen he joined the Socialist Party, and, after the Socialist split in 1920, he went Communist. He was Party secretary in the northern French industrial basin at the age of twenty-four. The next year he was elected to the national Politburo, and made his first pilgrimage to Russia.

Thorez got into his first real trouble with the French government on his return, agitating against the Riff war in 1927. For inciting soldiers to desert the army, he was given a jail sentence of six months. The day after his release from prison, he resumed his anti-government agitation. This time he escaped arrest, but spent two years in hiding.

In 1929 the police caught up with him again, and he stayed in jail until June 1930. By this time he was something of a national hero among French Communists. Thanks largely to the world economic crisis, membership in the Party increased rapidly. In 1930 he was elected Secretary General of the Party.

In 1936 he was elected to the National Assembly. It was the year of the Popular Front coalition, when fraternity was the order of the day. Thorez received the largest majority of any candidate.

The year before he had his first taste of the Soviet policy changes which were to become part of his life, and which he learned to justify with such glibness. Stalin concluded a non-aggression pact with France. And the man whom he dealt with was Pierre Laval, whom the Communists had hitherto been denouncing as Public Enemy No. 1. Four years later, after the glow of popular-front collaboration had dimmed, Molotov and Ribbentrop signed the shattering non-aggression treaty between Nazi Germany and the Soviet Union. The treaty caught the French Party in the middle of a violent campaign for the immediate punishment of "traitors" who were dealing with Hitler. As Thorez later admitted, the pact forced the Party to "modify its battle order overnight." The French government outlawed the Party and, for the first time, it suffered widespread defections.

Shortly after World War II began, Thorez was drafted in the French Army; but he managed to desert and escape to the Soviet Union. He was sentenced to five years' imprisonment *in absentia* for desertion.

Thorez left France a fugitive and came back in 1944 as something of a returning hero. In the interim the Communists had joined, and at one point threatened to absorb the French Resistance. The Party was legalized as its reward. Thorez, his jail sentence quashed, became Minister of State in De Gaulle's first post-war government.

For two years his Party trod lightly, giving a successful imitation of a national political organization dedicated only to its own country. But the presence of Communists in the government, constantly trying to worm their way into strategic positions, became increasingly hard for the non-Communist parties to endure. In May 1947, Paul Ramadier, a Socialist, dismissed the Communist ministers from his Cabinet. The Party resumed its role of revolutionary opposition, feeling the more comfortable for the change.

Through 1947 and 1948 Thorez tried militant tactics. Communists organized a series of strikes and demonstrations throughout France which put the country in an almost continual state of upheaval. They were repulsed due principally to the efficient counteraction of the police, under the direction of Jules Moch, then the Socialist Minister of the Interior. Having failed in this test of strength, Thorez put on his parliamentary suit again and began to re-explore the possibilities for a new Popular Front. His efforts foundered for a variety of reasons, principally the growing menace of the Soviet Union and clarity of the Party's Soviet connections. But the post-war years did produce a rich harvest of "useful idiots."

The 'forties marked a new, and probably an all-time, high in the development of drawing room Communism. It was fashionable to think, or at least talk "left," the more so since the presence of a large American Marshall Plan program offered a constant sitting target to Parisian intellectual wit. Jean Paul Sartre, his friend Simone de Beauvoir, *et al.*, developed the sort of "neutral" political existentialism that always seemed to end up only twenty versts away from Moscow. The literary output of Louis Aragon and others like him lent further intellectual lustre to Communism. Many remembered the heavy Communist role in the resistance and thought of the movement as the real wave of the future. Except for Mauriac and the Catholic intellectuals, at that time more beleaguered than later, the Communists found no cohesive body of thought or thinkers to oppose them. It took time for Albert Camus to make his famous break with Sartre and the pro-Communists and theorize his *L'Homme Révolté,* who found Communist totalitarianism at least as galling to the independent spirit as any other of the world's social systems.

Outside the drawing rooms and the study halls the Communists found their most powerful support in the General Labor Confederation (C.G.T.), the complex of unions which was then more powerful than it is at present. For some years the C.G.T., dominated by Communists and varieties of fellow-traveler, rode high, wide and handsome over French labor, calling out the workers with regularity for its protests against the Marshall Plan, its advocacy of various Communist "peace" fronts, and so on.

But for all his strength on the outside, Thorez and his assistants, Jacques Duclos, Andre Marti and others, were never able to wheedle their way into the sort of popular-front coalition for which they once hoped. Although the non-Communist political parties

of the Fourth Republic resembled an omelette in a state of transition, they managed to keep a united front in keeping the Communists out of government. To attain this aim against the largest
and best organized political party in France, they devised a pro-
portional representation electoral system of almost incredible complexity—one hesitates to call it "typically French"—in which the
non-Communist parties could combine their strength, even while
mutually opposed, to fight the Communists. Yet the considerable
number of Communist deputies who were returned to the National
Assembly managed to make the process of governing far more
difficult for French cabinets than it might have been.

In October 1950, Thorez suffered a stroke. Partially paralyzed,
he was flown to Moscow by Soviet military plane for treatment. The
treatment extended over a span of thirty months, during which he
virtually deputized his wife Jeanette Vermeersch to run the party
in his absence. He returned to France in April 1953. After several
purges of "deviationists" and "fractionalists" who seemed to have
sprouted in his absence, Thorez was ready to resume his work of
disrupting his country's political machinery.

The bulk of the French Communists' popular support—as with
its larger companion, the Italian Party—probably originated in
economic protest. Add to this the number of Frenchmen who
emotionally vote "left" in the happy delusion that they are storm-
ing the Bastille each time they walk to the polls. Add to this the
numbers of people impressed by the two issues which Thorez was
first able to capitalize on during the 'fifties: Indo-China and Algeria.

Since 1954 the Algerian question has been the Communists'
most powerful talking point. They have exploited the national
weariness with the war tremendously. Peace in Algeria committees
sprouted all over the country, many of them allied to the notorious
World Peace Council, run until his death by the Communist scientist, Frédéric Joliot-Curie. It was and still is hardly a difficult
thing to approach a group of factory workers and ask them if they
would like war or peace in Algeria. The answer is obvious. From
this start, the Communists begin collecting signatures and assem-

bling "petitions." Blown up by the Party and the fellow-traveling press, such petition movements, if on their face unobjectionable, serve to keep the electorate even more nervous and disturbed over the Algerian question than it would ordinarily be. Naturally, the Communists have also exploited to the full the dismal record of atrocities committed by French soldiers and *colons* in the course of a bitter war.

Yet such agitation, while of some effectiveness, is essentially negative. As such it is a good index of Thorez' capabilities. Communism in France has slipped badly since the first post-war days when the Party could boast one million dues-paying members. This was more than twice the present number. The impact of Hungary divided, if it did not wholly shatter, the Party's intellectual support. The surge in the economy has taken the political sting out of even the most solidly Communist-led unions. And finally De Gaulle, by his very presence, has been able to oppose to the Communists a polarized national sentiment such as they have never had to face in the history of the *Parti Communiste Français*.

Palmiro Togliatti, the perennial Secretary General of the Communist Party in Italy, is a far smoother article than his colleague, Thorez. Togliatti is no worker. He was born in Genoa to a poor family of the lower middle class on March 29, 1893 on Palm Sunday—hence his name Palmiro. On a scholarship he attended the University of Turin, where he studied law, theology and philosophy. He is a diplomatist of no mean ability. Although deceptively meek in appearance, he has a rare gift for bending people and movements to his will, through logic and persuasion as much as by force and exhortation. He is the perfect parliamentary Communist. It is a tribute to his tactical skill that after fifteen years of double-dealing, reversed Party lines and obvious direction from the Soviet Union, many Italians still believe that his is a truly national Party, that Italian Communism is something different.

Togliatti went into journalism after leaving the university and joined the Socialist party. He organized his first general strike in

1920 and a few years after bolted the Socialists with two other prominent leaders to form the new Italian Communist Party. At the time, however, there were too many black shirts in Italy for a new red banner. When Mussolini outlawed the Communist Party in 1926, Togliatti and his friends fled the country. He spent the next eighteen years in Moscow. There he performed various useful services for the old Comintern. Probably an even greater tribute to his diplomatic ability than his later triumphs in Italy was the fact that he stayed alive during this period, for hundreds of prominent foreign Communists perished in Stalin's purges of the 'thirties.

In 1944 he returned home—like Sanzo Nozaka in Japan—via an American military aircraft. He was speedily appointed Minister Without Portfolio in the Royalist government of Marshal Badoglio. He remained in office through the next four post-war cabinets, in a period of soaring growth and influence that even the most optimistic Italian Communists had hardly expected. As in France, the Italians had proved effective in the resistance movement and earned the temporary confidence of the Allied governments. In the confused political rubble of post-war Italy, when most of the prominent were either incapacitated or hopelessly tainted with Fascism, the Communists moved decisively. Communist mayors and other officials were appointed throughout the country, often by Allied military government authorities, because they seemed the only people eager and willing to take on the job. It was in these early years that the Party built up the layers of fat on which it could feed in the leaner times to come.

Togliatti moved cautiously. No one could ever accuse him of becoming "dizzy with success." His political platform was Communism dressed up in a neat business suit, wearing spectacles and carrying a few sober volumes of law and jurisprudence. He called for monetary stability, an end to wartime restrictions and the rejuvenation of industry. He made no frontal attacks on the Catholic Church. In fact in 1947 he supported reaffirmation of the Lateran Treaty linking the Catholic Church and the Italian state.

His party grew to a strength of well over 2,000,000. Communists gained control of the General Confederation of Labor, which in the early post-war years held within its ranks the overwhelming majority of Italian trade unionists. More importantly, Togliatti managed to graft his imported party onto the main body of Italian politics. As the humorous stories of the author Guareschi bore witness, the archetypical Communist mayor Peppone was as much a part of the local landscape as Don Camillo, the priest.

The front movements thrived throughout the 'forties. Italians flocked by the thousands to sign Communist petitions to abolish the Cold War, grant freedom to the "oppressed colonial peoples" or keep Italy out of alliances (with the West). The Communist Party headquarters on the Via della Botteghe Oscure became one of Rome's best-known and certainly its best-attended political monument. The Socialists were virtually colonized, through the years, by the persuasiveness of the Communists and the similarity of the causes for which both were "struggling."

To run its program the Party built up a complex of schools, cooperatives, unions, youth and women's organizations, nurseries, legal aid societies and businesses. (Just as in other Western countries the local Party makes a profitable concern out of trade with countries of the "Socialist camp.") There were, and are, presumed organizations of Communist militants, well supplied with weapons, who might be relied on to turn the balance in the Communists' favor if Italy were ever plunged into intense political and social disorder; but the exact shape of these units remains a matter of speculation.

The Communists came very close to using them in 1948—the same year they lost the critical elections to Alcide De Gasperi's revivified Christian Democrats. On July 14 of that year, a twenty-five-year-old medical student attempted to assassinate Togliatti, wounding him in three places. The angry Communists proceeded to stage a series of retaliatory riots and general strikes that stopped just short of an attempted *coup de main*.

The violence in 1948—which resembled a revolution called off just before the sticking point—was the only time the Communist

Party of Italy openly abandoned its "democratic" methods. Since then Togliatti has continued his temperate policy, concentrating on the appeal to economic discontent, anti-clericalism and, in his peace propaganda, the general fear of another war. But history has been unkind to him. The gradual improvement of economic conditions took away much of the Communist attraction on this score. And Hungary, as well as other instances of Soviet aggressiveness, drove thousands of potential sympathizers away from the Communists—to say nothing of the estimated 500,000 lost Party members, including some of the leadership. The original impression of Communist inefficiency and incorruptibility has long since vanished. In the first five post-war years, for instance, 588 Communist and left-wing Socialist mayors and city councillors were arrested on charges of corruption, financial manipulations, or other crimes.

Other parties awakened to the Communist domination of the unions. Here, as in France, the Communist hold has weakened, although it remains strong. By their own admission, membership in the Labor Confederation (C.I.G.L.) has gone down to 3,600,000 from its peak of five million (this figure was given out in January, 1959). There has been a corresponding rise in membership of the Christian Democratic Federation of Italian Labor Unions (C.I.S.L.) and the Socialist Union of Italian Workers (U.I.L.).

The Socialists have been backing away from their old close ties, at least somewhat. First came the bolt from the party of Giuseppe Saragat's group, on grounds of overmuch Communist influence. Since Hungary, there has been discontent even among the Nenni Socialists (so-called from their leader, Pietro Nenni, an old friend of the Communists) over their continuing ties with the Via della Botteghe Oscura.

The Communists remain strong through their continuing hold on their unions, cooperatives and various regions. In Sicily, Tuscany, the Aosta valley and Emilia-Romagna they are numerous enough to be in a position to control, or at least powerfully influence any local government. And a veteran gradualist like Togliatti has of course been aided greatly in mending his fences by the new image of Khrushchev's Communism.

Note the language of the report delivered at the Ninth Congress of the Italian Party, in January 1960: "The international situation today presents undeniable signs of the beginning of a new period. The Cold War has to end, leaving place for co-existence and pacific competition among the nations of socialism and capitalism."

Yet, the report continued, the Soviet Union has "largely beaten even the most advanced capitalistic states in the progress towards instruction, in the most advanced technics and in the field of space exploration . . .

"Before not a great many years, even the United States will be surpassed in per capita production. The general advanced economies of the Socialist countries and the jump forward by China assures that in 1965 the Socialist countries will have more than half of the entire world's industrial production. Capitalism in this way will cease to be an economic force . . ."

Having set forth this premise, Togliatti's Party went on to hammer away as usual at the weak spots in the Italian economy ("extensive areas of profound misery and poverty exist"). The old cry was not so effective as it had been, but still loud enough to attract and hold supporters—or some of them. Until the moment when, as and if the economy of Western Europe should deteriorate, or a war or other disaster takes place, Togliatti was doomed to fight a cautious Fabian struggle, trying to keep his own ranks together, while harassing as much of the enemy as possible.

Occasionally he would turn to strong-arm tactics, as in the riots of June, 1960, when he strove to overthrow a coalition government which depended partly on neo-Fascist votes for its survival. Such moments were few, carefully chosen, and of course dependent on temporary changes in the Party's Moscow direction—in this case the rash of violence following the U-2 and Summit breakdowns. Probably to Togliatti's regret, they served principally to remind Italians of the source of the Party's direction.

# CHAPTER X

# SPIES WITH A DIFFERENCE

"It is our task incessantly to strengthen the State Security organs."

—A. N. SHELEPIN,
Chairman of the K.G.B., 1959

THE least publicized aspect of Khrushchev's competitive coexistence campaign has been consistently one of the most effective. That is its intelligence arm. Not only is the scope of this activity known far less than it should be, thanks to the persistent tendency of humankind to believe Soviet denials, but its very nature is not appreciated. Other nations, whether through agents, military attachés, or spectacular reconnaissance like the American U-2 program, regard intelligence operations as primarily a means of finding out about the plans and resources of potential enemies. But ever since the old Polish Bolshevik, Feliks Dzerzhinsky, started to build the Cheka "security" system in 1918, the Soviet leadership has used intelligence officers and agents only partially to gather information. They have in addition the assignment of conducting a running guerrilla operation against the countries where they are sent or recruited. The Soviet intelligence officer is not so much a scout as a foreign body patiently inserted into the bloodstream of a society, with the object of doing as much damage as possible—whether through direct sabotage, recruitment, covert agitation, or "provocation."

The work of the Soviet intelligence was important enough in the Stalinist days, when Moscow still subscribed to the ideal of ultimate military conflict with the free world outside it. When

Khrushchev rejected the possibility of an armed showdown, basing his hopes on the doctrine that the capitalist world will of itself turn to "Socialism," the intelligence officers found themselves quite literally in the front lines. It is their job to speed along the "inexorable" process of Marxist dialectic by every undercover means at their command. Obviously, a country that seems to collapse internally is of infinitely more value as proof of Khrushchev's thesis than a country that has to be pressured into a Communist alliance by more or less overt threats.

The job of weakening and subverting non-Communist societies is known among Soviet intelligence officers as "decomposition" work. This is often their basic foreign assignment. Naturally, the pace of "decomposition" efforts will vary country by country. Often, as in Castro's Cuba and at least the earlier years of Kassem's Iraq, the Soviet Union and its allies have had no interest in subverting the local government; on the contrary, its agents are ordered to preserve a state of unrest highly favorable to Communism by keeping the local government in power. Then, too, "decomposition" involves more than sabotage against single governments and societies. One of the principal goals of Soviet intelligence since 1945 has been to loosen the brickwork of non-Communist alliances and international friendships. As the bulwark of most of these alliances and the rival power center, the United States in itself is a concurrent object of attack. Loss of trust in the Americans means a corresponding acquisition of faith in the Communist bloc, whether or not a country remains professedly neutral. So the basic targets of Moscow's decomposition experts are : 1) specific governments; 2) alliances; 3) the United States.

The two organs of Soviet intelligence are Military Intelligence (G.R.U.) and the Committee for State Security, the K.G.B. Although Military Intelligence has a large network of agents and under-cover "illegals" as well as formally designated attachés abroad, it is the State Security, direct successor to the N.K.V.D. and the G.P.U. of past Soviet history, which has traditionally held the dominant role. From Moscow the State Security plans the sabotage, political kidnappings, and "terror" operations that form the rougher side of "decomposition" work. The State Security's specialists also are responsible for forgeries, black propaganda, and other types of political misrepresentation which, as we shall see below, have enjoyed an alarming degree of success.

A certain percentage of Soviet diplomats abroad are officers of the State Security (or G.R.U.), notably cultural and press attachés whose "cover" occupations are conducive to intelligence work. So are selected members of Soviet trade missions, exchange cultural delegations, and a good percentage of Tass and Pravda foreign correspondents. The Soviet intelligence "Resident" in every embassy or legation is apt to have a cover diplomatic rank of Counsellor or First Secretary, although he is sometimes found in a more modest bracket. A typical middle-rank case was that of Colonel Mikhail Stepanovich Rogov, the Counsellor of the Soviet Embassy in Paris, who during 1958 and 1959 was responsible for a good deal of the Soviet undercover political "intelligence" operations there. In some sensitive areas, however, the diplomatic and the intelligence leaderships are united in one man. When Moscow announced its first ambassador to Fidel Castro's Cuba in July 1960, he proved to be none other than Sergei N. Kudriavtsev, a veteran officer of Soviet Military Intelligence, with past service in Austria and France.

Other Soviet officials, not officers of the K.G.B. or G.R.U. themselves, are recruited as agents. Like the officers, their identity is kept secret from their fellow-workers in the diplomatic service. One such agent, who later defected to the West, was recruited in Moscow in 1957 for undercover political work in the Soviet Embassy in Burma. He received a pseudonym for use in his reports and signed an agreement promising to fulfill his new tasks to the utmost. ("If I should reveal or betray any secrets that were given to me," it ran, "I am ready to meet any punishment, including death.") When he arrived in Rangoon, he was approached with the correct countersign by one Ivan Mikhailovich Vozniy, First Secretary of the Embassy, who was evidently the K.G.B. Resident. Outside of his normal working hours, he did jobs as translator and political reporter for Vozniy and later helped recruit local agents. One of the most important parts of his job was to dole out anti-Western and specifically anti-American newspaper articles written in Moscow, then sent to Rangoon to be inserted in local newspapers which Vozniy subsidized for this express purpose.

The diplomat in question was young, and well educated, with a broad knowledge of language and custom about the Far Eastern country where he had been slated to serve. His choice was typical of the new approach used by the State Security in the Khrushchev era, which has come a long way from the crudities of the old N.K.V.D. For one thing, the important people in Soviet intelligence are almost all Russian, members of the intensively trained Foreign Intelligence Directorate of the K.G.B. No longer do the Soviet security bosses rely so heavily on dedicated foreign Communists, as they did in the Comintern days. Indeed foreign Communists are often treated with great suspicion by the K.G.B. For certain kinds of work their use is frowned upon, as it is during certain periods of change in the international Communist movement. (In 1953, for example, during the turmoil following the death of Stalin and Beria's attempted seizure of power, K.G.B. officers in Vienna were instructed to purge from their lists of agents and contacts all but a few absolutely essential Austrian Communists.)

The Soviet K.G.B. regards its opposite numbers in the other countries of the Communist bloc—with the probable exception of the Chinese—as working subsidiaries of a single firm. In most foreign centers of espionage, various specialties are parceled out among the satellite intelligence arms, according to their proficiency. Where a Communist country happens to be in rather good odor with its capitalist hosts, as Poland in the United States after its October 1956 revolution, the Russians are quick to assign it peculiarly sensitive tasks. Ideally, the Communist-bloc foreign operatives in a given area are expected to act like members of a well-orchestrated unit.

The Soviet intelligence officer of the Khrushchev era is trained to mix with people rather than to avoid them, to court popularity rather than to shun it. To cite a typical instance of this type of action, take the case of Major Yuri Nikolaevich Paporov, who was not long ago unexpectedly "surfaced" in Mexico.

Paporov's cover was that of Second Secretary and Cultural Attaché at the Soviet embassy in Mexico City. Polished and extremely sociable, he spoke almost perfect Spanish, understood English and French and could be handy in Polish, Czech or German. People who met him on duty often mistook him for a non-Soviet European diplomat, which suited his purposes well.

Paporov studied philology and literature at Moscow University after the war, in which he had been badly injured. Apparently he did best in Spanish. He joined the State Security in 1946 and, after home training, was sent to Buenos Aires as a minor consular employee. This familiarization course, a common Soviet practice, lasted four years. After it he went home for more seasoning in Moscow. He married—his wife, conveniently, was also employed by the K.G.B.—and for a time earnestly cultivated the literati of the Soviet capital. A good writer, he had articles printed in *Sovestskaya Kultura* on a wide range of subjects, from ballet libretti to translations of Latin American literature.

As a result when he arrived at his Cultural Attaché's job in April 1954 he was considerably more believable in this function than others had been before him. It did not take Paporov long to become something of a literary lion in the leftist intellectual circles—the world of the "useful idiots" in front organizations is made to order for such operations. He became a frequent lecturer at two educational Communist front organizations, the Instituto de Intercambio Cultural Mexico-Russo and the Promoción Cultural A.C. in Saltillo. But, although he discoursed on the Russian drama, his principal interest was exclusively Mexican; the recruitment of selected members of his audiences. In Latin America, as we have seen, the Soviets have had considerable success in their aim of infiltrating student circles.

Paporov's immediate objective, in addition to long-term recruitment, was to foment dissatisfaction among Mexican student groups. One of the prime objectives of the new Soviet policy continues to be the instigation of strategically-timed riots or demonstrations. Students trained in the European tradition make good raw material for this kind of work. But Paporov was a little too obvious. In early May 1957, after a big student rising at Guadalajara, two Mexican City newspapers flatly accused Paporov and his fellow "attaché" Nikolai Trofimov of starting it. The hue and cry continued for several months, and reached the point where several student organizations formally asked the Mexican Government to demand Paporov's recall. In September 1957, suddenly and without explanation, he was put on a ship bound for the Soviet Union, to await further assignment.

This was not an isolated case. To get an idea of the persistence of the overseas Soviet intelligence effort, it is worth recalling similar incidents which have occurred in Latin America in the past few years. The Latin American example is used deliberately as an example of how widely Khrushchev has been able to cast his net. Historically, the area has always been a weak spot in the Soviet State Security network. The recent activity there, with Soviet, Chinese and satellite representatives working together, makes its own comment on Soviet designs for the 'sixties. Here is an incomplete chronology of the most notorious Soviet espionage incidents:

July 5, 1956: The assistant Soviet Naval Attaché was expelled from Argentina after an attempt to buy classified documents on U.S. Navy tactics from an Argentine naval officer.

May, 1957: Paporov and Trofimov were exposed in Mexico City as instigators of the May 12 student riots.

September, 1957: Czech Chargé d'Affaires Ludwig Horak and his Third Secretary were expelled from Quito because of "intolerable interference in the internal affairs of Ecuador." This followed discovery of their subversive activity among Ecuadorian student and labor groups. In the same year the Czech legation in Lima was closed by the Peruvian government and for the same reasons.

September 8, 1958: Vladislav Sidorenkov, a Soviet embassy

attaché in Montevideo, left Uruguay hastily when it was discovered that he had purchased secret documents from an employee of the Uruguayan foreign office.

September 25, 1958: Another satellite intelligence agent, a Pole, was unmasked as the real boss of an illicit Communist training school in Argentina.

March 31, 1959: Two more Soviet diplomats, Second Secretary Nikolai Arsenov and Naval Attaché Nikolai Remizov, were expelled from Mexico for their work in fomenting a needless strike of transportation workers.

April, 1959: Major Vasily Ivashov was declared *persona non grata* by the Argentine Government for inciting the dangerous street riots of April 6 in Buenos Aires. Although not so directly stigmatized, Ambassador Mikhail Kostylev, his Economic Counselor and the Romanian Chief of Mission were also heavily implicated. Police determined that the street riots had been organized by local Communists, supplied with funds—and directed—by Soviet diplomats.

April, 1959: Mrs. Vera Laskova de Zalka, Soviet wife of the Hungarian Minister to Argentina was implicated in local Communist disturbances in Bolivia, during a carefully planned visit there.

April, 1959: The Mexican Navy Department denounced the Soviet Naval Attaché, Nikolai Bykov, as a spy. He had been receiving confidential information from navy files.

June 8, 1959: The Bulgarian minister to Argentina was ordered expelled, after discovery of a secret radio transmitter on his legation premises. The radio furnished day-to-day communication between Argentine and Uruguayan Communist circles and Moscow.

To appreciate the significance of the preceding list, one must remember the small number of diplomatic missions allowed the Soviets and the satellites in all of Latin America—and the equally important fact that such incidents break surface only because of the faulty calculation or the isolated bungle, neither of them exactly encouraged in Soviet intelligence circles. These surfaced incidents are exactly analogous to the tiny projecting part of a huge iceberg.

Apart from the tightly disciplined freemasonry of the State Security and Military Intelligence, there are two other characteristics of Soviet intelligence work, and both of them in no small way responsible for its successes. The first is the available pool of local Communists and front members, who as we have seen constitute an ever-replenishing source of agent material. Khrushchev's efforts at pumping up international "good feeling" were a godsend for K.G.B. recruiters everywhere in the late 'fifties. Not only were more sympathizers available, but the new Soviet policy of mixing relatively freely with foreigners brought State Security officers into contact with people whom they had had to shun under the old Stalin dispensation. If "useful idiots" could no longer be found among brotherly European socialists, or inveterate Anglo-Saxon "causers," there were plenty of new recruits, particularly in the underdeveloped countries, whose original legitimate feelings against atomic war, colonialism, or racial prejudice were to lead ultimately to recruitment in the Soviet Union's espionage system.

Next to this impressive manpower pool * the great mark of the Soviet intelligence has been its ability to filter so much of its visible effort through intermediaries—either in the person of local Communists or satellite organizations. One of the great gains from the Soviet occupation of eastern Europe was the State Security's ability to spawn smaller-sized replicas of itself in each of the satellites, useful not only in keeping an eye on the local Party and government, but often extremely valuable in running risky intelligence operations of the sort that the Russians themselves did not wish to be associated with. Even where the State Security is directly in charge of a job, the "Center" in Moscow is scrupulous in avoiding any visible contact with it, especially if something goes wrong.

* By which I mean only the large supply of potential recruits on which local case officers could draw. The actual numbers of Soviet agents are relatively small. So is the size of the State Security itself, an elite group which has traditionally prided itself on its compactness.

A case in point is the contrast between the behavior of the United States Government, after the disclosure of the U-2 aircraft reconnaissance program in 1960, and that of the Soviet Union when faced with the 1958 arrest of one of its top agents in the United States, the man who called himself Colonel Rudolph Ivanovich Abel. When Francis Gary Powers, the pilot of the downed U-2 plane, was captured, the United States Government at its highest level admitted that he had been flying over Sverdlovsk, as an aerial spy, under Washington's orders. It is outside the scope of this book to examine the mixture of naïveté and incompetence that prompted the Eisenhower administration to accept this responsibility so readily, and in such a confused way. But the world was left in no doubt about both Powers' national and organizational affiliation.

Now consider the case of Colonel "Abel." At no point after his arrest or during his trial did Abel attempt to make contact with any Soviet official, other than to acknowledge his Soviet citizenship. And no official attempt was made by Soviet authorities to claim him—Moscow's response to the entire affair was silence. Abel did ask and receive permission to write letters to his "family," letters of a type not unknown in State Security communications. He said that his family could be reached through East Berlin, for the purposes of mailing, although in his conversations with Americans during his trial he made no bones of the fact that they lived in Moscow. When Abel was asked, hypothetically, whether he thought the Soviet Union would be willing to "exchange" him for Powers, he replied that all such questions would have to be taken up with his attorney, who was also in East Berlin.

All this may have seemed like palpable subterfuge, in the case of a confessed officer in the K.G.B. who had been caught in the act of spying for the U.S.S.R. in the United States. But it left Abel's bosses with absolutely no overt connection with his activities. The Soviet Union is true to this principle in all of its intelligence operations. Time and time again, the Russians will be caught with their fingers in someone's cookie jar. Without exception, they will insist that the fingers, if not the jar itself, were never really there.

Nowhere have intermediaries been so faithfully used as in one of the more interesting recent cases of Soviet "black" propaganda: their international chain of forged letters and documents. Since the first days of the Soviet intelligence one of its favorite instruments has been the use of "misinformation," i.e., planting false information, arranged to look as if it had come from legitimate sources. Forgery has always been a State Security strongpoint and the political warriors of the Khrushchev era have increasingly resorted to it. With so many satellite sources for originating forged letters or documents and so many neutralist countries, of varying opinion shades, with journalists—or governments—ready and able to disseminate them, forgery campaigns have become profitable as never before. Best of all, the ultimate Soviet source of the forgery can be at least officially hidden, thus leaving Moscow free to exhibit surprise, indignation or unconcern, as occasion demands.

From January 1, 1957 to July 1, 1959 the Russians put out a total of thirty-six forgeries—letters purporting to be from American or European officials, faked orders or circulars of the United State State Department, and the like. All but a few of them emanated ostensibly from non-Soviet sources. They varied in the competence of their invention. Some of them were obvious crudities, reminding one of the classic cartoon printed in the United States early in World War II, showing a group of Japanese soldiers laboriously learning the words: "Herro Bill, this are Joe. Please putting down honorable gun and come over here." For example, to quote from a typical case, the unknown stylists of the K.G.B.'s misinformation bureau have former Under Secretary of State Herbert Hoover, Jr., writing to an American engineer friend about a scheme to wrest control of the Sahara oil fields from the French. "Writes" Mr. Hoover: "Do you seriously believe there is someone else who would know how to grab and hold on to the good old Sahara Desert the way you would. They think highly of you in

Washington and give your abilities credit. I don't have to tell you about the importance of African oil." (In its replay of the Hoover "letter," Radio Moscow interpolated for the benefit of its French listeners the explanation that this proved "the desire of the U.S. monopolies to seize control of oil wherever it is found in the Middle East, and that the State Department gives them all possible aid.")

Or take the singularly un-American phrasing of another letter, written on a forged State Department letterhead, to Ambassador Robert McClintock in Beirut and "signed" by Deputy Under Secretary of State Robert Murphy: "You are right to note that we have nothing in common with Nasser and his kind. . . . However, I disagree with you that swords should be drawn ahead of time, particularly when our goals can be attained without resorting to arms. You certainly are aware of what I have in mind when I say that, after the snakes devour each other, the jungle becomes safer."

Other letters are misspelled, or abound in British spellings, or are obviously direct translations from the German or Russian. The official terminology used in forgeries purported to come from State or Defense departments is incorrect and even the numbering systems inaccurate. It would be a very dumb American or educated foreigner who could not spot them almost instantly for what they are.

The misinformation forgeries, however, are hardly intended for sophisticated audiences. They are designed to be printed, reprinted, and rebroadcast all over the world, in either the Communist press, neutralist papers with Communist sympathies and/or subsidies, or in publications which might like to run them for their sensationalist value. Particularly in the world's underdeveloped countries, newspaper readers have hardly yet developed even the relative discrimination of their Western counterparts. Anything in print is assumed to be some version of holy writ. Still more so in the case of broadcasting. Notably in Africa and the Middle East, illiterate masses of people listen to the local radio as a combination of information and entertainment. Because it is "official," they trust it. We could hardly expect Egyptian fellahin—or for that matter European factory workers—to notice that the State Department letter-head on one of the forgeries is obviously faked, or the official language palpably incorrect.

As a result, the well-planned forgery has become an important weapon of Soviet intelligence among the uncommitted and neu-tralist countries. It costs little, it can make a deep impression, especially among people who are only too happy to attribute Amer-ican politics to economic imperialism, in the Marxist tradition, or even to equate American and Soviet imperialisms as equally bad, in the neutralist vein. Best of all, it can be repeated almost *ad infinitum,* gaining in authenticity the further it is removed from its real source.

The "Rockefeller" letter is a fine illustration of how far and how fast a well-feathered forgery can fly. Originally, the "letter" appeared in the German Communist paper, *Neues Deutschland,* on February 15, 1957. It was heavily headlined as the "Secret Document of Rockefeller." "An authenticated writing of the Stand-ard Oil king to President Eisenhower," *Neues Deustchland* ban-nered, "Cynical Plan of the U.S.; goal for world domination; The Recipe: Economic aid—economic dependence—political domina-tion—military pacts—a blood-tax on peoples for the U.S.A. Hor-rible testimony of Imperialist inhumanity . . ."

The letter itself is a rambling document dated January 1, 1956 (despite the fact that it refers to an event which happened in February). It was researched with some care, however, and on the surface would seem plausible—at least to anyone unacquainted with the sender or his country. What "Rockefeller" advocates is a better-planned U.S. aid program, with the accent drifting from economic to military to economic. "Wherever possible," the letter runs, "we should emphasize the economic aspects of our alliances."

The word "emphasize" is of course the clue. For the letter goes on to develop a plan of economic penetration whose purpose would be more familiar to Bismarck or Machiavelli or for that matter Khrushchev. The plan, as "Rockefeller" unfolds it, is in fact an unconscious bit of Soviet self-revelation. It is the concept of an aid program, as they see it.

"In the past," the "letter" runs, "we have sometimes tied up the provisions of economic aid with demands to join one or other [sic] of our alliances in such a crude manner that many potential allies were allienated [sic]. It is necessary for us to act carefully and patiently and in the early stages confine ourselves to securing very modest political concessions in exchange for our economic aid (in some exceptional cases—even without any concessions in return). The way will then be open to us, but at a later stage, to step up both our political price and our military demands. . . .

"Intensive economic aid to all three groups of countries should always be presented as the expression of a sincere and disinterested desire on the part of the U.S. to help and cooperate with them. We cannot afford to economise [sic] in ramming home by every propaganda means available to us the disinterested nature of U.S. policy as regards aid to underdeveloped countries. We do not economise on our anti-Communist work. Meanwhile our investors, our technical experts and other specialists should make it their business to penetrate every branch of the national economy of backward countries, and to develop them with due respect for our own interests and encouraging [sic] the national ambitions of those native businessmen whose political loyalty is not in doubt.

"It seems to me that provided all these recommendations are carried out the result should be not only to strengthen the international position of the US as a whole but would [sic] also considerably facilitate to the fulfillment of any military tasks that may confront us in the future by strengthening existing military arrangements and breathing new life into them."

The mistakes of tone, grammar, and spelling in the above excerpts, e.g., anglicisms like "economize" with an *s,* are typical of the whole document. Many phrases used, e.g., "the hooked fish needs no bait," are also British, not American English. The typing is ragged, quite unlike the electrically typed letters which are turned out by the real Rockefeller office. (In fact, it was established that

the typewriter used was of East German manufacture.) Understandably, these nuances were lost on most of the audience for
whom the forgery was intended.

Here is the progress of the Rockeller "letter" as it was passed
around the Communist propaganda mill. On February 15, 1937
the text was published in *Neues Deutschland* in East Berlin and
the same day featured in East German satellite radio broadcasts.
On the same day in the finest traditions of Communist spontaneity,
Pravda reprinted *Neues Deutschland's* discovery. The next day it
was re-run in the Soviet provincial press. Also, on February 16
Radio Moscow began passing the ball in its transmissions to Southeast Asia, Indonesia, Vietnam, and Greece. The East German press
continued to adumbrate on its original story, now equipped with
Moscow's comments and, as early as the 16th, the Czech press
began to feature it. By the 17th New China News Agency was
distributing the news of the "letter" throughout the Orient, Tass
was running it on the wire, and Radio Moscow was busily re-
broadcasting the news to Latin America and the Middle East. On
February 18th, as Radio Moscow was translating the letter into
Turkish, Portuguese, Japanese, and Korean, Radio Peking was
playing the news big with its captive Chinese audience. By the
19th Romanians were hearing about it in the pages of the Party
newspaper Scinteia.

Moscow continued its broadcasts about the "letter" from February 19-22 and they were taken up by the East German press and
radio shortly thereafter, for another extended campaign, aimed
mainly at audiences in the Federal Republic. In March the forgery
was revealed to local Middle Eastern audiences by the Damascus
newspaper *Al Qabas*. On March 10 *Neues Deutschland* went back
into action with an article quoting Al Qabas on the same subject,
and revealing a new tidbit: a "secret memorandum" from Secretary of State Dulles to President Eisenhower which purported to
outline American aggressive proposals in the Middle East. By
March 11 the same process was in full swing with the Dulles

memorandum: heavy featuring in Tass, Radio Moscow and Radio Peking—plus two articles in the March 23 and April 13 editions of *Blitz,* the sensationalist and generally pro-Communist Indian magazine. (Evidently, the pro-Communist Indians were late in getting their signals.)

All this mileage from one inexpensive forgery on a typewriter.

The Rockefeller letter was a relatively simple matter for the Soviet misinformation specialists. The Berry letter, another Soviet forgery, was part of a more complicated effort, involving overt activity by the Soviets themselves. This was also surfaced by *Neues Deutschland;* the frequent surfacing of such documents in East Germany is a tribute to the excellent discipleship of the K.G.B.'s local subsidiary, the *Hauptverwaltung Aufklaerung,* which picturesquely translates as the "Chief Administration for Enlightenment." The "letter" was purportedly written by Assistant Secretary of Defense Frank B. Berry to Defense Secretary Neil McElroy. It was exposed to public view on May 7, 1958. The burden of its message was that the average U.S. bomber pilot was a hopeless psychoneurotic, as revealed by serious and extensive medical tests, hence not to be depended upon to take proper precautions with the nuclear weapons entrusted to his care. The "letter" is worth quoting in its entirety:

DEAR MR. SECRETARY:

I wish to inform you that the medical examination carried out in accordance with your instructions of all USAF officers and airmen stationed overseas and in the Internal Zone has been completed. I enclose here with the detailed report on this matter prepared by a group of experts.

Availing myself of the opportunity I wish to make several personal observations in this connection and draw your attention to the following:

1. According to the estimates made by the experts, 67.3 per cent of all crew members that have undergone the examination suffer from psychoneurosis. It is an impressive figure and cannot fail to cause alarm. The report indicates that the situation is especially adverse among the officers and airmen serving overseas as well as

among those in the Strategic Air Command of the Internal Zone. (My further observations will deal only with the latter category.)

2. Most striking in general is the condition of psychostenia which in majority of cases finds its expression in excessive impressionability, in actions inadequately controlled by the subject's will, in all sorts of phobias, particularly in "flight phobia" as well as hysterical syndromes and fits of unaccountable animosity.

3. After an additional thorough study of the data on this problem we have ascertained that the accidents that have occurred during the last six months on Midway Island, at the Cooke AFB (Calif.) and at the Patuxent River AFB (Md.) as well as opening of fire on the civil population (Wisc.) and a number of similar cases have occurred not so much for the reasons of technical failures as due to psychic deficiency of the crew members.

4. The study of the cases of the chronic overstrain of the nervous system among the pilots and navigators of the Strategic Air Command indicates that the chief factors conducive to such a condition are the following: a great strain particularly due to intercontinental flights; excessive and sytematic use of alcohol (quite often even in flight), use of narcotic drugs (particularly cigarettes containing opium and marihuana); sexual excesses and perversions, extreme fatigue due to constant card playing. At the same time moral depression is a typical condition of all crew members making flights with atomic and H-bombs. (See pp. 17-24, special section of the enclosed report.)

5. During the medical examination progress my colleagues and I consulted a number of representatives of the Air Force regarding the means on how to improve the physical condition of pilots and navigators. These representatives insist that the flight personnel must be thoroughly renewed. I believe you will agree, however, that this is practically impossible to do.

Our repeated attempts since early 1953 to raise the physical requirements of persons entering the USAF have encountered the resistance of the Air Force Command. The AFC fears, and I believe not without reason, that in that case the number of USAF personnel would be far below the necessary minimum of officers and airmen. Moreover the number of young men entering flying schools, as you are aware, has drastically decreased lately and the tendency is continuing.

6. I am no expert in aviation technique and engineering, yet I hold that certain measures proposed by experts i.e. further im-

provement of aircraft equipment, brighter lights of the ground signal system and beacons, installation of additional direction signs, etc. will no doubt decrease to some extent the number of accidents. On my part I would ask for more time to think over suggestions on how to improve medical service in the USAF. I must admit with all sincerity, however, that the proposed engineering measures as well as any possible measures concerning medical service will not solve the problem of radical improvement of the physical condition of the USAF personnel as a whole which according to the data supplied by the last medical examination is far below the contemporary requirements.

I would deem it expedient to acquaint the USAF Chief of Staff, the Commanders of Strategic and Tactical Air Commands, the USAF Commanders in Europe and the Pacific Zone as well as Commanders of the Units with the report of the experts and particularly with their conclusions and suggestions.

Sincerely yours,

FRANK B. BERRY, M.D.
Assistant Secretary of Defense
(Health and Medical)

Like all such documents, the Berry "letter" looked as fake as a three-dollar bill to anyone remotely acquainted with the facts of the matter. The general "examination" of U.S. flight personnel, for example, never took place. (And, as noted previously, the writer was away from Washington on March 27, when he was supposed to have signed his "letter.") The U.S. military terms used are inaccurate. No smart private first class, for instance, would use Internal Zone for the military term "Zone of the Interior." The term "Air Force Command"—another Germanism— is not used when referring to the U.S. Air Force. The "Patuxent River Air Force Base" mentioned is actually the Patuxent River Naval Air Station.

The ailment from which the fliers are supposed to be suffering —"psychostenia"—is an obsolete term rarely used by American psychiatrists, but its use might be expected from a Communist writer to whom modern psychiatry is by and large a closed and *verboten* book. Other inexact terms, e.g., "group of experts" or "further improvement of aircraft equipment" would have been made very specific, if the letter had been an authentic one.

Equipped with these and other failings, the letter was sent out in an obvious follow-up to a statement which Khrushchev had made to some American newspapermen in Moscow on November 22, 1957. In this he criticized the fact that a portion of the U.S. bomber force "is constantly in the air and always ready to strike against the Soviet Union." Said Khrushchev: "There is always the possibility of a mental blackout when the pilot may take the slightest signal as a signal for action and fly to the target that he had been instructed to fly to. . . . Does this not go to show that in such a case a war may start as a result of sheer misunderstanding, a derangement in the normal psychic state of a person, which may happen to anybody. . . . Even if only one plane with one atomic or one hydrogen bomb were in the air, in this case, too, it would be not the government but the pilot who could decide the question of war."

The *Neues Deutschland* letter was tailored to suit the cloth; and another political warfare campaign—it does their scope an injustice to call these efforts merely "propaganda"—was under way. The campaign was materially helped by a chance happening in Great Britain. An American aircraft mechanic named Vernon Morgan took a U.S. Air Force non-operational bomber into the air on a distinctly unauthorized junket—for he was not even qualified to fly. He was killed when the plane crashed just after the take-off. This happened on June 14, 1958. Four days later Radio Moscow was broadcasting this incident, as an illustration of the Berry "letter's" theme.

On July 3, 1958 the Soviet Embassy in London released another "letter" allegedly written by a U.S. Air Force pilot in Britain. The pilot threatened to drop a nuclear bomb into the North Sea in an effort to alert the British to the dangerous possibility that a nuclear war might start by accident, with so many dangerous bases and pilots in action. The letter was given wide publicity all over the world—so much so that the Russians with their characteristic combination of subtlety and hamhandedness, tried to release two more shortly afterwards. These were of course ignored.

While Moscow was busy making a packaged *cause celèbre* out of all three incidents, the East German subsidiary was converting the Berry letter into entertainment for the young. In a suggested culture program, sent out to both Germanies by the Culture Publishers for German Youth (*Kulterverlag der Deutschen Jugend*) this little ditty was included:

## THE FLYING PSYCHONEUROSIS

*By* WERNER BRAUNIG

There flies Jim from Alabama
there flies Jack from Tennessee
high above the city
wearing heated pants
with the bomb aboard
and the psychoneurosis,
and on the automatic pilot is printed: liberty.
And what can happen—
How does that concern us?
That does not concern us at all.
There flies Jim from Alabama
high over the state of Wisconsin
and there is a city
and people walk in rows,
and there is a nervous slip
and he shoots them up—
there were a few people killed
And if such a thing can happen
doesn't this concern someone?
doesn't this concern us at all?
There flies Jim from Alabama
over you, and over me

With death in his head
and then he sees red
and he pushes the button
And it's over for you and me
And because that can happen tomorrow
it does concern us
Mankind! it even concerns you.

The other forgeries were cut to much the same measure, with variations only in the subject and the artistry involved. There was the Frost "letter," purportedly written by Rear Admiral Laurence Frost, Chief of Naval Intelligence, to Colonel Kawilarang, one of the leaders of the 1958 revolt in Indonesia, which "establishes" American implication in the rebellion—this was released by the Communist Chinese. The Rountree "circular," purportedly sent by Assistant Secretary of State William Rountree to embassies in the Middle East on April 17, 1958, reaffirmed American hostility to the United Arab Republic and Washington's desire to "isolate" Nasser. Other alleged State Department communications discussed Washington's aim to overthrow the Sukarno regime in Indonesia or hinted at further aggressive machinations with Premier Kishi of Japan or Chiang Kai-shek. Then there were the faked G.I. letters, so beloved of Communist propagandists, professing the soldiers' disgust with the "intervention" in Lebanon —this was produced in the Beirut newspaper *Beirut al-Maasa* on August 25, 1958. Although some of them are written on stolen U.S. stationery, the same errors of fact and expression prevail as in the Rockefeller and Berry forgeries.

Primitive as some of these fakeries seem, they have their effect. As the editors of yellow newspapers have always known, a big lie tends to make an impression, however absurd the allegations and however well-documented the denials. As the new nations of Africa and Asia gain their independence, there will be more and more newspaper and radio audiences—and editors—ill equipped to distinguish between the lie and the true fact in these instances.

It may be of some comfort to know that the more informed newspaper editors and readers of Europe, Latin America and Asia place little credence in the palpable frauds of the Soviet State Security's misinformation specialists. Unfortunately, they are not aimed at the well-informed reader.

# CHAPTER XI

# THE BALANCE SHEET

IN the last decade—or, more specifically, in the five years since Khrushchev came to the fore in Moscow, the Communist world has completed that most difficult of military maneuvers: the redisposition of one's troops and the re-shuffling of one's objectives under the eyes of the enemy. The military analogy is used advisedly. Communism can only exist on the premise of its militancy. Of all the movements in past history it most resembles in this regard, as we have suggested, the classic struggle in Islamic belief. There the *Dar al Islam,* the world of peace, strove continually to enlarge itself at the expense of the *Dar al Harb,* the world of war and chaos, whose disturbances were made inevitable for want of the true belief. It was the duty of every true believer to push back the frontiers of the *Dar al Harb,* until the millennial time when it might be completely absorbed. No refinements of Communism in the last decade have changed the truth of this analogy, although Khrushchev's espousal of "peaceful" competition strikingly altered its tactics.

Both the redisposition and the re-shuffling were done under pressure of necessity. Ideological thinking was their byproduct, not their cause. Four factors conditioned the change: 1) the nuclear stalemate and the danger of general annihilation in nuclear warfare, a circumstance which made inevitable Khrushchev's break with the Leninist doctrine that armed conflict with the capitalist world was inevitable; 2) the rise of Communist China, to a point of near parity with the Russians in the world Communist alliances; 3) the growing mechanical and scientific aptitudes of the U.S.S.R. in the widest sense of the world, with the impetus they have given both

202

to consumer satisfaction and consumer demand at home; 4) the tacitly acknowledged bankruptcy of Communist idealism, as symptomized by the continuing desertion, rebellion or passive inaction of the intellectuals charged with expounding it.

These four main factors have combined to make the course of leadership in the Soviet world a difficult one both to plot and to steer in the 'sixties. Nikita Khrushchev proved his skill as a political man by adjusting his tactics to fit the new urgencies. To a great extent he adjusted the whole Communist world from his position of leverage in Moscow. His changes were often sweeping and they had to be. The problems which were released by Stalin's death were all the more difficult to handle because they had been so long concealed by the monolith of the dictator's power. (Once he was gone, they came quickly to a head.)

In the world Communist movement, as we have seen, the Khrushchev changes were especially noticeable. Not only did they produce effective revival of classic Communist "popular-front" techniques, through the new international calls for peace, science and solidarity. But they transformed the Soviet structure of alliances—on both the governmental and the party level—from one of outright domination, as it had been under Stalin, to a form of partnership. The partnership was spurious in that what Moscow took from the smaller partners was generally far out of proportion to the small amount it gave in return. (In instances, like the United Arab Republic and Afghanistan, where Moscow appeared to give economic assistance outweighing its direct return, the political advantages of splitting countries from the West or assuring their continued neutrality must also be considered. The same principle of political aid programs has been zealously followed by Communist China.) But the forms of partnership did exist, however fake they were. The enemies of Communism only gave these forms credence by insisting that the outright domination of the Stalin days was still in effect.

Thanks to Khrushchev's repairs, both emergency and relatively long-term, the world Communist movement emerged in far better condition in 1960 than it was in 1953. Its appeal had become wider for the practical approach used. The arguments of solidarity and physical progress made more sense to the underdeveloped nations than the old ideological appeals of the Marxist holy grail. "We are all together in this," ran the new theme, "and we are making great strides, so we must be right. We're winning. Join us—and, by the way, you'd better not be caught on the side of the losers."

At the same time the Khrushchev era showed the classic weaknesses of his system more clearly than ever. For one thing, events proved its dependence on the leader principle. Efforts at humanized Communism or collective leadership, or primitive fumblings towards democratic ruling processes result in one of two things: the break-up of the whole system or the imposition of a new Big Brother, after a period of factional struggle. This truism would explain the obvious dilemma of Khrushchev's opponents on the Central Committee in Moscow whose discontent was evident in the spring and summer shifts of Khrushchev's policies in 1960. They were far more powerful than the leader had imagined, powerful enough to force dismissal of some of his most trusted deputies; yet they were afraid to upset the leader himself, for fear the whole structure might collapse with it.

Sophisticated as the Soviet Union had grown, the leader principle and the police domination remained hallmarks of its policy. Students were taught the heroic deeds of "our beloved and respected Nikita Sergeyevich" and citizens found the new system of people's courts and commissions as restricting to personal liberties in some ways as the old uniformed jailers of the State Security. For that matter, the whole secret police arm—State Security, M.V.D. and Military Intelligence—was far from dismantled. It was Khrushchev who brought the detested and long-whispered word "Chekist" back into currency.*

* From *Cheka,* the first incarnation of the Soviet Secret police. The name *Cheka* was changed early in the 'twenties to O.G.P.U. and subsequently altered to N.K.V.D., M.V.D. and the present K.G.B. Through these changes the functions and personnel of the organization remained.

This is not to say that Khrushchev has revived the iron rule of Stalin. He could not do so, and he was too much of a realist to attempt it. For public opinion, or at least a certain amount of public pressure, has become a factor in the Soviet Union. A rising standard of education has brought with it a rising level of curiosity and questioning. Within the last two years Khrushchev has sharply cut down on liberal academic education in the U.S.S.R. in favor of narrowly set technical curricula and students' work programs. Not the least of his reasons for doing so has been the restlessness of Soviet students with the outworn Marxism which is still fed to them as official philosophy. The Soviet people on the whole are cynical about Communism, but accustomed to accept the inevitability of its system. An inbred caution discourages iconoclasts. Yet the old images are chipped and fragmented. The High Priest died in 1953 and the surviving clergy have had to make concessions to a people who no longer live in fear of his malediction, a people whose principal concern has been transferred from "how to survive" to "how to get fatter."

A signal weakness was also inherent in Khrushchev's revolutionary break with Communist orthodoxy: the denial that war with the capitalist world was inevitable. Not only had this practical reinterpretation disturbed the Communist Chinese, sometimes to the point of ill-concealed fury, but it doubtless worried many inside the Soviet leadership. It threatened the traditional carrot-and-stick system of Communist governance. Little by little the Soviet Union was becoming a society of Possessors. As material goods increased, so did the appetite for goods. And in the manner of Possessors, the Soviet people were growing concerned with keeping what they had and augmenting it. They had come a long way from the days when Soviet soldiers greedily snatched up watches in the captured cities of eastern Europe. In its muted but insistent way, Soviet public opinion was pushing to keep the *status quo*— and then some.

Now that the leadership had declared the world struggle was to be peaceful, there was no constant lurking danger to move these people to sacrifice, just as there was no real tabernacle of ideology left on the altar, to inspire political idealism. The lack of a visible danger from foreign enemies quite rightly disturbed many of the Party leadership. It threatened them. It threatened the Communist system. This explains why, when the chance came in the early part of 1960, they energetically tried to manufacture one.

There was another problem which faced the Soviet leadership and its friends abroad in their international dealings. Inevitably, the peoples of the underdeveloped countries have been developing their own sophistication about Communism. Having seen it in action and seen some of its effects they grow more or less wary —depending on their degree of familiarity. What is happening in Guinea in the summer of 1960 could no longer, for example, occur in Iraq; there Kassem has seen the Communists operate at uncomfortably close quarters. Again and again, even in the era of "peaceful coexistence," local Communist leaders had to reckon with the conflict between their particular Party programs and the always overriding needs or aspirations of the two large Communist states.

No local Communist leader has yet been able to get his heavy Trojan horse inside the walls quietly, to capture the city. As we have seen, the tactical desire to behave like good parliamentarians or act the part of the "forces of peace" in a country constantly runs into contradictions. On a local level, there is the need to keep the Party core zealous and united through non-compromising revolutionary action—the same problem which the Japanese Communists have encountered. Beyond this, there are the overriding directives from Moscow or Peking to stir up trouble according to the needs of their international planners, or the bad public relations that results from open Communist aggressions elsewhere. The cause of Communism in both India and Indonesia was badly set back by the aggression of the Chinese Reds in Tibet. (To this add, in the case of Indonesia, the bitterness over Peking's championship of the overseas Chinese.) To recall another example: the Communist-led riots in Japan of May-June, 1960, may have served the aims of Moscow and Peking by aborting President Eisenhower's planned visit. But the reaction against this violence, as had happened before, was badly injuring the local prospects not only of the Japanese Communists, but of their left Socialist allies.

For all these revelations of weakness in the Communist position, the era of "peaceful co-existence" had paid them big dividends. A position of weakness had been rebuilt into a position of strength. The "useful idiots" had multiplied throughout the world. Soviet influence had become apparent, sometimes even commanding in areas like the Middle East and Latin America where it had never before penetrated in strength. In many places in the West and in Asia, the longing for a peaceful settlement, cleverly stimulated by the Khrushchev pattern, had outrun the cautions of logic and prudence. Africa, confused though it was, lay open as well. In a word, Khrushchev had led his forces back to the high ground.

The new wave of aggressive behavior, begun in mid-1960, suggested that the climate of peaceful co-existence may have been softening Soviet spirits overmuch for the gains realized. With the artificial revival of the danger, discipline and solidarity could be the more easily restored. In the long run, the free peoples of the earth could probably thank their lucky stars that Communism's own inherent frailties had put an end to such a successful tactic.

Throughout this period the leadership of the non-Communist world, most notably the leadership of the United States, remained passive. It reacted sluggishly even to the most obvious and dangerous of the new Communist challenges. Despite its vast latent ability, the grouping of American, European and Asian countries which we often, for want of a better word, call "the West" time and time again neglected to exploit situations of Communist weakness to the advantage of free peoples. It is significant that none of the weaknesses in Khrushchev's Communism just noted resulted from any action of the West. They were either inherent in the system itself; or they arose as a result of Communist actions.

Even the West's most "aggressive" diplomat, the late John Foster Dulles, was forceful against Communism only in a posture of defense. The succeeding "soft" policy of President Eisenhower lacked even this strong point. It is a commentary on the lassitude displayed by the American leadership during this period that it produced not even a positive plan for solving the Berlin crisis, which festered throughout the six years 1953-1960. Even towards the end of this time, there were many Communist weaknesses in this position which could have been exploited—the weakness of the local Party governments in eastern Europe, the desire of the Poles for Western recognition of the Oder-Neisse western border, the lack of popular support for the Ulbricht satellite government in East Germany. In the earlier period 1953-1956, American planners might also have reckoned with Soviet indecision about the handling of German and the East European questions. Yet throughout the Berlin crisis, which continues in a latent form, Washington was content merely with rejecting Soviet proposals, or posing alternatives to them. It reacted. It did not act.

The free world must begin to act, instead of reacting: 1) in coordinating its own institutions, specifically its current economic patchwork; 2) in formidably reasserting its power base and power supremacy, which in turn can come only from realizing the changed nature of power elements in a necessarily peaceful struggle. It is the rocket-in-being, not the army-in-action that can sweep the military-political chessboard. Most important of all, its leaders must begin to preach sacrifice and dedication, instead of ease—and here again the charge rests most heavily on the United States.

There remain ample opportunities for the West to use Soviet weakness to freedom's advantage. Two newsworthy events can be anticipated, among others, and preparations should be made for them. They are the death of Khrushchev and the death of Mao Tse-tung. Khrushchev is 66 and Mao Tse-tung 67. Khrushchev has been the leader of the Soviet Union for six years. Mao Tse-tung has been the absolute reigning monarch of Chinese Communism for almost two generations, the last of the great Communist despots. If any law can be posited through the observation of

Communism in action, it is this one: the succession of the ruler is its weakest link and no succession in the history of Communism has yet been a peaceful one.

Even in the case where hand-picked successors exist—and they can be assumed—we can expect at the least a period of intense administrative confusion, a period of popular concern, particularly among Party members. It is more likely in both cases that the infighting among the Party's trustees will break out in the open, as it did after the death of Stalin. Having stood idly by and *watched* the Communist world shatter and reconstitute itself after Stalin's death, the democracies must be ready to take advantage of the next comparable crises in the Communist world. A weak or a squabbling committee of successors will accept many compromises over a conference table which a confident despot would reject out of hand. Plans should be ready for the eventuality.

Meanwhile the battle, if not for the minds of men, as the outworn phrase goes, at least for physical possession of their bodies and their property, will be fought bitterly by international Communism. Its front lines are already visible not only in the uncommitted countries of the world, but even within areas of the Western alliance. Whatever we may say about the agreed futility of nuclear war, it is a real political war the Communists are waging against civilization now, whether it be fought in the form of incited riots and downed American planes, or trade pacts and deceptive proposals over the conference table. The West would do well to remember that no army ever won a war by sitting safe in its trenches.

# APPENDIX:

*Guide to the Communist Parties of the World*

AFGHANISTAN
ARGENTINA
AUSTRALIA
AUSTRIA
BELGIUM
BOLIVIA
BRAZIL
BURMA
CAMBODIA
CANADA
CEYLON
CHILE
COLOMBIA
CONGO (Belgian Congo)
CUBA
CYPRUS
DENMARK
ECUADOR
EGYPT (United Arab Republic)
FINLAND
FORMOSA
FRANCE
GERMANY (Federal Republic)
GHANA
GREAT BRITAIN
GREECE
GUATEMALA
GUINEA
ICELAND
INDIA
INDONESIA
IRAN
IRAQ
IRELAND

ISRAEL
ITALY
JAPAN
JORDAN
KENYA
KOREA (South Korea)
LAOS
LEBANON
LUXEMBOURG
MALAYA AND SINGAPORE
MEXICO
MOROCCO
NEPAL
THE NETHERLANDS
NIGERIA
NORWAY
PAKISTAN
PANAMA
PERU
THE PHILIPPINES
PORTUGAL
SPAIN
SWEDEN
SWITZERLAND
SYRIA (Northern Region, U.A.R.)
THAILAND
TUNISIA
TURKEY
UNION OF SOUTH AFRICA
UNITED STATES OF AMERICA
URUGUAY
VENEZUELA
VIETNAM (South Vietnam)

# AFGHANISTAN

There is no known Communist Party organization of any description in Afghanistan. Soviet influence is considerable, however, primarily the result of the proximity of Soviet territories whose peoples are ethnically related to important groups in northern Afghanistan. Since 1956 the U.S.S.R. has managed to recapture the influence it enjoyed in the 1920's, and has developed extensive economic, military, and cultural cooperation programs. As the result of a $100 million loan in 1955, several hundred Soviet technicians are now stationed in Afghanistan, engaged in road, airport, dam and bridge construction, oil exploration and technical assistance. In 1959 a Red Army general came to Afghanistan to direct the Soviet program of re-equipping and training the Afghanistan armed forces. The U.S.S.R. and Communist China maintain active cultural contacts with Afghanistan, and a Soviet-Afghan Friendship Society was founded in Moscow in 1959.

Afghanistan, however, is still ruled by its royal family. It has no political parties and possesses no machinery for independent expression of public views. Although an Afghan parliament exists, the most important assemblage is the *Loe Jirgah,* a national forum summoned irregularly by the royal family to obtain public support for vital policy decisions. Membership in the *Loe Jirgah* is determined according to the traditions of tribal and religious influence and status.


# ARGENTINA

During the years of Juan Peron's rule in Argentina, neutral observers generally assumed that the Communist Party would be his natural heir. Peron was overthrown in September 1955 and since then the Communists have been straining every nerve to take his place. After failing to seize power on its own, the Party joined forces with the Peronistas (whose 2.5 million members remained faithful to their exiled leader), hoping to ride to power on a wave of violence. Although their unity consisted solely of a common desire to unseat the Government, the two groups warily combined into a common front called the United Workers' Movement and paralyzed Argentina with a general strike in January 1959. Emboldened by their success, they struck again in April and the resulting chaos and violence compelled President Frondizi to ban all Communist activity. At this moment, the Party is fighting for its life in the courts, while the Government is pressing hard to destroy it. Because Argentina's standard of living is the highest in South America, and its intellectual climate is not conducive to Communism, the Communists are not likely to achieve power in Argentina by other than violent means.

NAME: The Communist Party of Argentina; founded January 1918, affiliated with Moscow in 1919.

LEGAL STATUS AND MEMBERSHIP: Declared illegal in 1930 and 1943, repressed by Peron in 1950, and prohibited by President Frondizi in April 1959. Membership figures not known, but the Party in Argentina is believed to be the smallest in Latin America on a percentage-of-population basis.

LEADERS:

Vittorio Codovila—President of the Central Committee
Rodolfo Ghioldi—Secretary General of the Central Committee
Ernesto Guidice—Legal Representative of the Central Committee
Alcira F. De la Pena—Member of the Central Committee
Hector P. Agosti—Member of the Central Committee
Orestes Ghioldi—Member of the Central Committee

The aging Codovila and Ghioldi are still the titular heads of the Party, but Guidice has apparently assumed actual command.

OFFICIAL PAPER: Communist publications are now banned, but considerable propaganda enters the country from foreign sources.

POLITICAL STATUS: None under the present ban; in the elections of February 1958, the Party polled 191,538 votes, or 2.2 per cent of the total cast.

FRONT ORGANIZATIONS: International fronts apparently still active, although operating clandestinely, include the World Peace Council and the World Federation of Trade Unions. Dozens of national front organizations exist, but many are merely letterhead covers for propaganda purposes; among the more active fronts are the following:

The Argentine Peace Council
Movement for the Democratization and Independence of Trade Unions
Union of Argentine Women
League of the Rights of Man
U.S.S.R.-Argentina Cultural Relations Institute
Anielewicz Cultural Institute (to appeal to Slavs in Argentina)

In addition, the Communist Youth Organization provides youth activities for the Party.

DIPLOMATIC RELATIONS: Argentina maintains diplomatic relations with the U.S.S.R. and other Communist countries, but not with Communist China. The U.S.S.R.'s offer of $100 million worth of oil drilling and railroad equipment was accepted by Argentina in July 1958, as was last year's offer of a $329 million loan from the United States Treasury, the International Monetary Fund, and other sources.

# AUSTRALIA

The Australian Communist Party has grown so weak that it is often considered to be a spent force in the country's life. However, if its numbers have diminished, it still poses a serious threat to Australia through the power it holds over the nation's key labor unions. Defections and a slackening of number of youthful recruits have cut the number of Party members to a fifth of the 25,000 it claimed at the end of World War II, but most of these few thousand are fighting hard to maintain their strategic position. Control of key unions gives the Party the ability to cripple Australia in emergencies. During the Korean War, for example, ships headed for Korea were held up by Communist-led longshoremen and seamen striking over minor but technically legitimate issues. The Party's greatest opportunity for success, however, lies in the fact that the labor union movement controls the Australian Labor Party, and the Labor Party may one day again control the Australian federal government. The Labor Party is controlled, not by its federal and state Parliament members, but by its 36-member Federal Conference and its 12-member Federal Executive. The Communist Party, small as it is, already controls the coal-mining unions, most metal unions in heavy industry, sections of the transport unions and a number of building unions. If it can infiltrate the Labor Party's Federal Conference and Federal Executive in a similar fashion, it will be dangerously powerful. It is for this reason that the Communist Party is considered by government leaders to be stronger in Australia than in Britain or India.

NAME: Australian Communist Party; founded 1920.

LEGAL STATUS AND MEMBERSHIP: Now legal. It was banned from 1940 to 1942, and showed its skill at working underground at that time. In 1951, a constitutional amendment empowering the government to smash the Communist organization was submitted to a referendum, and rejected by 52,000 votes out of a total 4.7 million cast. Party membership is now estimated at 5,000, not all of whom are active.

Richard Dixon—President

Louis "Lance" Sharkey—General Secretary

Jim Healy—Secretary of Waterside Workers' Federation

E. V. Elliot—Secretary of Seamen's Union

OFFICIAL PAPER: *Tribune,* published weekly in Sydney; circulation about 16,500, at least 1,000 of which goes to anti-Communists keeping track of Party activities.

POLITICAL STATUS: The Party has no direct political influence; only one Communist has held a seat in a state parliament. No Communist has ever been elected to the federal legislature. In the elections of 1958, with voting compulsory in Australia, the Communists won only 26,337 votes—0.53 per cent of the total cast.

FRONT ORGANIZATIONS: The Australian Assembly for Peace, an affiliate of the World Peace Council, is the only international front active in Australia; however, the Communists control the 33,000-member Building Workers' Industrial Union; the 14,000-member Coal Miners' Federation; the 34,000-member Waterside Workers' Federation; the 4,000-member Seamen's Union; the 2,500-member Ship Painters' and Dockers' Union; the 44,000-member Australian Railways Union (except the autonomous New South Wales branch). In addition, Communists have federal control of the Amalgamated Engineering Union, with 59,000 members, and hand down decisions on state branches (some of them non-Red) of the 17,000-member Boilermakers' Society, the 23,000-member Sheetmetal Workers' Union, and the 11,000-member Blacksmiths' Union.

DIPLOMATIC RELATIONS: Diplomatic relations with the U.S.S.R. were suspended in 1954 following revelations of Soviet espionage, and resumed in 1959. Australia does not have relations with Communist China.

# AUSTRIA

Austria, divided in four zones of military occupation in 1945, nonetheless returned rapidly to a legally elected government which soon excluded Communists from policy-making posts. Thwarted in their attempt to win power through free elections, the Communists tried to overthrow the government with a general strike, supported by armed Communists and the Soviet occupation forces, in October of 1950. For a time, Vienna was cut off from the Western world, but the Austrians firmly resisted the Communist threats, the American commander warned the Soviet commander that further support of the Communist rebels would bring United States troops into the situation, and Austria escaped becoming a Soviet satellite. Five years later the U.S.S.R. agreed to end the occupation of Austria. The withdrawal of Soviet troops, as well as the Hungarian revolt in 1956, cut deeply into the Austrian Communist Party's waning strength. In the general elections of 1959, the Communists lost their last four seats in Parliament, and their only recent source of encouragement has been a minor resurgence in the last election of shop stewards.

NAME: Communist Party of Austria (*Kommunistiche Partei Oesterreichs*), founded in November, 1918.

LEGAL STATUS AND MEMBERSHIP: Legal; outlawed by the Dollfuss government after the Socialist-Communist putsch of 1934 was crushed; re-admitted as legal in 1945 by four-power Allied Council (as were

Socialists and conservative People's Party). Party membership estimated at about 50,000.

LEADERS:
> Johann Koplenig—Party chairman
> Friedl Fuernberg—Secretary

OFFICIAL PAPER: *Volksstimme* (People's Voice), published daily in Vienna, estimated circulation less than 40,000.

POLITICAL STATUS: The Party polled 3.26% of the votes cast in the May 1959 elections, but lost its last four seats in the Parliament since its percentage was not enough to earn it representation. The Party has not been represented in the cabinet since 1947, when it had one cabinet seat.

FRONT ORGANIZATIONS: International fronts include: The World Peace Council, the World Federation of Trade Unions, the World Federation of Democratic Youth, the International Union of Students, and the International Association of Democratic Lawyers. None of these is really significant in Austria. Local fronts include the Austro-Soviet Society, and the Communists are a major influence in the steel workers, construction workers, and the Vienna railway company.

DIPLOMATIC RELATIONS: Austria maintains diplomatic relations with the U.S.S.R., but not with Communist China, and has received no aid from the Soviet bloc. United States Marshall Plan aid to Austria has totaled approximately $1,300 million.

# BELGIUM

At the end of World War II, Communism was at its high point in Belgium, thanks to the deeds of the Soviet Army and the local Communist underground. In the 1946 post-war elections, the Communists won 13% of the votes, and 4 ministries in the resulting Socialist-Communist coalition government. With economic recovery and the pressures of the Cold War, the Communist Party fell into increasing disfavor, however. The Soviet suppression of the Hungarian revolution nearly destroyed it. Now, aided by the impressive Soviet exhibits at the Brussels World Fair in 1958, as well as the softer Soviet line since then, the Communists have begun a slow and painful climb back to a position of respect, if not of influence. The Party leaders concentrate on infiltrating the Socialist trade unions and keeping the Party's hard core intact and disciplined.

NAME: The Communist Party of Belgium (*Parti Communiste de Belgique—Belgische Communistische Partij*); founded 1919.

LEGAL STATUS AND MEMBERSHIP: Legal, never outlawed by the Belgians. Card-carrying membership estimated at 20,000.

LEADERS: Politburo: Gaston Moulin (Deputy), Frans Vanden Branden, Bob Wolsten; Secretariat: Edouard Burnelle, Rene Beelen, Gerard Van Moorkercke.

OFFICIAL PAPER: *Le Drapeau Rouge* (Red Flag), published daily, 5,000 subscribers—subscription only.

POLITICAL STATUS: The Party received 1.89% of the votes cast in the 1958 elections, has two of 212 seats in the Chamber of Deputies, one of 175 in Senate. It has not formed a part of the government since 1947.

FRONT ORGANIZATIONS: The International Association of Democratic Lawyers has an office in Brussels, but is not considered a significant organization. There are "Friendship Societies" with most of the Soviet-bloc nations represented; the Belgians regard them as primarily for business contacts, while the Communists use them for spreading propaganda.

DIPLOMATIC RELATIONS: Belgium has diplomatic relations with all the Soviet-bloc nations except Communist China; it has never received aid from the Soviet bloc or the United States, but about 5% of its trade is with the U.S.S.R.

# BOLIVIA

The peculiar characteristic of Communism in Bolivia is that it is camouflaged to look like democracy. Besides the Bolivian Communist Party and two Trotskyite groups, Bolivia's invisible Communism is represented by the part of the National Revolutionary Movement controlled by ex-President Victor Paz Estenssoro and the labor leader, Juan Lechin. This Titoist blend of nationalism and Communism has been behind all the revolutionary changes which have taken place in Bolivia since the victorious revolt of 1952. These include nationalization of the tin mines, agrarian reform, universal suffrage, the conversion of the regular army into a political machine, and the creation of a militia of the proletariat. These measures, combined with a policy of violence and terror, have vanquished the old traditional political parties and crushed most opposition to the regime; moreover, the regime can scarcely be defeated in an election since the votes of the illiterate peasants, workers, and miners represent a crushing majority, and this great mass of voters is easily led and maneuvered by the authorities in the Party hierarchy. The Bolivian Communist Party is working hard to infiltrate this national Communism and convert it into an international Communism ruled by Moscow, but its success cannot yet be accurately measured.

NAME: The Bolivian Communist Party; officially founded 1950.

LEGAL STATUS AND MEMBERSHIP: Now legal, though it only acts clandestinely; outlawed 1950-1951: The Party now claims 10,000 members.

LEADERS: Jorge Kello, secretary-general; other leaders, whose Party titles are unknown, include: Mario Monje, Felipe Iniquez, Alfredo Arratia, Sergio Almaraz, Ramiro Bedregal, and Sra. Carola de Iniguez.

OFFICIAL PAPER: *Unidad*, weekly, estimated circulation 2,000. Other Communist organs—though not controlled by the Party—include *El Pueblo, Lucha Obrera*, and *Masas*, which is the organ of the Trotskyite P.O.R. Party.

POLITICAL STATUS: The Communist Party got 2,500 votes out of 1,300,000 cast in the 1956 elections; their visible influence upon the national-Communist government is nil.

FRONT ORGANIZATIONS: The International Organization of Journalists is the only international Communist front showing any signs of life in Bolivia, and its influence is marginal.

DIPLOMATIC RELATIONS: Diplomatic relations with the U.S.S.R. have been authorized, but not yet begun. Bolivia has received $174 million in aid from the United States; it has received no aid from the Soviet bloc.


# BRAZIL

Brazil, which put down an armed Communist revolt in 1935, signed a three-year trade agreement with the Soviet Union in December 1959. This marked the first official contact between Brazil and the Soviet bloc since 1947; it was also an indication of Communism's progress in Brazil. Communist influence is disproportionately large in comparison with the small number of Party members. The Brazilian Communist Party, still theoretically outlawed, has had considerable success in the last two years by talking of nationalistic aims and avoiding mention of Communism itself. Reds have taken control of the Instituto Superior De Estudos Brasileiros, Brazil's most important graduate school, and are busily indoctrinating the future leaders of the country who are studying there, as well as influencing the government directly through the Institute's economic research projects. Communists have also infiltrated transportation, utilities and industrial unions, and are trying to organize a national workers' federation. The army has also shown some signs of Communist infiltration. Some explanation of Communism's recent successes can be found in Brazil's continuing economic difficulties, the Brazilian Communist Party's recovery from a post-Stalin split in 1956, and the absence of laws to counter Communist infiltration.

NAME: The Brazilian Communist Party (*Partido Communista Brasileira*); founded in 1922, allowed to function openly in 1945; presently called *Movimento Communista*.

LEGAL STATUS AND MEMBERSHIP: Outlawed in 1947, under constitution which prohibits the formation of anti-democratic parties. Estimated card-carrying party membership, 33,000.

LEADERS: Leader Luis Carlos Prestes now calls the Party the *Movimento Communista,* since he claims the Party itself is dissolved; for this reason also he has no Party title. Other Party leaders include Agildo Barata, Mauricio Grabois, and Diogenes Arruda, but Prestes is the only one still active in Party affairs.

OFFICIAL PAPER: The weekly *Novos Rumos* is considered to be the official Party newspaper; *Ultima Hora,* which follows the Party line faithfully, has a circulation of at least 115,000.

POLITICAL STATUS: Communist votes have apparently declined in the last three national elections; Communists and their sympathizers are believed to control 18 of the 326 seats in the Brazilian House, and none of the Senate's 63 seats.

FRONT ORGANIZATIONS: International fronts operating in Brazil include The International Federation of Teachers' Unions, The Confederation of Latin-American Workers, The World Peace Council and The International Association of Democratic Lawyers. Brazilian groups apparently dominated by Communists include the National Students' Union and the Parliamentary Nationalist Front.

DIPLOMATIC RELATIONS: Brazil does not maintain diplomatic relations with, or receive aid from, the Soviet bloc.

# BURMA

Burma regained its independence, after 124 years of British rule, on January 4, 1948; less than three months later, the Burma Communist Party was waging guerrilla war against the Burmese government, claiming that independence was a sham. Prime Minister U Nu proposed a compromise which would have taken Burma far to the left, but the Burma Communist Party rejected it, and in May its rival, the Communist Party of Burma, began an independent revolt. By 1949, at least five separate insurrections were in progress, and the government had lost control of most of central Burma. By 1956, Burmese Army pressure and internal dissension had weakened the Communist military position. The Communists put more effort into the leftist National United Front in an attempt to win politically what they could not gain by force. The National United Front captured a third of the popular vote in 1956 in a widespread public protest against the ruling Anti-Fascist People's Freedom League (A.F.P.F.L.), government corruption, bickering and misuse of power; and the A.F.P.F.L. soon split into rival camps. This split resulted in a weak government headed by U Nu and sustained by 45 Communist parliamentary votes; U Nu, determined to have peace at any price, began offering more and more concessions to the Communists. The situation deteriorated; the Communists, overjoyed by this unexpected reversal of fortune, grew arrogant and demanding. U Nu, clinging to power, led the country close to anarchy and Communism. Finally, realizing that the alternative was political suicide, U Nu turned the government over to General Ne Win in October 1958 and the army began restoring order. By February 1960 the country was ready for new national elections.

NAME: At least four Communist Parties: Burma Communist Party, founded 1939; Communist Party of Burma, founded 1946; Burma Workers' Party, founded 1950; and the People's Comrades Party, founded 1950, now merged with the People's Unity Party, which was formed in 1952.

LEGAL STATUS AND MEMBERSHIP: Burma Communist Party—illegal since 1953; Communist Party of Burma—illegal since 1947; Burma Workers' Party—legal since its formation; People's Comrades Party—illegal when founded, legally recognized when it withdrew from armed revolt before its merger with the People's Unity Party in 1959. Guerrilla membership of Parties down to about 1,400; other membership not known at present.

LEADERS:

Thakin Than Tun—Secretary General of Burma Communist Party
Thakin Soe—Secretary General of Communist Party of Burma
Thakin Chit Maung—Secretary General of Burma Workers' Party
Bo Zeya—Secretary General of People's Comrades Party
Thein Pe Myint—Head of the People's Unity Party

OFFICIAL PAPER: None at present.

POLITICAL STATUS: In the elections of 1956, the Communist-dominated National United Front polled 30% of the votes cast, won 47 of 250 parliament seats; since then the Communists have been at least temporarily disorganized by the army rule.

FRONT ORGANIZATIONS: Several fronts exist in Burma, but their activities came to a standstill during the army's rule. They include the following:

World Peace Council
World Federation of Trade Unions
World Federation of Democratic Youth
International Union of Students
Soviet-Burma Friendship Association
China-Burma Friendship Association
Afro-Asian Solidarity Committee

DIPLOMATIC RELATIONS: Burma maintains relations with the U.S.S.R. and Communist China; aid from the U.S.S.R., in the form of "gifts," amounted to about $40 million in 1957. The United States has provided perhaps $30 million in aid, plus other assistance.

# CAMBODIA

The Communist Party of Cambodia operates through the Pracheachon, a legal political-front organization. Cambodia's ruler, Prince Norodom Sihanouk, has officially labeled the Pracheachon a Communist organization, subsidized and directed by a "foreign power." Despite this, the Pracheachon has avoided governmental repression by supporting the Government's neutralist foreign policy and exploiting Cambodia's tense relations with neighboring Thailand and South Vietnam. Cambodia's diplomatic recognition of Communist China in 1958 facilitated the spread of Sino-Soviet influence throughout the country, particularly among Cambodia's 300,000 Chinese. The scope of Communist activity can be estimated from the fact that Communist propaganda comprised approximately 95% of all the reading material reaching the Chinese population of Cambodia. Through cultural, trade and aid programs, as well as propaganda, the Communists are exerting considerable and continuing efforts to extend their influence until neutralist Cambodia becomes a Communist state.

NAME: The Pracheachon; founded 1955 to replace the Khmer Vietminh movement, disbanded in 1954.

LEGAL STATUS AND MEMBERSHIP: Legal; members about 1,000 following about 30,000.

LEADERS: Not available.

OFFICIAL PAPER: *Pracheachon.* Other papers considered Communist-controlled are *Bkapheap, Mittapheap,* and *Meatophum,* and the French-language *Observateur.*

POLITICAL STATUS: All 62 seats in the National Assembly are held by Prince Sihanouk's People's Socialist Community party; no deputy is now affiliated with the Communists, but several are considered to have retained pro-Communist sympathies.

FRONT ORGANIZATIONS: Not Available.

DIPLOMATIC RELATIONS: Cambodia maintains diplomatic relations with the U.S.S.R. and Communist China. The Soviet bloc contributed $34 million in credits to Cambodia between January 1954 and June 1959; since then Soviet activities have expanded markedly.


# CANADA

Canadian Communists admit that Canada cannot be transformed into a Soviet state without the assistance of the Red Army and they do not even hope for mass public support in the near future. The main effort of Communism in Canada is in the realm of espionage rather than mass organization. Igor Gouzenko, the Russian code clerk whose defection in 1945 exposed the details of this plan, declared that the whole aim of Soviet espionage is to create a formidable Fifth Column under cover of a political party. Canada's strategic position between the United States and the U.S.S.R., and her long, undefended border with the United States, make her a key target for such activity. The Communist countries have had considerable success in Canada by making and withdrawing trade offers so as to create the impression that the United States is preventing such trade. A constant flow of Soviet artistic and cultural groups provides a ceaseless round of public gatherings at which the Communists reiterate their "peace and friendship" propaganda. Other Communists play on the discontents of the French Canadians, attempt to rouse the nostalgia of immigrants from Eastern Europe or invite journalists and commentators on bargain guided tours of the Communist world. In summary, it can be said that the Communist Party as a political party in Canada is unimportant; but Communism in Canada, operating through the Party, front organizations and the diplomatic representatives of Communist countries, is extremely active.

NAME: The Communist Party of Canada; founded clandestinely in 1921.

LEGAL STATUS AND MEMBERSHIP: Legal at present; was repressed from 1931 to 1936, banned in 1940, gradually returned to legal status; now claims 6,000 members.

LEADERS:

Tim Buck—General Secretary
William Kashtan—Member of the National Executive Committee
Leslie Morris—Member of the National Executive Committee
Bruce Magnuson—Member of the National Executive Committee
John Weir—Member of the National Executive Committee
Alfred Dewhurst—Member of the National Executive Committee
Nelson Clarke—Member of the National Executive Committee
John Boyd—Member of the National Executive Committee
Stanly B. Ryerson—Member of the National Executive Committee
Camille Dionne—Member of the National Executive Committee
Peter Prokop—Member of the National Executive Committee
James Harries—Member of the National Executive Committee

OFFICIAL PAPER: The official Party paper is *The Marxist Review,* but the weekly *Canadian Tribune* of Toronto, the weekly *Pacific Tribune* of Vancouver, and the bi-monthly French language *Le Combat* also follow the Party line. In addition, there are some two dozen periodicals aimed at minority groups; most of these are foreign language sheets and none has a circulation of more than 3,000.

POLITICAL STATUS: The last Communist member of Parliament, Fred Rose, was sentenced to jail as a Soviet spy in 1947. Communist votes in the national election of 1957 totaled 7,772, or .1% of the total vote—a sharp drop from the 1953 total of 61,703.

FRONT ORGANIZATIONS: Canadian fronts with some general influence include the Canadian Peace Congress, the Socialist Youth League and the Congress of Canadian Women. All of these are affiliated with international fronts.

DIPLOMATIC RELATIONS: Canada maintains diplomatic relations with the U.S.S.R., but not with Communist China.

# CEYLON

The Communists in Ceylon suffered setbacks in 1959. Moderates within the coalition government strongly opposed measures sponsored by the independent Communist ministers, and succeeded in forcing the independent Communists and most of the other leftists from the government in May. The ensuing government, dominated by moderates, subsequently adopted a hard line toward Communist-inspired strikes, and soon drove all three Communist political groupings into opposition. The strike policies of the Trotskyites have probably cost them popular support, and the ouster of the independent Communists from the government has divested that group of its major source of power. The three factional Marxist parties nevertheless continue to command strong support in the trade unions, with the Moscow-oriented party probably increasing its labor support at the expense of the other two. Foreign Communist propaganda is still widely circulated in Ceylon, but there has been a widespread reaction against the brutality of the Chinese Communists in Tibet, and enthusiasm for ties with the Soviet bloc has waned accordingly.

NAME: There are three Communist parties in Ceylon. The Communist Party of Ceylon is Moscow-oriented; the Lanka Sama Samaja Party is Trotskyite; the Lanka Sama Samaja Party-Revolutionary is independent.

LEGAL STATUS AND MEMBERSHIP: All are legal. C.P.C. membership is estimated at 4,000; L.S.S.P. at 1,500; L.S.S.P.-R. at 650.

POLITICAL STATUS: In the elections of 1956, the C.P.C. won 4.5% of the votes, the L.S.S.P. won 10.4%, and the L.S.S.P.-R. 5.1%. The L.S.S.P.-R. formed a part of the governing coalition front until May 1959.

# CHILE

Communism in Chile is fighting its way back to its former position of strength after ten years underground. In 1947 President Gonsalez Videla made three Communists members of his cabinet in recognition of Communist support of his candidacy; these three were the only known Communists ever to have held cabinet rank in South America. Subsequently Gonsalez Videla turned on his erstwhile allies as untrustworthy and the Defence of Democracy Law outlawed the Party at the end of 1947. Now the Communists are legal again and they and their many fellow-travelers are seeking power through the old Communist technique of the popular front. Their task is simplified by the large numbers of Chileans who fail to vote, as well as by harsh economic conditions in many areas of the country. Communist propaganda has it that the United States is keeping Chile from prosperity by preventing Chilean trade with the Soviet bloc and this line has proved convincing to many, including the Socialists. A gradual increase in the Chilean workers' standard of living has brought a corresponding decline in the power of the Communist Party; but Communism still presents a real challenge to democracy in Chile.

NAME: The Communist Party of Chile (*Partido Communista de Chile*), formed when the existing Socialist Party joined Lenin's Third International in 1920.

LEGAL STATUS AND MEMBERSHIP: The Party was outlawed from 1928 to 1931 and again from 1948 to 1958, for subversive activity; it is now legal again, and claims 40,000 members.

LEADERS:

> Elias Lafertte—President (purely honorary)
> Luis Corvalan Leppa—Secretary-General
> Galvarino Melo—Member of Executive Committee
> Jose Gonsalez—Member of Executive Committee
> Orlando Millas—Member of Executive Committee

OFFICIAL PAPER: *El Siglo,* published in Santiago, has a circulation estimated at 20,000; it is probably the best Party daily in Latin America.

POLITICAL STATUS: The Communists polled 110,000 votes in the 1958 elections, or 11% of the total number cast, and have six deputies in the Chamber of 147 seats. They are joined in the opposition coalition known as the Popular Action Front (F.R.A.P.), which polled 30% of the votes cast in the 1958 elections, and is numerically dominated by the Socialists. This strictly political alliance is strained by a fight between the Socialists and the Communists for control of the labor unions.

FRONT ORGANIZATIONS: Of the international front organizations, only the World Peace Council officially exists, and only the World Federation of Trade Unions is both active and influential. Other fronts and publications can be expected to emerge as the Party recovers ground.

DIPLOMATIC RELATIONS: Chile does not maintain diplomatic relations with nations of the Soviet bloc, nor receive aid from them; neither has she received aid from the United States Government.

# COLOMBIA

Communist activities in Colombia have continued to increase under the government's new policy of guaranteeing civil liberties. Communist influence is especially strong in the labor movement centered in the major cities of Cali, Barranquilla, Medellin, and Bogotá. Colombian politics generally have moved to the left in response to the stimulus of grave social problems, and the Communists have made use of the opportunity to increase their influence in intellectual circles. Although Liberal students at the Universidad Libre in Bogotá have petitioned for removal of Communist professors from the faculty, the Communist Party is working to infiltrate youth and student groups. In addition to the more or less conventional work of the Communist Youth movement, the P.C.C. maintains its own radio news program, and has made Bogotá one of the major Communist publishing centers for Latin America.

NAME: The Communist Party of Colombia (P.C.C.)

LEGAL STATUS AND MEMBERSHIP: The Party regained legal status in 1957; its membership is estimated at over 5,000.

OFFICIAL PAPER: The Latin American edition of the *World Marxist Review* began publication in Bogotá in 1959.

POLITICAL STATUS: The Party has no representatives in Congress, since Colombian political life is shared equally by the Conservative and Liberal parties, under the provision of the National Front agreement which was ratified as a constitutional amendment on December 1, 1957.

FRONT ORGANIZATIONS: Communist influence in the National Union of Colombian Students (U.N.E.C.) became so obvious that a new non-Communist University Students Association was recently formed. Other fronts include the Colombian Society of the Friends of China, The National Worker-Intellectual Front (F.M.O.L.), and the "7th of January" Worker-Student Movement. Communist sympathizers are trying to penetrate the Liberal Party through such local splinter groups as the Popular Liberal Movement in Barranquilla and the Popular National Union in Cali.

# CONGO (Belgian Congo)

The million square miles of Central Africa now known as the Belgian Congo became Africa's newest independent state on June 30, 1960. Although there is no Congo Communist Party, the trend of affairs since Independence has certainly offered Communism ample opportunity for penetration and expansion. The *Parti du Peuple,* a small party with a strong Marxist bent and no popular support, was assigned the task of drawing up an economic policy for the future independent Congo at the Conference of Federalist Parties held in December 1959. Not unexpectedly, this program had strong Socialist leanings. Another Congolese party, the *Centre du Regroupement Africain* (C.E.R.E.A.), was considered more likely to become the Congo Communist Party once independence was achieved, since its leaders have had more contacts with the outside Communist world. Present conditions, however, make prediction difficult. The Communists only began to take a serious interest in the Congo in 1958 and it was well repaid. Congolese nationalists, rejecting no assistance in the drive for independence, openly invited Soviet intervention, in a situation which by August 1960 had degenerated from nationalism to sectionalism into literal tribalism.

# CUBA

The emergence of Communism under Fidel Castro is a fact of national life in Cuba; that it is the most important fact is no longer open to question. Castro's revolution was at its inception a genuinely national revolt against the corrupt and oppressive Batista regime. The Communists, working from within Castro's 26th of July Movement, are doing their best to make it into an internationalist revolution which can only lead to a Communist Cuba. The Party, outlawed in 1952, emerged from underground in 1959 and is well on its way to becoming the most important single party in the country, but Communism's real power in Cuba depends upon the Communists and fellow-travelers who already control many of the country's important agencies. Chief supporter of the Party's aims is apparently Raul Castro, Fidel's younger brother and designated heir who holds the present post of Chief of the Armed Forces. A more capable organizer than his brother, Raul was a member of the Communist Youth Movement in Havana, studied and traveled in Eastern Europe as a guest of the Communists, and is instituting classes in Marxist theory in Cuban army posts. Raul's chief counsellor is Carlos Rodriguez, editor of the Communist paper *Hoy;* his private secretary, Joaquin Ordoqui, is a well-known Communist. Raul's wife is an avowed member of the Communist Party. Another leading Communist is Major Ernesto (Che) Guevara, Argentine-born commander of La Cabana Fortress in Havana, President of the National Bank of Cuba, and head of the industrial department of the Institute of Agrarian Reform. In his various capacities, he is Cuba's economic czar, and has already used his power to take over thousands of acres of arable land. Director of the National Institute of Agrarian Reform is Captain Antonio Nunez Jiminez, an aide to Raul Castro, whose book, *Geography of Cuba,* was banned as

Communist propaganda. Carlos Franqui, who worked for *Hoy* and published a clandestine weekly for the Party, is now editor of *Revolucion,* the official paper of the 26th of July Movement. David Salvador, with the aid of two Moscow-trained Communists, runs the Cuban Confederation of Labor. The list is long, and many middle-class Cubans find its meaning increasingly disturbing; but Castro still enjoys strong support among the mass of Cubans, and if Soviet aid offsets the losses resulting from nationalization and the damaging of economic relations with the United States, Cuba may have a Communist-oriented regime for some time to come.

## CYPRUS

The Communist Party of Cyprus, under the name of the Progressive Party of the Working People (A.K.E.L.), is a powerful influence in this former British Crown Colony torn by guerrilla war, now an independent republic. A.K.E.L. maintains the usual Communist youth group, a women's group, and a farmer's group; but its real strength lies in its control over the leadership of the Pan-Cyprian Confederation of Labor (P.E.O.). Although the A.K.E.L. itself claims roughly 6,000 members, the P.E.O., with some 40,000 members, comprises well over half the union membership on the island. In December 1955 British authorities banned A.K.E.L. and Communist groups other than P.E.O., and imprisoned many Party leaders. All Communist leaders have since been released, and now operate freely since A.K.E.L. was legalized in December 1959.

Communist strength in Cyprus is concentrated among the urban Greeks, finding little support in the rural centers which contain 80% of the island's population. A.K.E.L. has agreed to accept 5 of the 35 seats in the House of Representatives that are allotted to the Greek community in exchange for not contesting the election against the followers of President-elect Archbishop Makarios. The Turkish National Unity Party, led by Dr. Fazil Kutchuk, Vice President-elect of Cyprus, has no organized competition for the 15 seats allotted to the Turkish community. With 82 years of British administration ended, Cyprus begins its independence with one-tenth of its House of Representatives under Communist control.

## DENMARK

The Danish Communist Party, in common with others in Western Europe, has been in a steady slump since the days of victory in 1945, and now is suffering the additional turmoil of a split in the ranks of the Party. In the 1945 elections, the Party won a quarter of a million votes, or 12.5% of the ballots cast; by 1957 it had slumped to 3.2%, and in the 1960 elections it will probably lose the last of its parliamentary representation. In 1958, the Party expelled its popular leader, Aksel Larsen, for "severe violation of Party rules"; Larsen promptly founded the Socialist People's Party, and this Titoist group seems likely to draw much of the Communist Party's remaining strength. The future of any form of Communism seems dubious, however, in as prosperous and well-governed a social-democracy as Denmark.

NAME: Communist Party of Denmark (*Danmarks Kommunistiske Parti*); founded 1918 as a section of the Communist International, 1920 as a Danish party.

LEGAL STATUS AND MEMBERSHIP: Legal except from 1941-1945, when it was outlawed under Nazi pressure. Membership estimated at around 5,000.

LEADERS: Chairman, Knud Jespersen; Group leader in the Folketing (Parliament), Villy Fuglsang.

OFFICIAL PAPER: *Land og Folk* (Country and People), published in Copenhagen, circulation estimated to be below 7,000.

POLITICAL STATUS: Has 6 seats of 175 in the Folketing, will probably lose all of them in the elections this year. No influence in the government.

FRONT ORGANIZATIONS: The international World Peace Council and the local Danish-Russian Society for Cooperation operate with little influence.

DIPLOMATIC RELATIONS: Denmark has relations with the U.S.S.R. and Communist China, but has not received aid from the Soviet bloc. United States aid has totaled $145 million.


# ECUADOR

The Communist Party of Ecuador (P.C.E.), though it has only an estimated 1,000 members and is weak organizationally and financially, nonetheless has considerable influence among intellectuals and students. Its influence in the labor movement is also quite strong, and is bolstered by the P.C.E's policy of cooperation with the much larger Socialist Party. The Communists have managed to maintain their control of the Ecuadorean Student Federation despite a serious challenge to their position by non-Communist students. However, Communist influence remains negligible in the armed forces and government, and the P.C.E. won only 1.8% of the vote in the 1958 elections for the chamber of deputies.

# EGYPT (United Arab Republic)

Egyptian Communism has been faction-ridden since its beginning in the early 1920's, when it was smashed by the government after a brief existence. After World War II it began to emerge again, despite government crackdowns and continuing factionalism. Since the 1952 revolution overthrowing King Farouk, Egyptian Communism has survived alternating periods of tolerance and repression. The Communists opposed Nasser when he first came to power, but supported him when he veered away from the West in 1955. By 1958 the Communists had managed to unite briefly as the Egyptian Communist Party, and had a membership estimated at double that of 1954. The threat of a Communist takeover in Syria, however, led Nasser to form the United Arab Republic linking Syria and Egypt, and the next necessary step was the repression of Communism itself in both countries. As one of Nasser's confidants has phrased it: "The battles against Western imperialism are won and over. The battle of the future in the Middle East will be between Arab Nationalism and Communism."

NAME: Two main factions: The Egyptian Communist Party, and its principal rival, the Democratic Movement of the National Liberation (H.A.D.I.T.U).

LEGAL STATUS AND MEMBERSHIP: Both groups illegal, hundreds of their leaders in jail since January 1959, on charges of attempting the "forcible overthrow of the fundamental social and economic systems of the state." Party membership was estimated at 14,000 in 1958, before the crackdown.

LEADERS: All the following are jailed awaiting the verdict of their 1959 trial:

> Dr. Fouad El-Sayed Murzy, code name "Khaled," the name traditionally adopted by the Party Secretary General
> Ismail Sabry Abdullah
> Saad Abdel-Kawi Zehran
> Mohamed Hilmy Yassin

OFFICIAL PAPER: *Ittihad al-Shaab*, published clandestinely until 1959, now stopped entirely.

POLITICAL STATUS: None in its present state of suppression.

FRONT ORGANIZATIONS: There are no Communist fronts of any significance in Egypt at the present time.

DIPLOMATIC RELATIONS: Egypt maintains diplomatic relations with the U.S.S.R. and Communist China, and has received an estimated $658 million worth of aid from the Soviet bloc. Comparable aid from the United States has totaled $190 million.

# FINLAND

Finland enjoys an uneasy freedom. Situated next to the U.S.S.R., it keeps a wary watch for signs of a return of the "night frost," as President Kekkonen has called the local variant of the Cold War. The Soviet "night frost" appears whenever Finland seems to the Soviets to be drifting toward the Western Powers, but there has not been a full-scale attempt to upset the status quo. When a crisis developed in Finnish-Soviet relations in 1958, for example, the Soviet Ambassador in Helsinki took an extended "vacation," Soviet purchases came to a halt and the press of the U.S.S.R. blasted the Finnish Government. But the Communist Party of Finland itself caused no trouble, and the crisis was resolved by discussions. The process is both delicate and continuing. The Soviets are not permitted to dictate Finnish policy or to interfere in Finnish Parliamentary procedures; but at the same time the Finns must tread softly to keep from rousing the mistrust and anger of the Soviets. This situation complicates the problems of the Agrarians, who rule as a minority government. They would like to form a coalition with the Social Democratic Party and restore the stability of a majority government. Such action would almost certainly bring on a new "night frost," however, since the present leaders of the Soviets detest the Social Democratic Party who were, incidentally, reelected in April 1960. Despite these factors, the Communists do not seem likely to win control in Finland. The other parties are united at least in their opposition to the Communists, and the Soviets do not want to alarm Scandinavia by forcing their way into power. Apparently, the precarious balance has a good chance of continuing.

NAME: The Finnish Communist Party. Formed in 1918, in Moscow, from the remnants of the Red regime driven from Finland by Baron Mannerheim.

LEGAL STATUS AND MEMBERSHIP: Now legal. Banned in 1923, returned in 1924; banned in 1931, underground until made legal again in 1944. Membership about 30,000.

LEADERS:

      Aimo Aaltonen—Chairman of Finnish Communist Party

      Ville Pessi—Secretary of Finnish Communist Party

      Hertta Kuusinen—Chairman of People's Democratic Party
         Parliamentary group; member of Finnish Communist
         Party's Central Committee

      Yrjo Enne—Secretary of People's Democratic Party

OFFICIAL PAPER: *Kansas Uutiset* ("People's News"), daily, circulation about 50,000.

POLITICAL STATUS: The Party has not been included in a Finnish government since 1948, but the threatening possibilities of its presence influence most decisions of the government. The Party has 50 parliament seats; the divided Social Democratic Party has 51; and the ruling Agrarians have 47. The Communists received 23.2% of the national vote in the 1958 elections.

FRONT ORGANIZATIONS: The People's Democratic Party is the Communist Party's political front. The Defenders of the Peace is a branch of the World Peace Council. There is a Finnish-Soviet Friendship Society.

DIPLOMATIC RELATIONS: Finland has diplomatic relations with all the Soviet-bloc countries except East Germany. It has accepted $20 million in Soviet loans, since repaid, and $125 million in credits for industrialization. Loans from the United States have reached $59 million.

# FORMOSA

Communism on Formosa is limited to a few hunted secret agents. This is due in part to Formosa's island inaccessibility and in part to the anti-Communist security regulations which are stringently enforced by the Nationalist government. The Chinese Communists have sent agents to Formosa in the guise of refugees, merchants, tourists, students, and defectors. According to the Nationalists, many of these agents surrender voluntarily after seeing conditions on Formosa; agents who do not surrender are almost invariably caught as soon as they attempt overt action, for they have no underground organization and no popular support. Native-born Formosans, who at first resented the Nationalist "invasion," are now apparently prospering from it and show no interest in the Communist alternative. United States economic aid, totaling $920 million from 1951 to 1959, has contributed heavily to this economic well-being. Needless to say, Formosa has no relations with the Soviet bloc.

# FRANCE

The French Communist Party is numerically large, but isolated. Other leftist parties have rejected post-war Communist appeals for a Common Front, and De Gaulle's drive for greater financial and political stability and decolonization threatens to deprive the Party of many of its favorite sources of propaganda. Premier Khrushchev himself delivered a blow to the French Party in the fall of 1959 by backing the General's offer of self-determination for Algeria after the Party had attacked it. All this is a far cry from the Party's position in the years immediately following World War II. By the end of 1946, the Communists held 25% of the seats in the all-powerful National Assembly, and in 1947 and 1948 they nearly paralyzed the country through a series of general strikes. The exhausting wars in Indo-China and then in Algeria provided a continuing source of bitterness which the Communists could exploit with little difficulty. The Party vote in France did not drop significantly until De Gaulle returned to power in June 1958. Today, however, there are indications that the Party may regain many of the more than one million votes it lost in the November 1958 general elections. The reason: the Algerian war, with its heavy toll in blood and money, is still, in De Gaulle's own words, "blocking the nation's future."

NAME: French Communist Party (*Parti Communiste Français*); founded 1921.

LEGAL STATUS AND MEMBERSHIP: Now legal; outlawed in 1939 in retaliation for the Nazi-Soviet pact. Membership about 425,000 as of 1959.

LEADERS: Maurice Thorez, Secretary General; Jacques Duclos, Secretary.

OFFICIAL PAPER: *L'Humanité*, published daily in Paris, circulation about 170,000.

POLITICAL STATUS: In the 1958 elections, the Party received 20.7% of the vote; they now control 10 of 552 seats in the National Assembly, and 14 of 320 seats in the Senate. The Party forms a coalition only with the tiny Progressivist group.

FRONT ORGANIZATIONS: The General Labor Confederation (C.G.T), an affiliate of the World Federation of Trade Unions, is by far the largest and most powerful Communist front in France; the World Peace Council's influence has dwindled lately, but is still a significant factor. Local fronts include the usual Soviet-bloc friendship societies; the Union of French Women; the Union of Valiants (a youth organization); the National Federation of Deportees, Internees and Resistance Patriots; and the Republican Association of Former Combatants.

DIPLOMATIC RELATIONS: France maintains relations with the U.S.S.R., but not with Communist China; she has received no aid from the Soviet bloc, while Marshall Plan aid totaled about $6 billion.

# GERMANY (Federal Republic)

The Communist Party organized rapidly in West Germany in the years following World War II, and seemed to be on its way toward winning a substantial role in the first Federal government; but the Soviet blockade of Berlin turned public opinion against it, and it won only 4.9% of the votes in the first elections in 1949. In Parliament the

Communists were unable to form any sort of alliance with the Socialist opposition, and found themselves limited to creating nuisance opposition on their own. The East German Communists apparently realized the futility of supporting their West German cohorts before the elections of 1953, with the result that the West German Party fell to 2.2% in the balloting, and exhausted most of its remaining funds in the process. When it was declared illegal in 1956, the Party had already moved underground to take up its new task of agitation and troublemaking. The anti-Semitic incidents of late 1959 are considered by West Germans to be the work of Communist agents busy stirring up old enmities; at the moment this kind of incident would seem to be the most the Communists can hope for.

NAME: German Communist Party (*Kommunistische Partei Deutschlands*); founded 1919 by friends who had sheltered Lenin during his exile in Germany before World War I.

LEGAL STATUS AND MEMBERSHIP: The Party was repressed by the Nazis, and declared illegal in 1956 by the Federal Supreme Court. Estimated membership now 30,000.

LEADERS: Max Reimann, Chairman, only known leader.

OFFICIAL PAPER: *Volksblatt* (People's Sheet), a mimeographed sheet distributed clandestinely in Hamburg, is the only known Communist paper.

POLITICAL STATUS: None.

FRONT ORGANIZATIONS: The World Peace Council exists under surveillance in seven of the ten West German states, and the once-legitimate Association of Victims of the Nazi Regime has become a Communist front, and is now banned in four states.

DIPLOMATIC RELATIONS: West Germany has diplomatic relations with the U.S.S.R., but not with Communist China; it has received no aid from the Soviet bloc, and United States aid ceased in the early '50's, when Germany became self-sufficient again.

# GHANA

There is no Communist Party in Ghana, and no history or tradition of Communism there. The British prohibited it during their reign and since Ghana achieved its independence in 1957 the ruling Convention People's Party has shown no inclination to tolerate the formation of rival parties. Ghana has established diplomatic relations with the U.S.S.R., Czechoslovakia and Poland, and the Russians are busily but quietly distributing literature and going the social rounds. Prime Minister Kwame Nkrumah looks to Britain and the United States for capital to finance major projects, while the country's gold and cocoa exports keep its treasury in a healthy state. The United States has provided a million-dollar program of technical and agricultural assistance, and many Ghanaians, including the Prime Minister, have studied at universities in the United States. The Communist bloc is working hard to increase its trade with Ghana and Ghanaians are to be offered 150 scholarships to Eastern European universities in 1961, but this will not necessarily spread the Communist gospel. Ghanaians, like many African nationalists, see Communism as just another brand of imperialism, and are hardly likely to relinquish any of their new-found freedom for a little trade and aid.

# GREAT BRITAIN

The British Communist Party presents an extraordinary contradiction. Politically, it is a ludicrous nonentity which time and again has been able to win no more than some 1% of the total vote in national elections. Among the trade unions, however, the Party is an active and enterprising force displaying considerable acumen and a disturbing ability to take advantage of opportunities to improve its position, as well as to foment strikes and discord within industries vital to the country. Control of key British trade unions could give the Party tremendous power, for the unions are unquestionably the largest cohesive political force in the country. The Communists are well aware of this, and miss no chance to extend their influence in the unions, particularly by working to control as many Joint Shop Stewards' Committees as they can. Working from this vantage point, Party members have time and again blown a minor dispute into a paralyzing wildcat strike, defying union leadership in the process. Of the 20,000 Shop Stewards' Committees in Britain, some 1,200 are affiliated with the Communist-controlled Engineering and Allied Trades Shop Stewards' National Council, the Communists' most powerful weapon in the trade union movement. Communism's success in this area has been the result of its own initiative, the apathy of the average union member towards union politics, and the ineffectuality of the Communist Party in national politics, which makes it seem more harmless than it is. Ironically, the increasing economic well-being of the average worker makes him less interested in union affairs, so that for once the Communists are aided by prosperity. The illegal procedures with which the Party has achieved and maintained power in the unions have lately aroused many Britons; but it will take a great deal of continuing effort to dislodge the Communists from their positions of power in a country which has no basic sympathy for Communism.

NAME: The British Communist Party; founded 1920.

LEGAL STATUS AND MEMBERSHIP: The Party has been legal since its founding; it now claims 26,000 card-carrying members.

LEADERS:

William Gallacher—President
Harry Pollitt—Chairman
Rajani Palme Dutt—Vice-Chairman
John Gollan—General Secretary
William Alexander—Assistant Secretary

OFFICIAL PAPER: *The Daily Worker,* London, claimed 56,000 circulation in 1959.

POLITICAL STATUS: Practically nil; the Party has not polled more than 0.1% of the vote in the last three national elections.

FRONT ORGANIZATIONS: Organizations which are Communist fronts or are under Communist control or influenced include the following:

The British Peace Committee, connected with the World Peace Council, is a growing influence due to its skillful manipulation of the campaign for nuclear disarmament; has 300 to 400 "peace committees" throughout Britain at present.

The Engineering and Allied Trades Shop Stewards' National Council, already mentioned, extremely powerful and responsible for most wildcat strikes in Britain.

Science For Peace, the British representative of the World Federation of Scientific Workers, has some significance in scientific circles.

The Electrical Trades Union—leadership is Communist-dominated.

The Fire Brigades Union—leadership is Communist-dominated.

Other unions are influenced by Communists, but not dominated by them.

Minor fronts include many societies for friendship with Communist countries.

DIPLOMATIC RELATIONS: Great Britain maintains diplomatic relations with the U.S.S.R. and Communist China; it has not received aid from the Soviet bloc or from the United States.

# GREECE

The Communist Party of Greece (K.K.E.) has staged three armed revolts in the last seventeen years, and gives every indication of being ready to try a fourth time. The Party made its first bid for power in 1943 and 1944, during the Nazi occupation; the Communists rallied many patriots to their side, and ruthlessly suppressed rival resistance organizations. Between August and December of 1944 the Party negotiated to join the legitimate Greek government then forming in Cairo, but in December it rebelled again. This second rebellion collapsed after 33 days, since only 10,000 hard-core Communists joined it, and British troops were on hand to aid the legal government. The third revolt, from 1946 to 1949, was a protracted guerrilla war, and might have dragged on indefinitely but for the United States aid and Yugoslavia's break with the Cominform in 1948. In 1949, thousands of defeated Greek Communists fled to Albania and Bulgaria; today the official Party headquarters are located in Romania. Communism is once again active in Greece, however, and the party called the "United Democratic Left" (E.D.A.), founded in 1951, is the Communist Party of Greece in its present legal guise. Most of its support derives from the Greek middle class; most of its leaders are Communists who escaped prosecution or were released by various acts of clemency after the revolt. During its nine years of existence, the E.D.A. has faithfully followed the principles and slogans of the exiled K.K.E.; it came as a shock to Greece and the free world, therefore, when the E.D.A. polled 24.4% of the votes in the elections of 1958. Some of these votes were doubtless protests against the government; but nonetheless the E.D.A. is now the largest party in opposition, and as the K.K.E. in Romania recently said with unconscious irony in a manifesto, "... there can be no doubt that Greece faces the danger of new tragic adventures."

NAME: The Communist Party of Greece (*Kommounistikon Kommatis Ellados*—K.K.E.); founded 1918, now in exile; the "United Democratic Left" (E.D.A.) is its legal guise in Greece today.

LEGAL STATUS AND MEMBERSHIP: The Party was declared illegal in 1925, and again in 1936; in 1947 it was made illegal again, and has been illegal ever since. Party membership within Greece is not known; some 30,000 members fled in 1949.

LEADERS: Leaders of the K.K.E. in its Romanian exile include:
A. Grozos
D. Partsalidis
K. Kolijannis
L. Stringos
P. Roussos

OFFICIAL PAPER: *Neos Kosmos* ("New World") published monthly in Bucharest; in Greece, the E.D.A. publishes a morning daily called *Avghi* ("Dawn"), which faithfully reports the Party decisions, and claims a paid circulation of 12,000.

POLITICAL STATUS: For the K.K.E., none; however the E.D.A. is the largest single opposition party, despite having distributed some of its 79 Parliament seats to new front parties, and it won almost a million votes (24.4%) in the 1958 elections.

FRONT ORGANIZATIONS: The World Peace Council is the only international front operating in Greece. It operates under the name of the Committee for International Relaxation and Peace, and has little influence. Other minor fronts include friendship societies with some of the Soviet-bloc nations; but the only important Communist front in Greece is the E.D.A. itself, together with its affiliates.

DIPLOMATIC RELATIONS: Greece maintains diplomatic relations with the U.S.S.R., but not with Communist China. It receives no aid from any country at the present time.

## GUATEMALA

The Guatemalan Communist Party, under the name of the Guatemalan Labor Party (P.G.T), was extremely powerful during the Arbenz regime. When that administration was overthrown in June, 1954, the P.G.T. was driven underground, its ablest leaders were exiled, and for three years the Castillo Armas administration rigidly suppressed the remnants of the P.G.T. within Guatemala. Restrictions against the Communists relaxed after the assassination of President Castillo Armas in July 1957, however, and since then their organizational and other activities have increased. Except for a small number of hard-core leaders still in exile, principally in Mexico, the majority of exiled Communists and sympathizers have been permitted to return to Guatemala by the Ydígoras government. The Communists have made strong efforts to infiltrate the moderately left-wing Revolutionary Party, but have had little success so far. They have met with somewhat more success among certain ultra-nationalist groups of intellectuals, students, and workers, but they are still far from the position of power they held in 1954.

## GUINEA

There is no Communist Party in Guinea. The very few local Communists have no direct influence. The country, which became independent in October 1958, is governed in practice by its sole political party, the *Parti Démocratique de Guinée* (P.D.G.). French assistance was rapidly withdrawn after Guinea became independent, and Soviet-bloc offers of substantial aid were soon made and accepted. Numerous Communist technicians are active in Guinea; Czechoslovakia has provided arms to replace those withdrawn by the French; the U.S.S.R. has granted a long-term loan of $35 million; and a substantial portion of Guinea's foreign trade has been consigned to the Communist bloc through a series of bilateral barter agreements. By the end of 1959, Guinea had established diplomatic relations with the U.S.S.R., Communist China, Bulgaria, and Czechoslovakia. Cultural agreements have been signed, and a Soviet offer to build a 2,500-student technical institute—Guinea's first institution of higher learning—has been accepted. Soviet and Communist Chinese correspondents are assigned to Guinea, and the country has become a meeting-place for international Communist-front organizations stressing African affairs and dealing with labor, youth, and educational circles. The second plenary session of the Afro-Asian People's Solidarity Conference was scheduled for Guinea in April 1960, and Guinea is also to be the site of the 1960 Third World Conference of Teachers under the auspices of the Union of Teachers for a World Peace and Democracy. At least 80 Guineans are presently studying in Soviet-bloc schools. 30 Guinean delegations, composed chiefly of government, trade, labor, and youth representatives, went to Soviet-bloc countries in 1959, and 27 Communist delegations paid return calls. Guinea, in brief, has accepted Communist assistance wholeheartedly; it remains to be seen whether it can continue on this course without falling under Communist influence.

# ICELAND

The strength of the Communist Party in Iceland has declined noticeably in the last few years. Among the causes of this decline have been: the revulsion stirred by Soviet suppression of the Hungarian revolution; vigorous joint action by the Conservatives and Social-Democrats against Communists in the labor unions; and a rise in the standard of living, which has increased the resistance of Icelandic workers to demagogic and inflationary Communist demands for wage increases. The Social-Democratic government of 1959 instituted an anti-inflationary program which won general labor support despite Communist attempts to wreck the program through strikes. However, the Communists managed to hold their membership in the trade unions, and even slightly increased their control of Dagsbrun, Iceland's largest union. The Communist electoral front organization, Labor Alliance, won 16% of the votes in the October 1959 elections, a fall of 3.2% from the 1956 totals, and the Party's smallest share of the vote since World War II.

# INDIA

The Communist Party of India has constantly swung between the alternatives of revolutionary violence and parliamentary infiltration. This old dilemma was clearly posed by the results of the elections in the State of Kerala in February 1960. In 1957 the Party won 60 of 120 seats in the parliament of the newly formed Kerala State; with the support of five Independents, the Communists had an absolute majority, and thus became the British Commonwealth's first Communist government. In the 1960 elections, the Party and its allies lost 36 of their 65 seats despite a 50% increase in Communist votes cast.

This extraordinary result was apparently due to an opposition which united to defeat the Communists at the polls. For many Communists, the Kerala episode proved the futility of the policy of peaceful methods, adopted in 1958 after years of dedication to the violent overthrow of the Indian government. The Party's long career of violence, however, has not proved notably successful either; continuing Communist outrages failed to shake the government, but prompted Prime Minister Nehru to warn in 1948 that the Communists were trying to introduce chaos throughout the country. Several states banned the Party at that time. Rather than return to a policy of violence, the Party will probably continue working by reasonably peaceable and legal means. It suffers heavily from the aggressive deeds of the Chinese Communists.

NAME: The Communist Party of India; founded in 1924.

LEGAL STATUS AND MEMBERSHIP: The Party was banned by the British government from 1934 to 1942, and was banned for a time by some Indian states in 1948. The Party's present membership is estimated at 300,000.

LEADERS:

> Ajoy Ghosh—General Secretary
> B. T. Ranadive—Member of the National Council of the Communist Party
> E. M. S. Namboodiripad—Member of the National Council of the Communist Party
> M. Basava Punniah—Member of the National Council of the Communist Party
> Jyoti Basu—Member of the National Council of the Communist Party

OFFICIAL PAPER: *New Age,* published weekly in Delhi; circulation 12,000.

POLITICAL STATUS: The Communist Party is the second largest party in India—Nehru's Congress Party is the largest. In the last national elections, in 1957, the Communists received 8.92% of the total vote, or over 10 million. This gave them 30 of 494 seats in Lok Sabha (lower house) and 14 of 232 in the Rajya Sabha (upper house). The Party does not participate in any coalitions.

FRONT ORGANIZATIONS: Important international fronts in India include the All-India Peace Council, connected with the World Peace Council; The All-India Trade Union Congress, a member of the World Federation of Trade Unions; The Indian Committee for Afro-Asian Solidarity; the Association of Scientific Workers; and the All-India Students' Federation. Local fronts of some importance include the Indo-Soviet Cultural Association, the India-China Friendship Association, the National Federation of Indian Women, and the All-India Progressive Writers' Association.

DIPLOMATIC RELATIONS: India maintains relations with the U.S.S.R. and Communist China. Soviet bloc aid has totaled approximately $700 million; United States aid has totaled $1.7 billion.

# INDONESIA

The Communist Party of Indonesia, after twice failing to seize power through armed revolt, is now achieving considerable success through less violent methods. The Party's first attempt at revolution was directed against the Dutch administration in 1926; the revolt failed, and the Party was effectively suppressed until the Indonesian revolution of 1945 restored it to legality. In September 1948 the Party rebelled again; armed Communist units seized the city of Madiun in central Java, only to be crushed by Indonesian Army units under Col. Abdul Haris Nasution when the revolt failed to spread. The Party fell into disgrace and disorganization, but in 1951 a twenty-seven-year-old Communist named Aidit wrested control of the Party from its older leaders, and instituted radical changes in Party policies. He began mass organization, cooperation with "anti-imperialist" parties, and most importantly, thoroughgoing nationalism and support for President Sukarno. This policy paid off handsomely; riding Sukarno's coattails, the Party polled over six million votes in the elections of 1955, and soon extended its influence to control the S.O.B.S.I. labor federation and the B.T.I. peasant front. The Party continues to attack Sukarno's ministers, blaming them for interfering with the progress of his "guided democracy"; other favorite targets are the United States, the Netherlands, and the Western-owned oil companies in Indonesia. The army, now led by Gen. Nasution, has been struggling with considerable success to keep the Communists in check, and Sukarno's "guided democracy" has also deprived the Communists of some of their power; but they are still a force to be reckoned with in Indonesia's future.

NAME: The Communist Party of Indonesia (*Partai Komunis Indonesia*—P.K.L.); founded May 1920.

LEGAL STATUS AND MEMBERSHIP: Now legal; banned by the Dutch administration from 1927 until it ended in 1945. Membership not known, but it is the largest vote-getting Communist Party outside the Soviet bloc, and one of the few supporting a non-Socialist government.

LEADERS:

Dipa Nusantara Aidit—Chairman, Central Committee
M. H. Lukman—First Vice-Chairman, Central Committee
Njoto—Second Vice-Chairman, Central Committee
Sudisman—Member, Central Committee
Jusuf Adjitorep—Chief, "Agitprop" department

OFFICIAL PAPER: Strictly speaking, none; however, *Harian Rakjat* (People's Daily) is controlled by the Party, edited by Njoto; circulation about 55,000, making it one of the largest in the country. In addition *Bintang Timur* (Star of the East) pushes the Communist line, and has a circulation of about 45,000.

POLITICAL STATUS: The Communist Party won 6,176,914 votes in the first (and last) national elections, held in 1955, about 17% of the total. The Party has 39 seats in the 263-seat parliament. There are Communists in various government organs, and 3 of 44 cabinet members have Communist ties, but under "guided democracy" government members must renounce party ties, and at any rate they are appointed by the President and can be removed by him.

FRONT ORGANIZATIONS: International Communist fronts active in Indonesia, together with the names of the local branches, include the following:

World Peace Council (National Committee for World Peace); World Federation of Trade Unions (S.O.B.S.I. labor federation, largest in Indonesia, is affiliated); World Federation of Democratic Youth (and other youth groups); International Union of Students; Afro-Asian Solidarity Committee. All these groups are at least moderately powerful, and S.O.B.S.I. is so powerful that only the army holds it in check. Local fronts include the B.T.I, (Indonesian Peasant Front), the People's Youth Corps, and the Sino-Indonesian Friendship Society.

DIPLOMATIC RELATIONS: Indonesia has diplomatic relations with the U.S.S.R. and Communist China, and has received about $204 million in Soviet-bloc aid, as compared with more than half a billion dollars in United States aid since Indonesia gained its independence in 1945.

# IRAN

The Communist Tudeh ("Masses") Party in Iran once very nearly made that nation into a Soviet satellite, but now its remaining members are underground and inactive. The Tudeh got its start in 1941, when Britain and Russia occupied Iran to provide a supply line for American aid to the Soviet Army. The Soviets missed no chance to spread Party influence throughout Iran; "autonomous democratic states" were founded in the provinces of Azerbaijan and Kurdistan while they were still occupied by Soviet troops. Iran complained to the United Nations in 1946 about the continuing Soviet occupation, and the Soviets reluctantly withdrew. Iran then took control of its provinces again, and the Tudeh, claiming trickery, did not try to keep its nine seats (of 136) in the Majlis (lower house), when elections were held at the end of the year. The Soviets then launched a violent propaganda campaign against the Iranian Government. In February 1949 an attempt to assassinate the Shah failed, but led to the banning of the Tudeh. The Tudeh lay low for a year, until Mohammed Mossadegh began denouncing the Anglo-Iranian Oil Company. Then the Tudeh helped make Mossadegh Prime Minister in 1951, in time to nationalize the oil. The Tudeh then pushed for power on its own, and in the critical days of mid-August 1953, when the Shah's supporters were overthrowing Mossadegh, the Tudeh offered to destroy the Shah's adherents if Mossadegh would give it arms. Mossadegh refused, and the Communist missed their chance to seize the country. Before they could organize another coup, the Shah's forces suppressed them sternly and executed twenty-six of their leaders in 1954. Since then, Tudeh activity has been carried on only outside the borders of Iran. Communism has not recovered its losses despite a peaceable Soviet approach.

NAME: The Tudeh Party; founded 1941.

LEGAL STATUS AND MEMBERSHIP: Illegal since 1949; repressed effectively since 1954; present membership unknown, since party is underground and inactive.

LEADERS: Dr. Reza Radmanesh and other titular Party leaders are in the Soviet bloc; present leaders of the Party in Iran, if any, are unknown.

OFFICIAL PAPER: *Sobhe Emrouz* is printed in East Germany and smuggled into Iran.

POLITICAL STATUS: None; in 1952, while backing Mossadegh, the Party got only 0.1% of the vote, but was more powerful than this would indicate.

FRONT ORGANIZATIONS: None operate in Iran now; before 1953 there were literally hundreds of fronts of various types and sizes.

DIPLOMATIC RELATIONS: Iran has diplomatic relations with the U.S.S.R., but not with Communist China. The only Soviet aid so far accepted has been five tons of insecticides. United States aid to Iran has totaled almost one billion dollars since its inception.

# IRAQ

In the spring of 1958 no Near Eastern government stood more firmly allied with the West than Iraq's. In no other Near Eastern country were the Communists more persecuted, or the government more despised for its persecution. After the successful overthrow of the monarchy in 1958, they gained what seemed an unchallengeable position. Events since then have disclosed flaws in the Party's façade of strength. Internal disagreements which had plagued the movement since its beginnings in Iraq have reappeared. Yet Iraq's Communists remain the country's best-organized, best-disciplined and most potent political force. By 1960, the government had signed trade and cultural agreements with virtually every nation in the Soviet bloc, and Communist technicians and advisors were spread across the country. Premier Major General Abdul Karim Kassem, however, seemed determined to keep friendship with the Communists within bounds. A Communist massacre of their enemies in Kirkuk in July 1959 shocked many Iraqis, and marked the beginning of a decline in their popular regard. Kassem's attempts to tighten his control over both Communists and nationalists were slowed when he was wounded in an assassination attempt in October 1959, but in 1960 the government managed to split the Communist ranks, by encouraging a dissident faction headed by Daud Sayigh. The orthodox Communists, led by Abdul Qadir Ismail, applied for a license as the Unity of the People Party, but the government rejected the application. Such government moves are helping to keep Iraq from becoming a Soviet satellite. It has been suggested that the Soviets themselves are tacitly in sympathy with this aim, for they desire Iraq as a client state rather than an uncomfortably conspicuous satellite.

NAME: Communist Party of Iraq, legal faction; Unity of the People Party, illegal faction; Party originally founded in 1934.

LEGAL STATUS AND MEMBERSHIP: Legal for the first time as of February 9, 1960 (one of two factions only); membership not known.

LEADERS:

Daud Sayigh—Head of legal Party
Zakki Khairi
Abdul Qadir Ismail (al-Bustani—last name seldom used) ⎫
Hussein Ahmad al-radhi (alias Salem Adil) ⎬ Leaders of illegal faction
Aziz Sherif—Secretary General of Partisans of Peace ⎭

OFFICIAL PAPER: *Al-Mabda,* for legal Party; *Ittihad al-Shaab,* for illegal faction. Both published in Baghdad; circulation of each estimated at under 10,000.

POLITICAL STATUS: Although the Communists' influence on Iraqi policy is large, it is unofficial, since Kassem has ruled under martial law since 1958.

FRONT ORGANIZATIONS: Powerful Iraqi branches of international fronts include:

Partisans of Peace (branch of the World Peace Council)
General Federation of Iraqi Trade Unions (branch of World Federation of Trade Unions)
Iraqi Democratic Youth (branch of World Federation of Democratic Youth)

Significant local front groups include the following:

League for the Defense of Women's Rights

General Students' Union
General Union of Peasants' Associations
Soviet-Iraqi Friendship Society
Chinese-Iraqi Friendship Society
Iraqi Journalists' Association

DIPLOMATIC RELATIONS: Iraq maintains relations with the Soviet-bloc nations, and receives loans and technical aid from the U.S.S.R., as well as technical aid from Poland, Czechoslovakia, and East Germany. Iraq receives no United States aid.


# IRELAND

The Irish Workers' League, founded in 1942, denies having Communist ties, but is generally considered to be the Irish branch of the British Communist Party. Although its influence is negligible, its troubles are not; Ireland's traditional conservatism and devout Catholicism combine to make the Irish almost totally unreceptive to Communist ideas, despite long-standing poverty and underemployment. One of the League's former leaders has left it to join a Catholic Action group, while another recently became a Trappist monk. The League, though legal, can claim only about 700 members and has never won more than 255 votes even when running on a Socialist ticket. The Party paper, *The Irish Democrat,* is printed in England and imported at the rate of about 800 copies a month. The only known Communist front operating in Ireland is the Irish Workers' League itself.


# ISRAEL

The Communists are a dwindling influence in Israel. Arab nationalists in Israel, who once saw the Israeli Communist Party as a legal means of opposing the state from within, now realize it is an ineffectual means as well. Israel's Jews generally dislike Communism's anti-Zionism and subservience to the U.S.S.R's national interest. The state of Israel, bolstered by $47,400,000 in United States aid in 1959 alone, is hardly likely to slip into the economic chaos on which Communism thrives.

NAME: Israeli Communist Party (*Miflaga Komunistit Yisraelit,* or M.A.K.Y.), founded in 1919 as the Palestine Communist Party.

LEGAL STATUS AND MEMBERSHIP: The Party has never been outlawed; it claims a membership of 15,000, which includes perhaps 5,000 Arabs.

LEADERS:

Shemuel Mikunis—Secretary-General of M.A.K.Y.; Deputy in Knesset

Twefik Toubi—Christian, No. 1 Arab in M.A.K.Y.; Deputy in Knesset

Moshe Sneh—Newcomer to M.A.K.Y. leadership; Deputy in Knesset

Meir Vilner—Extremist, fading from leadership of M.A.K.Y.

Emil Habibi—Arab, also a Christian; Editor of *Al-Ittihad*

OFFICIAL PAPER: *Kol-Ha-Am,* a Hebrew daily with about 3,000 readers, and *Al-Ittihad,* an Arabic weekly with a circulation of a few hundred.

POLITICAL STATUS: The Party lost three of its six seats in the Knesset (Parliament) in the November 1959 elections, winning less than 3% of the votes cast; it has no part in the coalition government.

FRONT ORGANIZATIONS: The international World Peace Council and the local Israel-Soviet Friendship League manage to survive but have insignificant influence.

DIPLOMATIC RELATIONS: Israel maintains diplomatic relations with the U.S.S.R., but not with Red China. It receives no aid from the Soviet bloc, but received $47 million from the United States in 1959.

# ITALY

Italy, like France, was very nearly submerged by a wave of Communist strikes and violence in 1947 and 1948. Only a hard-fighting Christian Democratic Party under the late Premier Alcide de Gasperi, aided by a tough police force, kept Italy out of the Soviet bloc in those years. The Communists still pose a major threat, and a number of unsolved problems simplify the Communists' task of subversion. Unemployment and poverty are still widespread in overpopulated Italy. Their presence increases the regional jealousies which tend to divide the country into antagonistic fragments, since some regions (notably the South) are far poorer than others. The Communist Party is working hard just to win local control in the more underprivileged districts, then to increase the autonomous authority of these regions vis-à-vis the central government. The Party has made political capital out of the many postwar scandals involving businessmen and politicians. The Party's propaganda also influences many Italians, including non-Communists, by its attacks on monopolies and on United States missile bases on Italian territory. As in most Latin countries, there is a considerable segment of Italian opinion that is strongly anti-clerical, not without historical reason. The Communists lay heavy stress on this anti-clericalism in their propaganda, since the Catholic Church is one of the most effective opponents of Communism. The Party's basic problem in Italy is that it must sell two totally different lines: 1) it must convince the anti-Communist, anti-Soviet part of the population that it is not a revolutionary party; 2) at the same time it must persuade its sympathizers that it is determined to use revolutionary means to improve their lot. Despite this basic split, the Communists are more than holding their own in Italy today.

NAME: The Italian Communist Party (*Partito Communista Italiano*); founded 1922.

LEGAL STATUS AND MEMBERSHIP: Legal; outlawed by Mussolini in 1926, restored to legal status by the Allies in 1944. The Party now lists 1,787,338 members.

LEADERS:

> Palmiro Togliatti—Secretary (actual head of Party)
> Luigi Longo—Vice-Secretary
> Giorgio Amendola—Secretariat member, Deputy in Parliament
> Pietro Ingrao—Secretariat member, Deputy in Parliament
> Giancarlo Pajetta—Secretariat member, Deputy in Parliament
> Anelito Barontini—Secretariat member, Deputy in Parliament

OFFICIAL PAPER: *L'Unita*, published in Rome and Milan, estimates of circulation range from 180,000 to 400,000; in addition, *Il Paese* ("The Country"), a morning paper, and *Paese Sera* ("Evening Country"), its evening equivalent, follow the Communist line faithfully.

POLITICAL STATUS: The Party was represented in every post-war government until it joined the Socialist Party in opposition in 1947. The Communists and their allies, the far left-wing Socialists, have been polling up to a third of Italy's vote since the end of World War II. The Hungarian revolution shattered the Popular Front alliance in 1956, but the two parties still cooperate in Parliament. Since the elections of 1958, the Communist-Socialist bloc has controlled 224 of 596 seats in the Chamber of Deputies, and 93 of 253 seats in the Senate.

FRONT ORGANIZATIONS: The following fronts are influential in Italy:

> The C.I.G.L. Labor Confederation (very powerful)
> The Italian Movement for Peace—member of the World Peace
>     Council
> World Federation of Democratic Youth
> International Union of Students
> International Association of Democratic Lawyers
> International Association of Democratic Jurists
> International Union of Agricultural Workers
> National College of Unions
> Women's International Democratic Federation
> Italy-U.S.S.R. Association (branches in most big cities)

DIPLOMATIC RELATIONS: Italy maintains relations with the U.S.S.R., but receives no Soviet-bloc aid. United States aid since the war is estimated at $5.3 billion, which includes all forms of assistance.

# JAPAN

The Japanese Communist Party, despite its small and declining numbers, still wields considerable influence; but in a country that has seen devastating war losses, atomic bombings, occupation by the victorious American forces, and chronic unemployment and over-population, it is perhaps surprising that Communism has had such limited success. Many Socialists, who have cooperated with the Communists in the past, have grown disgusted with Communist violence and lack of democracy, and have broken their ties to the Party while still espousing many of the same causes. The violent excesses of the Zengakuren "students" in riots against the United States—Japan Security Treaty in 1959 and 1960 offended many Japanese as well. The Communists still have friends, however; one of the most important is Kaoru Ota, head of SOHYO, the 3½ million-member leftist union combine, which ironically was founded in protest over the leftist domination of its predecessor. Communists under Ota have infiltrated SOHYO and now manipulate its policy although they are still a minority faction; SOHYO is showing signs of strain, however, since conservative unions average higher wages. Another Communist friend is Kaoru Yasui, head of the Japan Council Against Atomic and Hydrogen Bombs (GENSUIKO), a front which is known for its ability to overlook the U.S.S.R.'s atomic weapons tests. Despite strong feelings against atomic weapons, the Japanese are looking on this group with increasing suspicion. In Japan generally, Communism has sold many of its ideas by capitalizing on natural fears and natural longings; but it has failed to sell its own organization as the means to meet these fears and longings.

NAME: Japan Communist Party (*Nippon Kyosanto*); founded 1922.

LEGAL STATUS AND MEMBERSHIP: Now legal; suppressed by the Japanese government from its founding until 1945, when the Occupation authorities legalized it. Membership estimated at 60,000, slowly dwindling.

LEADERS:

Sanzo Nozaka—Chairman, Central Committee of upper house of Diet
Kenji Miyamoto—Secretary General
Yoshio Shiga—Central Committee Member
Shoichi Kasuga—Central Committee Member
Satomi Hakamata—Central Committee Member

OFFICIAL PAPER: *Akahata* (Red Flag), published in Tokyo; circulation estimated at 50,000 to 60,000.

POLITICAL STATUS: In the 1959 elections, the Party received votes enough to receive 1 of 467 seats in the lower house, and 3 of 250 in the upper house; they frequently support Socialists, however, in close campaigns, so their total votes would be higher than indicated. They do not form part of the government.

FRONT ORGANIZATIONS: Branches of international fronts include: the Liaison Council of International Jurists; the Democratic Scientists' Association; the Japan Journalists' Congress; Japan Peace Committee; and the Japan Afro-Asian Solidarity Committee. These fronts are of little significance. Local fronts have more influence; these include: GENSUIKO, SOHYO (mentioned above) and Zengakuren, the National Federation of Student Self-Government Associations, whose leaders include many "students" in name only. Less important fronts include: the All-Japan Federation of Women's Organizations, the Women's Democratic Club, and the Japan-Soviet Society.

DIPLOMATIC RELATIONS: Japan maintains diplomatic relations with the U.S.S.R., but not with Communist China, which has been linking trade relations with diplomatic recognition. Japan has received no aid from the Soviet bloc; United States aid has totaled almost $2 billion, but negotiations are now under way concerning Japanese repayment of perhaps a third of this sum, which was the percentage agreed upon when Germany repaid United States aid.

# JORDAN

Although the Communist Party of Jordan is illegal, it survives as a capably led and well disciplined hard core. In the past it has found support among students, intellectuals, dispossessed Palestinians, and a small labor group which took the place of the old Palestine Workers' Party. Its major strength lay in its ability to exploit anti-Western and anti-monarchic Arab nationalist elements; but in mid-1957 it alienated the Arab nationalists by attempting to seize control of the joint effort to overthrow King Hussein. Events in Iraq, together with U.A.R. President Nasser's attacks on Communism, have since deepened the rift between nationalists and Communists. The Party's diminished capabilities have been further hindered by continuing police raids and the imprisonment of Party personnel, including several members of the Central Committee. Nevertheless, the Party still retains the potential for rapid regrowth in the event of a change in the political climate.

# KENYA

Communism is not banned in Kenya because it does not exist there. The government keeps the colony under strict control and African nationalist leaders generally look on Communism as just another brand of foreign imperialism. Even Jomo Kenyatta, the leader of the Kikuyu tribe which began the Mau Mau revolt, showed few evidences of Communist control or indoctrination despite his eighteen months of education in the Soviet Union. The only known Communist Kenya has ever possessed has been languishing in exile for ten years in a remote village in the northern reaches of the colony. Makan Singh, a Sikh printer, was put away in May 1950 before he had recruited any members for a Communist Party, but not before he had laid a solid foundation for the present trade-union movement in Kenya. The young nationalist leader, Tom Mboya, combined this trade-union movement with the nationalist movement and the result has been a unified force strong enough to demand, and perhaps to enforce, a large measure of self-government in the near future. At the present time, it seems most unlikely that self-government will bring with it any appreciable Communist influence.

# KOREA (South Korea)

The first Communist Party in Korea was founded in 1925, but was soon disbanded by the Japanese occupation authorities. A new Party was organized in 1945 and soon merged with other leftist parties to form the South Korean Labor Party in 1946. This was outlawed in 1948 by the National Security Law because the Communists were by then engaged in guerrilla warfare and subversion against the Republic of Korea (South Korea). The Communists, at their peak strength in this period, had an estimated 400,000 Party members, 50,000 of whom were carrying on guerrilla warfare. The Korean War, between 1950 and 1953, purged the Republic of Korea of Communists and Communist organizations and persistent North Korean attempts to infiltrate Communist cadres into South Korea since then have apparently met with little success. The R.O.K. government's vigilance and the South Korean people's painful knowledge of Communist ways make a revival of Communism most unlikely in South Korea despite a strong sentiment for reunification of the long-divided country.

# LAOS

The Communist threat still remains greater in Laos than in any other country of Southeast Asia. Communist insurgents resorted to armed warfare against the Royal Laotian government in mid-1959, and while the arrival of a United Nations Fact Finding Subcommittee brought temporary peace to Laos, the Communists retain the capacity to renew warfare at any time. Laotian Communists, strongly supported by Communist China and neighboring North Vietnam, maintain a continuing propaganda barrage against the Laotian government in an attempt to undermine its authority and convert it to a neutralist course. This campaign is reinforced by radio broadcasts from Communist China and North Vietnam, stressing the dangers of contacts with the West and picturing the Pathet Lao as the "true champions" of Laotian independence. Apparently this campaign has had considerable success in spreading anti-government feeling in the rural areas and among the primitive minority tribes which comprise nearly half the population.

NAME: Neo Lao Hak Xat (N.L.H.X.) is the legal political front for the Communists, formed in 1957 to replace the militant Pathet Lao movement.

LEGAL STATUS AND MEMBERSHIP: The N.L.H.X. is legal; membership figures are not available.

LEADERS: Prince Souphannouvong and fourteen other N.L.H.X. leaders recently escaped while awaiting trial on charges of treason; other leaders are not known since they operate clandestinely.

OFFICIAL PAPER: *Lao Hak Xat,* weekly until its recent suspension, was the Party paper of the N.L.H.X. It is now being published clandestinely.

POLITICAL STATUS: Three parties—the N.L.H.X., the Santiphap, and the Democrats—usually vote as a bloc in the National Assembly. Together they gained 40% of the popular vote in the May 1958 elections. However, the Prime Minister presently governs under special powers, and several N.L.H.X. and Santiphap leaders are in prison or in hiding.

FRONT ORGANIZATIONS: The N.L.H.X. is the chief political Communist front in Laos; the Pathet Lao is the military arm of the Communist movement.


# LEBANON

In the past ten years the Communist Party of Lebanon has dwindled into insignificance from the country's most potent political force. Its leaders are experienced, however, and a sudden change of the Near Eastern political scene could thrust the Party into a position of importance. Although swift changes are commonplace in the Arab world, Lebanon's complex political maze of religious and clan loyalties makes a general change less likely and more difficult to organize. The five-month revolt against Camille Chamoun's government in 1958, together with the United States intervention, should have been an ideal opportunity for Lebanon's Communists; but they could neither take credit for the revolt nor profit by it. The Party has had somewhat better luck in its efforts to infiltrate Lebanon's trade unions, although its successes so far have been minor. The trade unions are among the few organizations in which religious and clan loyalties have become blurred, and this fact may prove to be the key to political power in Lebanon. At present, however, the Communist Party of Lebanon is struggling to preserve and expand its organization in a country that is strongly inclined to maintain its ties with the Western world.

NAME: The Communist Party of Lebanon; founded about 1928.

LEGAL STATUS AND MEMBERSHIP: The Party has never been licensed by the Lebanese government, but has been allowed to operate with only moderate interference, except for a period of suppression following the outbreak of World War II in 1939. Membership is estimated at 2,200, about 200 of whom are diehards.

LEADERS:

Khalid Bakdash—Secretary General of Party in Lebanon and Syria

Antun Thabit—sometimes Secretary of Party; President of Partisans of Peace

Elias Habre—President of illegal Communist Federation of Labor Unions and powerful Hotel, Restaurant and Coffee House Workers' Union

Nikola Shawi—title unknown, prominent in Party activities

Moustafa al-Aris—Head of Communist Printers' Union; Party activist

OFFICIAL PAPER: *Al-Akhbar,* weekly and *Al-Nida,* daily, published in Beirut; both have estimated circulations of between 3,000 and 4,000.

POLITICAL STATUS: No Communist has even been elected to office in Lebanon. The Party's influence on the present government is negligible.

FRONT ORGANIZATIONS: The World Peace Council, through the local Partisans of Peace, is the only front that exerts any influence in Lebanon at the moment; the World Federation of Trade Unions and the World Federation of Democratic Youth maintain a shadowy existence, but local fronts are practically nonexistent.

DIPLOMATIC RELATIONS: Lebanon maintains relations with the U.S.S.R., but not with Communist China. It has received a total of $54 million in aid from the United States, and none from the Soviet bloc.

# LUXEMBOURG

Although the Communist Party of Luxembourg gained 9.1% of the votes cast in the February 1959 elections, Party membership is estimated at less than 600, and the Party's influence on national life is not strong. Communist strength is concentrated in the southern industrial area, where the Communist-dominated labor organization has a membership of approximately 3,500 in the steel mills and the mines. Despite a general political shift to the right, the Party gained a fractionally larger percentage of the vote of 1959 as compared to the previous parliamentary elections in 1954.

# MALAYA AND SINGAPORE

The eleven-year war between the Malayan Communist Party's Liberation Army and the authorities in Malaya drags on still, but only an estimated 600 guerrillas remain deep in the forests, harried by Malayan and British Commonwealth troops. The Communist revolt never succeeded in winning even the first-phase objectives of the planned campaign to undermine the country's administration through incessant guerrilla raids. Perhaps the main reason was that the Malayan Communist Party is composed predominantly of Chinese, who blended their Communism with Chinese nationalism and thereby alienated the Malayan people from whom they expected support. What the revolt did accomplish was to awaken the Malays politically, with the result that in 1957 the Federation of Malaya became independent under a Malayan nationalist government. This step ruined the Communists' few remaining hopes of victory through armed revolt, and since then they have been trying to make peace in order to work their way into the Malayan government itself. Meanwhile, in Singapore, the Malayan Communist Party has abandoned its policy of violence and the exploitation of discontent in order to cooperate with the dominant People's Action Party, which won a heavy majority in Singapore's first fully independent elections in June 1959. This new spirit of cooperation is partially a result of the new international Communist line of peaceful progress; a more practical reason is that the People's Action Party is dedicated to a merger of Singapore and the Malayan Federation. The Communists, who also desire the merger, can best accomplish their ends by lying low for the present, and this is exactly what they are doing.

NAME: The Malayan Communist Party; founded 1931.

LEGAL STATUS AND MEMBERSHIP: Illegal; was considered legal from 1942 to 1948, when it was declared illegal because of armed revolt. Present membership is unknown, although the "Liberation Army" is now down to approximately 600 men.

LEADERS:

    Chin Peng—Secretary-General
    Musa Ahmad—Chairman
    Rashid Maidin—Assistant Secretary-General
    Chin Tien—Head of Politburo
    Balan—Member of Central Committee

OFFICIAL PAPER: None now circulating.

POLITICAL STATUS: The Party has never contested an election.

FRONT ORGANIZATIONS: Although the Party is busily trying to infiltrate trade unions, political parties, and other democratic institutions, it has closed down its known front organizations in Malaya and Singapore.

DIPLOMATIC RELATIONS: Neither state has diplomatic relations with the U.S.S.R. or Communist China, or receives aid from the Soviet bloc. The United States has given no aid to Singapore, and only small-scale technical assistance to Malaya.

# MEXICO

The political, economic, and social climate of Mexico today is unfavorable to the growth of Communism. As a result, the Communists in Mexico are being driven to the use of camouflage tactics by which they try to advance their basic aims without revealing themselves. They follow the general Communist line for the hemisphere by trying to break up whatever cooperation may be achieved between Mexican and United States groups or individuals, and by advancing the line of a "neutralism" ostensibly aimed at supporting neither East nor West. The Communists also are busy exploiting the dissatisfaction of industrial workers whose entrenched union leaders no longer fight for their rights. The strikes and stoppages of 1958 and 1959 were a high mark of recent Communist activity; they provoked forcible suppression of protest gatherings by both the outgoing and incoming presidents of Mexico, creating an anti-government reservoir of ill-will which the Communists hope to tap in the future. The strikers were government workers drawn from the unions in the oil, railway, school, and telegraph systems. The subsequent crackdowns were the most radical and violent Mexico had seen since the Communist Party was outlawed in the late 1920's, and they had the effect of driving the Party underground again. The Party, however, will not be easily suppressed. Marxism has deep roots in Mexico, and the movement is helped greatly by the prestige of Communist artists like Siqueiros and the late Diego Rivera. Moreover, it is assisted by a long history of anti-United States sentiment, which tends to come to the surface in times of stress. The Soviet Embassy, with a giant staff of 120, is present headquarters for the Communist program in Latin America, and provides considerable support for the local Communists. In addition, many Mexican workers and peasants have legitimate causes for complaint, and the Communists have the experience to exploit such discontent.

NAME: The Mexican Communist Party (*Partido Comunista Mexi-*

*cano*); other Marxist parties are the Popular Party and the Party of Mexican Workers and Peasants. The Party was founded in 1919.

LEGAL STATUS AND MEMBERSHIP: Legal, but not registered as a political party, as it lacks strength to meet minimum registration requirements. Outlawed for a time following 1929 revolt. Membership now estimated at 30,000.

LEADERS:

> Vincente Lombardo Toledano—head of Popular Party, labor leader, probably the No. 1 Communist in Latin America
> Dionisio Encina Rodriguez—Secretary General of Mexican Communist Party
> Jose Valdez Ochoa—Secretary of Mexican Communist Party
> Juan Jose Meraz—Secretary of Finance of Mexican Communist Party
> Juan Pablo Sainz—Director of *La Voz de Mexico*

OFFICIAL PAPER: *La Voz de Mexico,* published clandestinely in Mexico City since the government repressed the Party in 1959, circulation about 2,500.

POLITICAL STATUS: The Party has been unable to qualify as a registered party since 1946, due to insufficient strength.

FRONT ORGANIZATIONS: International fronts operating in Mexico include:

> World Peace Council—Mexican Peace Movement
> World Federation of Democratic Youth
> International Union of Students
> World Federation of Trade Unions—Confederation of Workers of Latin America (Vincente Lombardo Toledano one of founders)
> The People's Youth—youth group of the Popular Party
> Various Soviet-bloc friendship societies

DIPLOMATIC RELATIONS: Mexico has diplomatic relations with the Soviet Union, but not with Communist China.


# MOROCCO

The Moroccan Government's recent ban on the Communist Party of Morocco will probably have little effect on the future of Communism in this country. The Party is devoting its energies to the task of infiltrating the National Union of Popular Forces (U.N.F.P.), a left-of-center party which dominates the present coalition government, and also the *Union Marocaine du Travail* (U.M.T.), the leading labor federation. Such infiltration has no need of a legal Communist Party. Communism's success in Morocco will depend to a large degree on whether the revered King Mohammed V and his supporters can lead the country out of the vast economic recession and widespread unemployment and poverty that has followed the withdrawal of about $500 million in French capital since 1956. The Algerian war, which has already generated severe pressures in Morocco, could cause unpredictable upheavals in the future, especially if the Chinese Communists should intervene as they have threatened to do.

NAME: The Moroccan Communist Party; created from Moroccan cells of the French Communist Party in 1936, formally founded in 1943 as the *Parti Communiste du Maroc.*

LEGAL STATUS AND MEMBERSHIP: The Party is once again banned in Morocco. The French Protectorate banned the Party twice, in 1939 and 1952, and the Moroccan Government banned it in September 1959, after having tolerated it since the end of the Protectorate in November 1955. Party membership is now estimated to be about 6,000.

LEADERS:

Ali Yata—Secretary General
Abdsalem Bourquia—Assistant Secretary General
Abdallah Layachi—Secretary and Chief of the Politburo
Hadi Messaouak—Central Committee Member
Abraham Serfaty—Politburo Member

OFFICIAL PAPER: *Hayat ech-Chaab,* in Arabic, and *Espoir,* in French, reach an estimated 5,000 readers through clandestine routes.

POLITICAL STATUS: The Party, being illegal, has no members in the government, though it has alleged sympathizers in posts under the present régime.

FRONT ORGANIZATIONS: There are no significant Communist front organizations operating in Morocco at present.

DIPLOMATIC RELATIONS: Morocco maintains diplomatic relations with both the U.S.S.R. and Communist China. The United States has contributed $105 million in aid to Morocco since 1956; the Soviet bloc has contributed no assistance of any kind, although the U.S.S.R. has made at least one offer.

# NEPAL

The Communist Party of Nepal, though numerically small, has gained some influence among students and peasants. It controls Nepal's largest peasant organization, and continues to appeal to peasants by opposing the present landholding system and supporting measures designed to benefit farmers. Other issues the Communists attempt to capitalize on are India's position of dominance in relation to Nepal; periodic food shortages; and continuing British recruiting of Gurkha troops within the country.

NAME: The Communist Party of Nepal; founded in 1949.

LEGAL STATUS AND MEMBERSHIP: The Party has been legal since April 1956; membership estimated at 3,500.

POLITICAL STATUS: The Communist Party won 129,434 votes in Nepal's first national election in the spring of 1959. Although this vote was 7.2% of the votes cast, the Party won only 4 seats (3.7%) in the House of Representatives and no position in the government. However, the Party won 20% of the vote in the Katmandu Valley, Nepal's cultural and intellectual center, and 15% in five districts along the Indian border.

DIPLOMATIC RELATIONS: The United States and the U.S.S.R. established diplomatic missions in Katmandu in 1959; India and the United Kingdom also maintain diplomatic missions there.

# THE NETHERLANDS

The Communist Party of The Netherlands, bolstered by a desire for change and feelings of comradeship generated by the Russian struggle against the Nazis, polled half a million votes in The Netherlands' first postwar election in 1946, which came to 10% of the votes cast. Since that time, Communist influence in The Netherlands has been diminishing constantly to its present low estate. With a Party almost destroyed by outward and internal causes, deeply distrusted, even hated, by the vast majority of the population, without sizable support from labor, with only a tiny parliamentary representation, with a newspaper ignored by all but Party diehards and kept alive only with outside support, the Party leadership faces an apparently hopeless task in its isolation. Despite all this, the Party struggles on, trying to stir up labor troubles and preserve itself for a future which holds little promise for it.

NAME: Communist Party Netherlands (*Communistische Partij Nederland*); founded in 1919 as Communist Party Holland.

LEGAL STATUS AND MEMBERSHIP: Legal; outlawed only by Nazi occupation government. Membership unknown; Communist Party and dissident Communist group together polled 179,288 votes in the national elections of 1959.

LEADERS:

    Paul de Groot—Secretary-General and Party leader

    Marcus Bakker—Editor of *De Waarheid*

    Harry Verhey—Secretary General of Communist trade union

    Joop Wolf—Editor of *De Waarheid*

    Theun de Vries—Chairman of The Netherlands-U.S.S.R.
        Association

OFFICIAL PAPER: *De Waarheid* (The Truth), published in Amsterdam; estimated circulation 15,000 daily.

POLITICAL STATUS: The Party and the dissident Communists together polled 2.99% of the vote in the 1959 elections, and won 3 of 150 seats in the Lower House. The Communists' political influence is practically nonexistent.

FRONT ORGANIZATIONS: International fronts operative, if insignificant, include the World Peace Council, the World Federation of Trade Unions, the World Federation of Democratic Youth, and the International Union of Students. The Netherlands-U.S.S.R. Association is a local front, and equally insignificant.

DIPLOMATIC RELATIONS: The Netherlands maintains diplomatic relations with both the U.S.S.R. and Communist China, and has received no aid from either the Soviet bloc or the United States.

# NIGERIA

Nigeria, whose 35 million citizens make it the most populous country in Africa, has no official Communist party and is in no real danger of Communist infiltration at the present time. It does have a small, furtive band of Marxists, composed mainly of junior civil servants, with a few trade-union leaders and at least one university intellectual in the group. They are generally regarded more as a social grouping of the misguided than as a real political force. Their chief activity consists of passing around dog-eared Communist literature, and the Nigerian Federal Government makes strenuous efforts to keep such tracts from entering the country. (The British Colonial Office had assisted the Nigerians in this task until Nigeria became independent on October 1, 1960.) Despite the efforts of the authorities, some Communist literature enters Nigeria; much of it reportedly comes from Red China rather than Russia. This propaganda trickle, however, has had negligible effect upon Nigerian life up to the present time.

# NORWAY

The development of Norway into a modern Social-Democratic welfare state has made Communism virtually homeless there. After a brief period of progress following World War II, when the Communist Party profited by its wartime record of anti-Nazi underground resistance and also by the Soviet liberation of northern Norway, the Party fell back into the insignificant and sectarian position it had held before the war. Its political influence today is practically nonexistent, and its influence in the trade unions is marginal as well. The Communists' decline has been hastened by Soviet violations of liberty and national independence in other parts of the world, as well as by a social and economic situation in Norway which has deprived the Communists of issues. In addition, the strongly individualistic Norwegians resent the notion of blindly obeying a distant leadership and the native Communists have failed to produce competent leaders of their own.

NAME: Communist Party of Norway (*Norges Kommunistiske Parti*); founded in 1923.

LEGAL STATUS AND MEMBERSHIP: Never outlawed by any legitimate Norwegian government; outlawed by German occupation authorities, 1941-1945. Present membership roughly 7,000.

LEADERS:

>    Emil Lvlien—Chairman, sole representative in Storting (Parliament)
>
>    Just Lippe—Secretary General
>
>    Reidar Larsen—Chairman of Communist Youth League; Editor of *Friheten*

OFFICIAL PAPER: *Friheten,* published in Oslo; circulation roughly 8,000.

POLITICAL STATUS: The Party controls one Parliament seat out of 150; it was represented in the "Liberation government" of 1945, but has never been part of any other before or since, nor has it formed part of any opposition coalition.

FRONT ORGANIZATIONS: The World Peace Council is the only international front operating with even mild success in Norway. There are several societies for the promotion of friendship between Norway and various Communist countries, but they exert very little influence outside the circle of Communist believers.

DIPLOMATIC RELATIONS: Norway maintains diplomatic relations with the U.S.S.R. and Communist China, but does not receive aid from the Soviet bloc.


# PAKISTAN


Communism in Pakistan has found many obstacles in its path. The Communist Party of Pakistan was formed as an extension of the Indian Party at the time of partition in 1947; the Pakistani Party soon dissociated itself from the Indian Party, but had neither the funds nor the organization to make any progress for some time thereafter. It was further hindered by the intrinsically anti-Communist feelings of the Moslem Pakistanis, by the lack of a large trade-union movement to exploit, and by governmental suppression, beginning in 1951, which has forced the Party underground. Pakistan's poverty and unemployment demand reforms, but legal political parties have stolen much of the disorganized Communists' fire by advocating social and economic reforms as sweeping as those advanced by the Communists. During the political turmoil of 1958, the powerful and popular fellow-traveler, Maulana Bashani, nearly persuaded the government to legalize Communism. But after the imposition of martial law, he was put in jail instead, in East Pakistan. The government of General Ayub Khan has no intention of letting him out.

NAME: The Communist Party of Pakistan; founded 1947.

LEGAL STATUS AND MEMBERSHIP: The Party was outlawed in 1954; membership unknown.

LEADERS: Unknown, since the Party is underground; however, one prominent leader, Aziz Ahmed Kahn Gwaliori, recently defected from the Party.

OFFICIAL PAPER: None.

POLITICAL STATUS: None. Party is illegal; country is under martial law.

FRONT ORGANIZATIONS: All are banned by the martial law regime.

DIPLOMATIC RELATIONS: Pakistan maintains diplomatic relations with the U.S.S.R. and Communist China; it has trade relations with the Soviet bloc, but has not received any aid from it. United States aid has been considerable.

# PANAMA

The Communist Party in Panama, under the name of the People's Party (P.D.P.), was outlawed in December 1953. Its finances and organization have been in an almost continual state of crisis ever since. Moreover, P.D.P. members are denied employment in education and in the Canal Zone, where many Panamanians are employed. All these factors have contributed to the decline of Communist influence over the past few years. Panamanian nationalist claims of sovereignty over the Canal Zone led to rioting against the United States in November 1959, however, and even in its weakened condition the P.D.P. can be expected to make the most of such opportunities.

# PERU

Despite the demonstrations against Vice-President Nixon in 1958, the Peruvians generally are firmly pro-Western and anti-Communist. The Catholic Church is strong in Peru and militantly anti-Communist, and the Reds suffer as well from lack of funds, lack of official recognition and lack of contact with the main stream of Communism. The Peruvian social system, however, is vulnerable to Communist penetration; there are great disparities in the distribution of wealth, and the Indian half of the population, speaking little or no Spanish and existing in poverty beyond the pale of national life, may some day be awakened to the possibilities of political disorder.

NAME: The Peruvian Communist Party (*Partido Communista Peruano*); founded in 1928 as Peruvian Socialist Party; became the PCP in 1929.

LEGAL STATUS AND MEMBERSHIP: Not outlawed, but its legal existence is "not recognized" under the terms of the Peruvian Constitution, which withholds legal recognition from internationally organized political parties. Communists claim almost 40,000 Party members. Anti-Communists say the number is nearer 2,000.

LEADERS:
> Raul Acosta Salas—Secretary General
> Jorge del Prado Chavez—Press and Propaganda Secretary
> Enrique Flores de Paz—Finance Secretary
> Jose Reccio Gutierrez—Labor Secretary
> Alfredo Abarca Abarca—External Affairs Secretary

OFFICIAL PAPER: *Unidad,* published infrequently in Lima.

POLITICAL STATUS: In the present Government, three of 49 Senators and six of 182 Deputies are considered to be Communist or pro-Communist, though they were elected under other party labels because of the constitutional proscription; no known Communist holds a policy making post.

FRONT ORGANIZATIONS: No international fronts operate in Peru, but there are several local fronts, including the following:
> United Workers' Front
> Progressive Women's Union
> Intellectual Group of Peru
> Peruvian Movement of Peace Partisans
> Committee Against Nuclear Arms
> Committee for the Defense of the Cuban Revolution
> Revolutionary Students' Front
> Several "cultural" societies with ties to various Communist countries

DIPLOMATIC RELATIONS: The Peruvian Government does not maintain diplomatic relations with any Soviet-bloc nation, nor does it receive aid from any of them.

# THE PHILIPPINES

The Communist party, decisively defeated by the late President Ramon Maysaysay in the early 1950's, is struggling to make a comeback. Supported by heavy Communist Chinese financing and under Soviet intellectual guidance, the Party appears to be making some headway. The Communists, who once nearly swept to power on the strength of the "Huk" armed peasant rebellion, have lately switched tactics in their new bid for dominance. The emphasis is on careful infiltration of educational institutions, labor unions, the two million unemployed, and the restless intellectual class. Although illegal, the Party is hardly inactive. It has taken up the cry of nationalism, assails graft and corruption in government, instigates troubles at United States military bases, and presses for closer ties with the U.S.S.R. and Communist China. It is aided by Communist Chinese agents, a nearly bankrupt national economy, and a widely disproportionate division of wealth throughout the islands of the country, as well as by the anti-American feelings of many sincere nationalists. The Communist attempt at armed revolt in the early 1950's was serious. Some 20,000 armed Huk revolutionaries, backed by as many as two million sympathizers, nearly seized control of the country. However, Magsaysay, as Defense Minister, revitalized the army to beat the Communists decisively, and later as President contained them. He went into the Communist rural strongholds offering land, jobs, and pardons, beating the Communists at their own game. He was killed in a 1957 plane crash and thus far no strong leader has appeared to replace him.

NAME: National Liberation Army (*Hukbong Mapagpalaya Ng Bayan*); founded as the Communist Party in 1927.

LEGAL STATUS AND MEMBERSHIP: Illegal since 1957; membership now punishable by death sentence; present membership about 700, plus 19,000 supporters.

LEADERS:

> Dr. Jesus Lava Supremo—in hiding in mountains somewhere in Philippines
>
> Casto Alejandrino—second-in-command, also in hiding
>
> Alfredo Saulo—jailed after surrendering to authorities
>
> Nicanor Mayupayo—jailed following capture; was chief of national organization
>
> Mateo Castillo—finance officer, rumored killed by his own men

OFFICIAL PAPER: None known.

POLITICAL STATUS: The Party is outlawed.

FRONT ORGANIZATIONS: There are no known Communist fronts in the Philippines.

DIPLOMATIC RELATIONS: The Philippines does not recognize any Communist country, nor receive aid from any of them. United States aid since the end of World War II has totaled about $2 billion.

# PORTUGAL

The Portuguese Communist Party, outlawed for almost thirty years, is a small, tough, tightly knit underground organization with virtually no political significance at present. Portugal has not had a parliamentary government since 1926, and the regime of Dr. Antonio Oliveira Salazar, now in its fourth decade, has kept Portuguese Communism under stern control since 1931. The Party, fighting hard for its existence under these conditions, seldom emerges to test its political strength; but in the 1958 presidential elections, it took advantage of the chance to influence public opinion at little risk to itself, by supporting the opposition candidate. Some rioting took place, and the government blamed the Communists, but popular discontent with the regime was the more likely cause. Portuguese Communism's great opportunity will arise when the 70-year-old Salazar leaves office.

NAME: Portuguese Communist Party (*Partido Comunista Portugues*); founded 1921.

LEGAL STATUS AND MEMBERSHIP: Has been illegal since 1931; estimated to have 8,000 members at most, of a population of almost ten million.

LEADERS: Alvaro Cunhal, Party Secretary General from 1940 to 1949, when he was jailed; escaped from jail in January 1960, and is expected to try to resume Party leadership. Other leaders are underground and unknown.

OFFICIAL PAPER: *Avante,* published clandestinely; usually manages to put out about 5,000 4-page copies every two weeks.

POLITICAL STATUS: None.

FRONT ORGANIZATIONS: None are permitted.

DIPLOMATIC RELATIONS: Portugal does not have relations with the U.S.S.R. or Communist China; it has received no Soviet aid, and negligible United States aid.

# SPAIN

June 18, 1959 was an extraordinary day in Spain, because nothing really unusual happened. The explanation of this paradox lies in the fact that Spain's Communists had done their best to organize a nationwide strike on that day as a "National Front" protest against the Franco regime. The strike failed; the other opposition parties wanted no part of the Communist stigma attached to them, and did not participate in the strike. The police rounded up the Communist leaders, and the Communist rank-and-file was too small and disorganized to make itself heard. The non-Communist opposition parties were delighted with this turn of events, for it provided indisputable proof of their contention that there was another alternative besides "Franco or Communism," as Franco's Falange had been saying for twenty years. The truth seems to be that, contrary to widespread opinion, the Communists have never won really widespread support among the anarchistic, individualistic Spaniards. Even during the Spanish Civil War, the heavily-financed Communists were welcomed more because they were anti-Fascist than because they were Communist, and their stern discipline did not go well with the Spanish temperament. Communism's only chance to achieve power in Spain would seem to depend on a really violent revolt against the Franco regime, in which Communist discipline might give it control of the anti-Franco forces despite its numerical inferiority.

NAME: The Spanish Communist Party (*Partido Comunista Espanola*); founded 1921.

LEGAL STATUS AND MEMBERSHIP: Franco declared the Party illegal in 1936, and his triumph in 1939 made the ban nationwide; the Party now exists in exile, and underground in Spain, where estimates of its membership range from 3,000 to 10,000.

LEADERS: Simon Sanchez Montero, a self-admitted top party leader, was sentenced to twenty years' hard labor last September (1959); others underground, unknown.

OFFICIAL PAPER: *Mundo Obrero* (Worker's World), edited in France and smuggled into Spain; also a radio station, "Radio Espana Independiente," which claims to broadcast from the Pyrenees, but is really located in Prague.

POLITICAL STATUS: There have been no elections for twenty-four years; no known Communists are in any government office.

FRONT ORGANIZATIONS: None.

DIPLOMATIC RELATIONS: Spain does not have diplomatic relations with the U.S.S.R. or Communist China, nor has it received aid from the Soviet bloc; United States aid and loans have totaled more than $2 billion so far.

# SWEDEN

The Swedish Communist Party, despite its small size, was twice able to save the country's Social-Democratic government in 1959. This was the first time in eleven years that the Communists had been of any importance in national politics, and their votes in the second crisis may cost them more than they have gained, since the bill they helped to pass set up an unpopular purchase tax. The Communists, acting under Kremlin orders, have persisted in their cooperation with the Social-Democrats for the last five years, despite the Social-Democrats' refusal to cooperate with the Communists even if it meant the end of their leadership of the government. In common with most Swedes, the Social-Democrats do not want to associate themselves with a Party which is so slavishly following the line set down by a foreign power. This Communist dependence on Moscow's orders, the violence of the Soviet Cold-War actions in Hungary and elsewhere, and Sweden's well distributed high standard of living, have all combined to reduce the Swedish Communist Party to a position of minor influence.

NAME: Swedish Communist Party (*Sveriges Kommunistiska Parti*); founded 1921.

LEGAL STATUS AND MEMBERSHIP: The Party has always been legal, though its papers were banned during part of the Russo-Finnish War of 1939-1940. The Party claims 30,000 members, but other sources call this figure exaggerated.

LEADERS:

> Hilding Hagberg—Chairman of Party; Member of Parliament (lower chamber)
> Knut Tell—Party Secretary
> Erik Karlsson—leading Party theoretician
> C. H. Hermansson—editor of Party paper
> Gunnar Ohman—Member of Parliament; leader of Communists in the upper chamber

OFFICIAL PAPER: *Ny Dag* ("New Day"), published in Stockholm, estimated circulation 15,000 to 20,000.

POLITICAL STATUS: The Communists polled 4% of the total votes in the 1958 elections, giving them five seats in the lower chamber and two in the upper chamber; except in the unusual circumstances noted above, they have not been an influence in the government for over a decade.

FRONT ORGANIZATIONS: Communist fronts include the Swedish Peace Committee, a branch of the World Peace Council; Democratic Youth, a chapter of the International Federation of Democratic Youth; the Swedish Clarte Federation, originally a Socialist internationalist organization; and a Soviet friendship society. None of these has wide influence.

DIPLOMATIC RELATIONS: Sweden maintains diplomatic relations with the U.S.S.R. and Communist China; it has not received aid from the Soviet bloc or the United States.

# SWITZERLAND

The Swiss Communist Party still has not recovered from the tremendous blow dealt it by the Hungarian revolution in 1956. The brutal suppression of Hungarian freedom caused feelings of revulsion among the Swiss, including many Party members, that have not subsided with the years. Even today, Communist support of a cause is enough to discredit that cause in the eyes of most Swiss; the Communists, therefore, can do little but provide discreet and indirect support to the left wing Socialists and any others who take up a cause which may fit the Communists' objectives. Adding to the Communists' difficulties are a lack of leadership and organization and an unprecedented economic boom which has created a continuing labor shortage, as well as a steady rise in wages and purchasing power. The Communists play quietly on the resistance of many Swiss to increased defense expenditures and try to create dissension between the French and German-speaking sectors of the population. They have also had some success in infiltrating the unskilled labor force and the local consumer's cooperatives and are the biggest party in the French-speaking Canton of Geneva. In general, however, the Communists in Switzerland are outcasts both politically and socially.

NAME: The Swiss Labor Party (*Parti Suisse du Travail/Partei der Arbeit*), founded in 1921 as the Swiss Communist Party.

LEGAL STATUS AND MEMBERSHIP: Legal; outlawed in 1940 for subversive activities; the Labor Party, founded as a substitute in 1944, became the successor to the Party when the ban was lifted in 1945. Party now has an estimated 4,000 members.

LEADERS:

> Edgar Woog—Secretary General of Party
>
> Jean Vincent—Member of Parliament; leader of Geneva branch, which is the largest in Switzerland
>
> André Muret—Leader of Vaud Cantonal branch (second largest) and member of Swiss Politburo
>
> Marino Bodenmann—Leader of Basle branch; member of the Politburo
>
> Armand Forel—Member of Parliament

The Party has switched to "collective leadership," and bestows no titles except Woog's.

OFFICIAL PAPER:

> *Voix Ouvrière* ("Worker's Voice"), French daily, Geneva; circulation 8,000.
>
> *Vorwarts* ("Forward"), German weekly, Basle; circulation about 10,000
>
> *Il Lavoratore* ("The Worker"), Italian weekly; Lugano; circulation 2,000

POLITICAL STATUS: The Party received 26,248 votes in the 1959 national elections, or 2.6% of the votes cast. This gave the Party three seats out of 196 in the National Council, and none of 44 in the States Council (upper chamber). The Party forms no part of the Government or of any coalition.

FRONT ORGANIZATIONS: There are many front organizations in Switzerland, but since the other parties and papers devote considerable effort to unmasking them, they seldom achieve a membership higher than that of the Party itself—about 4,000—and their influence is similarly restricted. The principal fronts are:

> The Swiss Movement for Peace

The Switzerland-Soviet Union Society
The Association of Culture and People
Swiss Women's Organization for Peace and Progress
Swiss Workers' and Peasants' Assistance
Book Retailing Cooperative
Free Youth of Switzerland
DIPLOMATIC RELATIONS: Switzerland maintains diplomatic relations with both the U.S.S.R. and Communist China.


# SYRIA (Northern Region, United Arab Republic)

In 1957, Communism in Syria seemed well on its way toward transforming the country into a Soviet satellite; by the end of 1958 Syrian Proconsul Abdel Hamid Serraj was saying of Communism that "its attitude is treason to the Arab cause..." The very success of the Communists in Syria was responsible for their defeat. At one point they had collaborated with non-Communist Arab nationalist parties; but ultimately the Socialist Ba'ath Party grew so afraid of the possibility of a Communist takeover that it spearheaded the drive for the union of Syria with Egypt in the United Arab Republic. The U.A.R. union in February 1958 marked the beginning of the Communist Party's decline in both countries. Since the beginning of 1959 the Party has been suppressed altogether, but the Syrian Communist Party, like the Egyptian, has managed to survive suppression several times in the past. Syrian Communism began its upsurge in 1954, when it emerged from a period of harassment to vote its leader, Khalid Bakdash, into the Parliament of Syria. The U.S.S.R., sensing its opportunity, launched a cultural invasion of Syria, and a trade agreement signed in 1955 opened the way for rapid Soviet economic encroachment. The Syrian Party founded a national front in 1956, and its hold on the government quickly increased. By 1957 the Ba'ath Socialists, who had cooperated with the Communists against the conservative elements, were organizing the union with Egypt. Bakdash fled in 1958. In the July 1959 elections, the Ba'athists themselves were soundly defeated by Nasser's supporters, and the suppressed Communists did not show at all.

NAME: Communist Party of Syria; founded 1928.

LEGAL STATUS AND MEMBERSHIP: Illegal. The Party was outlawed in 1939, dissolved in 1948, suppressed in 1959 by the U.A.R. Membership unknown at present.

LEADERS: Khalid Bakdash, Secretary General; in exile at present. Other leaders unknown due to clandestine nature of Party.

OFFICIAL PAPER: None.

POLITICAL STATUS: None; the Party is suppressed.

FRONT ORGANIZATIONS: Most of the major international fronts

functioned in Syria, but fronts have ceased to function since Party activities ceased in January 1959.

DIPLOMATIC RELATIONS: The United Arab Republic maintains diplomatic relations with both the U.S.S.R. and Communist China. Before union with the U.A.R., Syria received much aid of various kinds from the Soviet bloc, and did not accept United States aid. Since the union, Syria has received some of the United States and Soviet aid accepted by the U.A.R.

# THAILAND

Communism is, and always has been, a negligible force in Thailand. The present ruler of the country, Field Marshal Sarit, made a great event out of the destruction of a Communist cell in Bangkok in 1959, but this action only served to underline the rarity of such occurrences. Even in the period from 1955 to 1958, when political parties were allowed to flourish, the Communists failed to put in an appearance, and the leftist Socialist United Front could not manage to provide an effective opposition party. Marshal Sarit has ruled Thailand under martial law since October 1958, and all political parties except his own Revolutionary Party have been banned since then. Under these conditions, Communism has all but vanished.

NAME: The Communist Party of Thailand; founded 1928.

LEGAL STATUS AND MEMBERSHIP: Illegal; was legal from 1928 to 1933, and from 1946 to 1952. Membership is not known.

LEADERS: Secretary General believed to be Prasong Vongvivat; others unknown.

OFFICIAL PAPER: None.

POLITICAL STATUS: The Party has never contested an election.

FRONT ORGANIZATIONS: None operate in Thailand.

DIPLOMATIC RELATIONS: Thailand has diplomatic relations with the U.S.S.R., but not with Communist China; it has received no aid from the Soviet bloc. Aid from the United States has averaged $23 million a year over the past ten years.

# TUNISIA

Communism has made little headway in Tunisia since the country became independent in March 1956. The Tunisian Communist Party, with an estimated 400 members, managed to win only 3,461 votes in the November 1959 elections, while the ruling Neo-Destour Party and its affiliates won over a million votes. Communism's lack of success apparently stems from the fact that most Tunisians regard it as an alien influence. The General Federation of Tunisian Workers (U.G.T.T.) is strongly anti-Communist, and maintains an affiliation with the International Confederation of Free Trade Unions (I.C.F.T.U.). Tunisia established diplomatic relations with Czechoslovakia in November 1959, and President Bourgiba has proposed the establishment of diplomatic relations with the U.S.S.R. in 1960; but this seems unlikely to benefit the Tunisian Communist Party appreciably.

# TURKEY

Turkey, a nation which has fought eleven wars with the Russians over the past two hundred years, continues to view its northern neighbors with acute suspicion. Moreover, this feeling is apparently strong in all classes of the population. Some Turks say that Communism might have had a chance in Turkey if it had come from a Western nation, but that, associated with Russia, its cause is hopeless. There was a period after World War I when Mustafa Kemal (Ataturk) temporarily joined forces with the Soviets during the Turkish war of independence, but once the Turks had won their struggle, he suppressed the Communists without hesitation. Relations with the U.S.S.R. remained cordial, however, until the late 1930's, when they grew distinctly chilly. Since then, except for brief periods in 1946 and 1950, all left-wing activities have been suppressed in Turkey, including some movements that would hardly be considered leftist in the West. But if Communism's influence is negligible in Turkey at present, its opportunities are growing. Land reform is urgently needed to prevent agrarian chaos, and industrialization is creating the urban proletariat which has so often provided the seedbed for Communism. The Kurdish minority in eastern Turkey is another possible source of trouble for the Turks; Soviet and Iraqi propaganda, directed at these two million tribesmen continues to fan the flames of Kurdish nationalism. Despite these threats, few people in Turkey have much knowledge of Communist methods of subversion, and this lack of information, together with a complacent assumption that Turkey is safely aligned with the West, sharply increases the Communists' opportunities.

NAME: Founded in 1920 as the Angora Communist Party.

LEGAL STATUS AND MEMBERSHIP: Now illegal. Banned in 1938, legalized and banned again in 1946; legalized and banned again in 1950.

LEADERS: Unknown in Turkey. The poet Nazim Hikmet, a Communist since the 1920's, fled Turkey in 1951 and now broadcasts from the U.S.S.R. He is the best known Turkish Communist, but his influence is more literary than political.

OFFICIAL PAPER: None.

POLITICAL STATUS: None; the Party is illegal.

FRONT ORGANIZATIONS: None known.

DIPLOMATIC RELATIONS: Turkey maintains diplomatic relations with the U.S.S.R., and has since 1920; it does not maintain relations with Communist China.

# UNION OF SOUTH AFRICA

Former members of the banned Communist Party of South Africa find themselves in an intricate situation which leaves them little opportunity to exert political influence. Some of them now work in the Negro Congress movement, where they preach racial cooperation in contrast to the extremists among the African National Congress, who believe the whites will have no place in an African-controlled South Africa. The Communists are thus in the unaccustomed position of preaching non-violence, since they believe violence at this stage can only result in further repression—a belief which recent events have tended to support. Some former Communists are active in the Congress of Democrats, which is now all-white and therefore no longer in contact with the powerful African National Congress. Nationalist movements have also suffered from banning imposed under the Suppression of Communism Act, but this has not made them feel that the Communists are their brothers. Indeed, one of Communism's chief problems in South Africa is that the African nationalists tend to distrust *all* whites and *all* foreign movements, regardless of their origins and professed beliefs.

NAME: The Communist Party of South Africa; founded in 1921.

LEGAL STATUS AND MEMBERSHIP: Outlawed by the Suppression of Communism Act in 1950. This Act provides jail sentences of up to ten years for any person who declares himself a Communist or advocates anything which the Act describes as the aims of Communism, or who is merely deemed to be a Communist by the Governor-General. At the time that the Party went into voluntary liquidation in 1950 the membership was estimated at 2,000.

LEADERS: Many former leaders of the C.P.S.A. are still active in legal organizations open to them; among these are the following:

Dr. Yusuf M. Dadoo—Indian; former Chairman of the Transvaal section of the C.P.S.A.

Moses M. Kotane—African; former General Secretary of the C.P.S.A.

Isaac Horowitz—white; former National Chairman of the C.P.S.A.

Sam Kahn—white; Communist member of Parliament from 1948 to 1951, when he was put out of office by the Suppression of Communism Act

Brian Bunting—white; Managing Editor of *New Age*

OFFICIAL PAPER: Despite its wide powers, the government has not suppressed the Communists' weekly newspaper, presently called *New Age,* which has an estimated circulation of 90,000; the editors changed the name each time the paper was banned, until the government abandoned the game.

POLITICAL STATUS: None at present.

FRONT ORGANIZATIONS: Communist fronts cannot operate in South Africa because of the Suppression of Communism Act.

DIPLOMATIC RELATIONS: South Africa broke off diplomatic relations with the U.S.S.R. in 1956, and has never established relations with Communist China.

# UNITED STATES OF AMERICA

Communism in the United States of America has fallen a long way in the years since the end of World War II. In the 1930's, many Americans looked on Communism as a promising means of solving the manifold problems of the depression world, and during World War II Soviet Russia's heroic struggle with the Nazis won it the admiration of the Allies. However, the U.S.S.R. abandoned the policy of friendship after 1945, and Communist aggressive actions in Eastern Europe, Berlin, China, Korea and elsewhere effectively doomed the Communist Party of the U.S.A. before 1950. Revelations of espionage on the part of U.S. Communists, and charges of Communist infiltration of the government, led to measures designed to destroy the effectiveness of the Party in the U.S.A. In 1949, eleven leaders of the C.P.U.S.A. were convicted of conspiracy to advocate the violent overthrow of the U.S. government, an action punishable under the Smith Act of 1940. Lesser Party leaders were convicted in the next four years, and the Party had no younger leaders to replace those in jail. In 1953 several Communists were convicted of transmitting atomic weapons secrets to the U.S.S.R.; Julius and Ethel Rosenberg received death sentences, and other conspirators were jailed. In 1954 the Communist Control Act subjected Communists and the C.P.U.S.A. to the Internal Security Act of 1950, thereby requiring the Communists to register with the Attorney General as agents of the U.S.S.R. and putting them under the supervision of the Subversive Activities Control Board.

Pressure on U.S. Communists has diminished somewhat in recent years. Two U.S. Supreme Court decisions in 1957 limited the scope of Congressional investigating committees and of the Smith Act, and the latter decision reversed the convictions of fourteen secondary leaders of the C.P.U.S.A. The leaders of the C.P.U.S.A. completed their jail sentences and returned to wrangle over the remnants of their Party; public opinion was not aroused, for the C.P.U.S.A. was clearly ineffectual.

In the words of Earl Browder, Party National Chairman until ousted from the post in 1945, U.S. Communism has "long been politically dead. There is no hope of it ever being revived."

NAME: Communist Party of the U.S.A.; founded 1919 as Workers' Party of America, soon changed to Communist Party of America. After World War II, the Party changed to its present title, the Communist Party of the U.S.A.

LEGAL STATUS AND MEMBERSHIP: The C.P.U.S.A. claims it is no longer Moscow-dominated, and is therefore no longer subject to the supervision of the Subversive Activities Control Board. The Board reaffirmed its control in 1959, however. The Party claims 10,000 members; other sources estimate membership at about 3,000.

LEADERS:

Gus Hall—General Secretary
Benjamin Davis—National Secretary
Eugene Dennis—National Chairman
William Z. Foster—Chairman-Emeritus
Claude Lightfoot—Vice-Chairman
Elizabeth Gurley Flynn—Vice-Chairman

OFFICIAL PAPER: *The Worker;* weekly, estimated circulation 10,000. Formerly the *Daily Worker,* but financial difficulties forced the change to weekly publication.

POLITICAL STATUS: Although Communism itself is a dominant national concern in the U.S., the C.P.U.S.A. has dwindled to a state of insignificance. No known Communist holds any governmental position in the U.S., and the Party's influence on national affairs is nonexistent.

FRONT ORGANIZATIONS: There are no significant Communist-front organizations in the U.S.; the Communists set up paper fronts from time to time for propaganda purposes, but these are generally identified and isolated in short order by the Attorney General's office.

DIPLOMATIC RELATIONS: The U.S. has diplomatic relations with the U.S.S.R. and most of the Soviet Bloc nations, but has never recognized Communist China.

# URUGUAY

The Soviet embassy in Uruguay operates with a staff of more than seventy, and it imports Spanish-language propaganda into the country at the rate of a hundred tons a month. Although much of this propaganda effort is directed toward other parts of South America, it indicates the freedom that Communism enjoys in Uruguay, and makes its failure to exert important influence more difficult to understand. Part of the explanation lies in the fact that Uruguay has been living for decades under a regime of paternal socialism which has stolen the

Reds' thunder. Moreover, Uruguay is one of the most prosperous and best educated nations in Latin America and its citizens have tended to look with indifference upon Communist appeals, despite the problems of continuing inflation and unemployment. It remains to be seen whether the Uruguayan Communists' present campaign to penetrate the ranks of labor and universities will meet with anything other than the customary indifference.

NAME: The Communist Party of Uruguay (*Partido Communista del Uruguay*), founded in 1920.

LEGAL STATUS AND MEMBERSHIP: Has always been a legal party; membership now about 7,000.

LEADERS:

Rodney Arismendi—Secretary General

Enrique Pastorino—Secretary

Enrique Rodriguez—Member of Executive Committee

Julia Arevalo de Roche—Member of Executive Committee

Alberto Suarez—Secretary

OFFICIAL PAPER: *El Popular,* of Montevideo, estimated circulation 10,000.

POLITICAL STATUS: The Party has polled less than three per cent of the vote in the last three elections, has formed no coalitions, and its influence in the government has been marginal.

FRONT ORGANIZATIONS: The following are among those active in Uruguay: Workers' Single Central (*Central Unica de Trabajadores*) is trying to organize labor in competition with democratic organizations.

National Board of Partisans of Peace

Feminine Union of Uruguay

Student Section (Communist secondary students)

House of Spain (group of Spanish republicans)

The Uruguayan-Soviet Cultural Institute

DIPLOMATIC RELATIONS: Uruguay maintains diplomatic relations with the U.S.S.R., but not with Red China; almost a fifth of its trade is with Soviet-bloc nations. This trade is in dollars and is not regulated by treaties or accords. Uruguay has not received aid from either the Soviet bloc or the United States.

# VENEZUELA

The Venezuelan Communist Party was outlawed and persecuted during the dictatorship of Marcos Pérez Jiménez in 1952-1958, but polled 150,000 votes in the December 1958 elections following the overthrow of that régime. Since then, Communists have gained open or indirect power in the universities, in journalism and in radio. They are agitating for immediate, all-out agrarian reform, on the pattern of

Fidel Castro; they also decry high rents and unemployment, and do their best to undermine public confidence in business and commercial interests. Operating without governmental restrictions, they are exerting an increasing influence upon communications and the future leadership of this nation, which is second only to the United States in oil production.

NAME: Venezuelan Communist Party; founded clandestinely in 1933 as Venezuelan Revolutionary Party, legally in 1945 under present name.

LEGAL STATUS AND MEMBERSHIP: Legal; estimated membership 125,000.

LEADERS: Gustavo Machado, Director of Party; Pompeyo Marquez, Jésus Faria, members of Party Political Bureau with Machado.

OFFICIAL PAPER: *Tribuna Popular,* a weekly tabloid published in Caracas; estimated circulation 35,000.

POLITICAL STATUS: The Party polled 150,000 votes in 1958 elections, controls two seats in Senate (0.8% of total) and six seats in Deputies (4.9% of total). Not in any coalition, forms no part of present government.

FRONT ORGANIZATIONS: The World Peace Council, the World Federation of Democratic Youth and the International Association of Democratic Lawyers operate as fronts in Venezuela. Other familiar international fronts are run there as letterhead organizations, to spread propaganda. Domestic fronts are being organized as well.

DIPLOMATIC RELATIONS: Venezuela does not have diplomatic relations with the U.S.S.R. or Red China, or receive aid from them. The United States has provided some Point Four technical assistance, but no economic aid.


# VIETNAM (South Vietnam)

Communism in South Vietnam is working to undermine the population's confidence in the government, and to accomplish this objective the underground organization, known in South Vietnam as the *Viet Cong,* resorts to terrorism. For the past several years the Communists have been assassinating rural government officials, destroying agricultural machinery, burning provincial administrative offices, and on one occasion assassinating American military advisors. In addition, they have been carrying on a high-powered propaganda campaign. Frequently they seize an isolated village at dusk, and spend the night indoctrinating their prisoners and playing on their discontent. The *Viet Cong* has little trouble receiving supplies and reinforcements across the long, inaccessible borders of South Vietnam, so that its activities can hardly be stopped for good by the South Vietnamese forces, which are hindered by primitive communications in the outlying areas. The *Viet Cong* also does its best to create instability in South Vietnam's political life. The South Vietnamese elections in August 1959 were carried out in the face of an ingenious variety of Communist harassments.

NAME: The Vietnam Workers' Party (*Lao Dong*), founded in 1951; replaced the Indo-Chinese Communist Party, which had been founded in 1930.

LEGAL STATUS AND MEMBERSHIP: Illegal in South Vietnam since that republic was founded in 1955; membership cannot be estimated in South Vietnam.

LEADERS: In North Vietnam, the Party leaders are:
Ho Chi Minh—President
Pham Van Dong—Premier
General Vo Nguyen Giap—Army Commander

OFFICIAL PAPER: *Nhan Dan,* published in Hanoi; none published in South Vietnam.

POLITICAL STATUS: There is no Communist vote in South Vietnam.

FRONT ORGANIZATIONS: None.

DIPLOMATIC RELATIONS: South Vietnam does not maintain diplomatic relations with the Soviet bloc. United States aid has totaled $1.2 billion.

# INDEX

General Union of Workers and Peasants (Mexico), 94
Gensuiko (Japanese Council Against Atomic and Hydrogen Bombs), 142, 247, 248
Germany; *see also* East Germany
    Communist Party of, 233
Ghana, 12, 14, 152-53, 233-34
    National Union of Students, 152
    People's Convention Party, 152
Gómez, Juan Vincente, 82
Gomulka, Wladyslaw, 27, 30
Gordeytchik, Peter, 15
Gouzenko, Igor, 222
Great Britain, 8, 38, 46, 51, 60, 129, 131, 234-35
    Communist Party of, 234-35
    Engineering and Allied Trades Shop Stewards' National Council, 234-35
Greece, Communist Party of, 235-37
Guatemala, 61, 99, 104, 237
    Communist Party of, 237
Guevara, Alfredo, 97-98
Guevara, Ernesto, 62, 95, 98, 100, 226
Guidice, Ernesto, 213
Guinea, 148, 150, 206, 237-38
Guzman, Jacob Arbenz, 99
Gwaliori, Aziz Ahmed Khan, 259

HADITU (Egypt), 57
*Hauptverwaltung Aufklaerung* (East Germany), 195
Havana University, 99
*Hayat ech Chaab* (Morocco), 162
Hikmet, Nazim, 268
Ho Chi-minh, 110
*Hoy* (Cuba), 97
Hungarian revolution, 1956, 22, 27, 32
Hungary, 4-5, 10, 26, 28, 68, 70, 138, 165-66, 176, 179
Hussein, King, 248
Hyderabad, 130

Ibrahim, Abdullah, 147, 162
Iceland, 238
India, 13, 15, 33, 108, 110, 124-35, 168, 238-40
    Communist Party of, 128-34, 239-40
Indian Congress Party, 129, 131-32
Indo-China, 110, 175
Indonesia, 14-15, 33, 111, 113-19, 206, 240-41
    Communist Party of, 114-19, 240-41
Indonesian Labor Federation, 116, 118
Institute for Sugar Stabilization, 100
Instituto de Intercambio Cultural Mexico-Russo, 185
Instituto Superior de Estudos Brasileiros, 72, 217
Inter-American Congress for Democracy and Freedom, 96
Inter-American Organization of Anti-Communist Journalists, 103
Inter-American Regional Labor Office, 75
Inter-American Regional Workers' Organization, 90
International Association of Democratic Lawyers, 73

International Confederation of Free Trade Unions, 71, 90, 153
International Democratic Women's Federation, 73
International Federation of Trade Unions, 140
International Organization of Journalists, 84
International Union of Students, 72, 152
Iqbal, Muhammed, 39
Iran, 15-16, 241-42
    Communist Party of, 242
Iraq, 13-15, 36-38, 40-41, 45-55, 58, 182, 242-44
    Communist Party of, 45-55, 243-44
    Friendship societies, 50
    Ministry of Education, 53
    Ministry of Guidance, 53
    National Democratic Party, 46
    Railway Workers' and Employees' Trade Union, 51
Iraqi Democratic Youth, 243
Iraqi revolution, 45-46, 58
Iraqi Trade Unions, General Federation of, 50
Ireland, 244
Israel, 41, 44, 244-45
    Communist Party of, 244-45
Israeli-Arab dispute, 41
Istiqlal Party, 46, 160-61
Italian Labor Unions, Christian Democratic Federation of, 179
Italian Movement for Peace, 246
Italy, 5, 82, 166, 168-69, 176-80, 245-46
    Communist Party of, 176-80, 246
    Labor Confederation, 179
*Ittihad al Shaab* (Iraq), 50
Ivashov, Vasily, 187

Japan, 6, 8, 14, 82, 106-08, 113, 124, 126-28, 135-46, 206-07, 247-48
    Communist Party of, 135-45, 247-48
Japanese Council Against Atomic and Hydrogen Bombs (Gensuiko), 142, 247, 248
Japanese Federation of Labor (Sohyo), 140-41, 247, 248
Japanese League of Industrial Organizations (Sambetsu), 140
Japan Teachers' Union, 141
Jara, Heriberto, 91
Java, 116
Jemali, Fadhil al, 54
Jewish state, 41
Jiménez, Marcos Pérez, 81, 272
Jiminez, Nunez, 97, 99, 226
Joliot-Curie, Frédéric, 175
Jordan, 36, 44, 58, 248
    Communist Party of, 248
Journalists, International Organization of, 84
Juliao, Francisco, 72

Kadar government (Hungary), 28
Kaganovich, L. M., 22
Kassem, Abdul Karim, 47-50, 53-55, 243
Kato, Mrs. Shizue, 145

277

Katyn massacre, 10
Kelly, Guillermo, 80
Kenya, 148, 154-56, 158, 248-49
Kenya African Union, 155
Kenyatta, Jomo, 149, 155, 249
Kerala, 130-34
K.G.B.; *see* Soviet State Security
Khrushchev, Nikita S., 3-5, 7-10, 14, 18-19, 21-35, 37, 58-60, 62, 64, 67, 107, 111-12, 125, 171, 181-82, 202-05, 207-08
Kikuyu Independent Schools (Kenya), 154
Kishi, Nobusuke, 144-45
Koinange, Peter Mbiu, 154
Korea, 73, 108, 110, 138, 143, 249
    Communist Party of, 249
Korean armistice, 20
Kostylev, Mikhail, 187
Kotane, Moses, 156-57, 269
Kubba, Ibrahim, 52-53
Kubitschek Juscelino, 68
Kudriavtsev, Sergei N., 183
Kuwait, 51

Laos, Communist Party of, 249-50
Larrazabal, Wolfgang, 82
Larsen, Aksel, 166, 228
Lateran Treaty, 177
Latin America, 8, 15, 62-105, 185-87, 207
    Confederation of Trade Unions of, 75, 90
Laval, Pierre, 173
Lavin, José Domingo, 92
League for the Defense of Women's Rights (Iraq), 48
League for the Rights of Man, 66, 213
Lebanon, 36, 38, 42, 45, 58, 250-51
    Communist Party of, 251
Lechin, Juan, 217
Lenin, Vladimir, 3, 4, 8, 18, 23, 29, 74
Leninism, 3, 4, 21, 23, 29, 32, 34, 202
*L'Humanité* (France), 171
Liu Shau-chi, 121
Llada, Jose Pardo, 96
Lu Ting Yi, 34
Luxembourg, 251-52
Luzon, 108

Machado, Gustavo, 62, 64, 81-84, 273
Machine tractor stations (U.S.S.R.), 18, 24
Magsaysay, Ramon, 108, 260-61
Mahdawi, Colonel, 53
Malaya, 15, 108, 110, 112-13, 124, 252-53
    Communist Party of, 112, 252-53
Malenkov, Georgi, 5, 20-22
Malenkov plan, 20, 23
Mao Tse-tung, 6, 30, 32-33, 106, 109-11, 135, 208
Marin, Luiz Munoz, 96
Marinello, Juan, 98-99
Marshall Plan, 167, 174
Marti, Andre, 174
Marxism, 29, 30, 64, 226
Masetti, Jorge, 104
Mateos, Adolfo Lopez, 86, 89, 93

Matos, Hubert, 101
Mau Mau revolt (Kenya), 148, 154-56
Maung, Thakin Chit, 123
Mboya, Tom, 148, 156, 249
Mercader, Raymond, 88
Messaouak, Hadi, 162, 255
Mexican Labor Federation, 90
Mexican Workers and Peasants, General Union of, 94
Mexico, 62-64, 66-67, 86-96, 104, 185-87, 253-54
    Communist Party of, 89-95, 253-54
    Partido Popular, 90
Middle East, 6, 12, 36-60, 191, 207
Mikoyan, Anastas, 87, 95, 102
Military Intelligence (G.R.U.), 182-83, 188
Miranda, Victor, 98
Missiles, 14, 167
Moch, Jules, 173
Modiera, Frota, 70
Mohieddine, Khaled, 56
Mohieddine, Zacchariah, 56
Molotov, Vyacheslav, 22, 173
Montera, Simon Sanchez, 263
Morocco, 159-64, 254-55
    Communist Party of, 159-63, 255
    Democratic Independence Party, 161
Moscow purge trials, 1938, 5
Moslem Masjumi Party, 117
Moslems, Soviet, 40
Mossadegh, Mohammed, 242
Movement for the Democratization and Independence of Trade Unions (Argentina), 213
Muslim League (Kerala), 133
Mussolini, Benito, 177
Mutual Economic Assistance, Council for, 29

Namboodiripad, Elamkulam Mana Sankaran, 131-35, 239
Nasser, Gamal Abdel, 36-37, 40, 44, 49, 55-60, 123, 161-62, 229
Nasution, Abdul Haris, 115, 240
National Confederation of Industrial Workers (Brazil), 70
National Democratic Party (Iraq), 46
National Federation of Student Self-Government Associations (Japan); *see* Zengakuren
National Institute for Agrarian Reform (Cuba), 97, 100
National Maritime Union (Brazil), 70
National United Front (Burma), 122-23
Nazi Germany, 173
Nehru, Jawaharlal, 126, 133, 239
Nenni, Pietro, 179
Nepal, Communist Party of, 255-56
Neruda, Pablo, 66, 76
Netherlands, Communist Party of, 256-57
*Neues Deutschland*, 192, 194-95
New China News Agency, 51, 53
Ne Win, 120, 122-23, 220
Niemayer, Oskar, 66, 76
Nigeria, 153, 257
Nigerian Trade Union Congress, 153
Nishio, Suehiro, 143

278

Soviet (cont.)
consumer goods, 31-32
credit program, 15
forgeries, 190-200
intelligence, 181-201
loans and credits, 14
Ministry of Health, 16
press, 33
purges, 5, 10, 22
science, 6, 25
*Soviet Bloc: Unity and Conflict, The*, 29
Soviet Moslems, 40
Soviet State Security (K.G.B.), 19, 22-23, 63, 88, 182-90, 195, 204
Soviet-Yugoslav declaration, 1956, 27
Space and missiles, 14
Spain, 9, 166, 262-63
Communist Party of, 263
Sputniks, 6, 14, 25
Stalin, Joseph, 5-7, 10, 19-23, 25-34, 37, 42, 62, 110, 173, 177, 205
Stern, Alfred and Martha Dodd, 93
Stockholm Peace Appeal, 43
Students' Union, International, 72, 152, 219
Suez Canal, 56
Sugar Stabilization, Institute for (Cuba), 100
Sukarno, Achmed, 106, 114-15, 117, 119, 240
Sultan, Leon, 159
Summit meeting, 1960, 4, 30, 33, 169, 180
Supremo, Jesus Lava, 261
Sweden, 166, 263-64
Communist Party of, 264
Switzerland, Communist Party of, 166, 265-66
Syria, 15, 36-38, 40, 42, 58, 151, 256-67
Communist Party of, 266-67

Tahir, Fasfi, 53
Tamayo, Jorge, 91
Taruc, Luis, 108
Tass news agency, 51, 53
Thailand, 114, 267
Communist Party of, 267
Thanarat, Sarit, 114
Thorez, Maurice, 82, 165, 169-76, 232
Tibet, 33, 111, 138, 169, 206
Tito, Josip B., 26-28, 33
Togliatti, Palmiro, 82, 161, 168, 176-80, 246
Toledano, Vincente, 62, 75, 90-91, 254
Touré, Sekou, 148-50
Trade Unions
Movement for the Democratization and Independence of (Argentina), 213
World Federation of, 6, 11, 13, 50, 90, 141
Trotsky, Leon, 66, 88, 159
Trujillo, Rafael L., 65
Tunisia, 267-68
Turkey, Communist Party of, 268-69
Twentieth Congress of the Communist Party of the Soviet Union, 4, 5, 10, 22, 26, 111

U-2 aircraft, 4, 25, 30, 34, 180-81, 189
U.A.R.; see United Arab Republic
Ukraine, 21
Union of South Africa; see also Africa
Communist Party of, 156-58, 269-70
United Arab Republic, 15, 47-48, 151, 203; see also Egypt
United States, 6, 9, 23, 47, 51, 58-60, 65, 69, 71, 73, 91-93, 104, 110, 139, 142-43, 167, 169, 174, 181-82, 184, 189-92, 208, 270-71
Communist Party of, 271
Senate, Foreign Relations Committee, 19
U-2 aircraft; see U-2 aircraft
*United States in the World Arena, The*, 24
United Nations, 104
United Workers' Movement (Argentina), 79
U Nu, 219-20
Uruguay, 187, 271-72
Communist Party of, 272
U.S.S.R., 4, 6, 14-34, 43, 45, 51-52, 57-58, 62-63, 67, 76-77, 82, 87, 90, 95, 103, 165, 168-69, 173, 181-209
U.S.S.R.-Argentina Cultural Relations Institute, 213

Vallejo, Demetrio, 93
Venezuela, 62-64, 67, 81-85, 96, 272-73
Communist Party of, 81-84, 273
Venezuelan Association of Journalists, 83
Videla, Gonsalez, 75, 224
Vietnam, Communist Party of, 273-74
*Voices of the People* (Mexico), 91
Vozniy, Ivan Mikhailovich, 183-84

Western Europe, 166-80
W.F.D.Y.; see World Federation of Democratic Youth
W.F.T.U.; see World Federation of Trades Unions
Women's Rights, League for the Defense of (Iraq), 48
World Council of Physicians, 73
World Federation of Democratic Youth, 8, 12
World Federation of Trade Unions, 6, 11, 13, 50, 90, 141
World Peace Council, 12, 40, 73, 175

Yagoda, Genrikh, 23
Yasui, Kaoru, 247
Yata, Ali, 160-62, 255
Yemen, 15
Yugoslavia, 27-28
Yukawa, Hideki, 143

Zayas, Jorge, 101
Zengakuren (National Federation of Student Self-Government Associations—Japan), 138-40, 247, 248
Zhdanov, Andrei, 5, 108
Zhukov, Georgi, 21, 22

280